Industrial Capabilities
Report To Congress
Fiscal Year 2020

By law, the Secretary of Defense must submit an annual report to the congressional armed services committees on the actions, investments, and assessments conducted in support of the U.S. defense industrial base (DIB). The FY 2020 Industrial Capabilities Report satisfies the requirements pursuant to title 10, U.S. Code., Section 2504, and provides context to the challenges facing the U.S. DIB.

It is published as a convenience to those who may wish to have a quality professionally printed copy of the manual.

Edited 2021 Ocotillo Press
ISBN 978-1-954285-77-4

Ocotillo Press
Houston, TX 77017
Books@OcotilloPress.com

TABLE OF CONTENTS

FOREWORD

FOREWORD

A 21ST CENTURY DEFENSE INDUSTRIAL STRATEGY FOR AMERICA

Introduction to the Fiscal Year 2020 Industrial Capabilities Report to Congress

In many ways, Americans have every reason to be confident about our national security future.

The American military is still the most powerful in the world. Its leading defense industry companies are still global leaders in weapons innovation and production. Likewise, the Department of Defense is still the colossus of the federal system, i.e., the single biggest buyer of goods in the U.S. government. But unless the industrial and manufacturing base that develops and builds those goods modernizes and adjusts to the world's new geopolitical and economic realities, America will face a growing and likely permanent national security deficit. Our offices, the Under Secretary of Defense for Acquisition & Sustainment and the Office of Industrial Policy, have the primary responsibility for assessing this challenge, and are the authors of the 2020 Industrial Capabilities Report.

America's defense industrial base was once the wonder of the free world, constituting a so-called "military-industrial complex" that, regardless of criticism, was the model for, and envy of, every other country – and the mainstay of peace and freedom for two generations after World War II. Today, however, that base faces problems that necessitate continued and accelerated national focus over the coming decade, and that cannot be solved by assuming that advanced technologies like autonomous systems and artificial intelligence (AI) and 5G and quantum will wave those challenges away, and magically preserve American leadership.

On the contrary, those advanced technologies themselves rely on a manufacturing complex whose capability and capacity will have to be trusted and secure to protect the Pentagon's most vital supply chains. These include microelectronics, space, cyber, nuclear, and hypersonics, as well as the more conventional technologies that make up our legacy defense equipment.

What will be required is a defense industrial strategy based on a four-part program to:

1. Reshore our defense industrial base and supply chains to the United States and to allies, starting with microelectronics, and restore our shipbuilding base.

2. Build a modern manufacturing and engineering workforce and research and development (R&D) base.

3. Continue to modernize the defense acquisition process to fit 21st century realities.

4. Find new ways to partner private sector innovation with public sector resources and demand.

All these steps will be necessary to create a robust, resilient, secure, and innovative industrial base. As the National Security Strategy noted, a "healthy defense industrial base is a critical element of U.S. power."[1] The defense industrial base is the key to preserving and extending U.S. competitive military dominance in the coming century and, with it, deterrence that will keep Americans safe and keep the peace. Realizing a defense industrial strategy will require a substantial commitment of capital investment and resources, as well as continuing and extending the reforms to the Defense Department's industrial base that have been underway in the past several years.

*****

The issues confronting our defense industrial base can be viewed in the context of four major evolutions stretching over more than a half-century, each of which requires us to accelerate change and reform.

The first has been the steady deindustrialization of the United States over the past five decades, including workforce and manufacturing innovation. From 40 percent of the U.S. gross domestic product (GDP) in the 1960s, manufacturing has shrunk to less than 12 percent today, while shedding more than five million manufacturing jobs from 2000 to 2015 alone. Just fifty years ago, manufacturing industries employed 36 percent of male workers. Today, manufacturing employs fewer than 11 percent of all workers.[2]

While total manufacturing output has grown during this period, thanks in part to labor-saving technologies, the workforce on which a defense

industrial renaissance would depend has become, in effect, an endangered species.

Together, a U.S. business climate that has favored short-term shareholder earnings (versus long-term capital investment), deindustrialization, and an abstract, radical vision of "free trade," without fair trade enforcement, have severely damaged America's ability to arm itself today and in the future. Our national responses – off-shoring and out-sourcing – have been inadequate and ultimately self-defeating, especially with respect to the defense industrial base.

Manufacturing Employment (Millions of Workers)

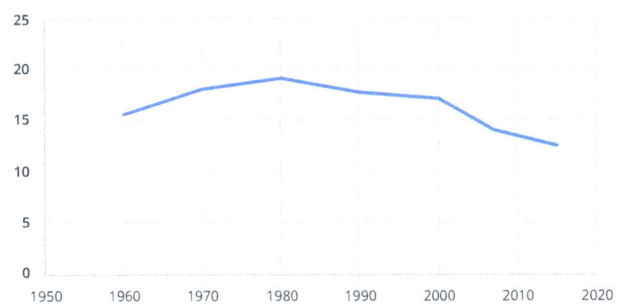

Net Output ($100 billions, 2009 dollars)

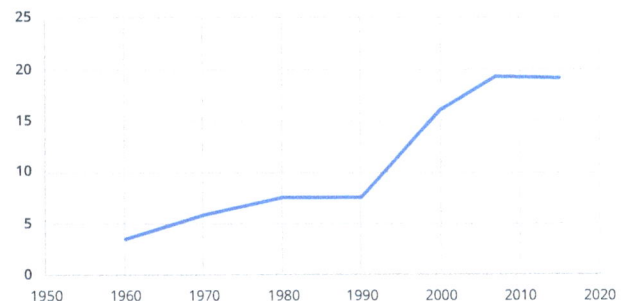

Manufacturing's Share of Total Employment

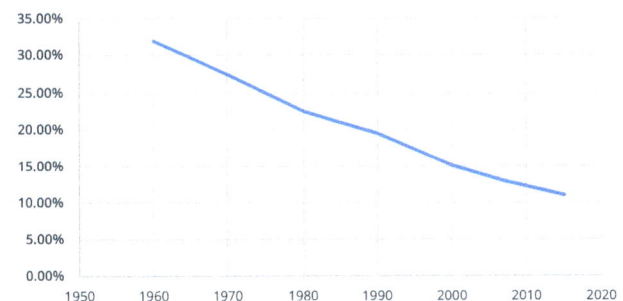

These trends have had particular impact on the core element of a successful manufacturing economy: the machine tool industry. Of the world's top twenty-one machine-tool makers, only two today are American: Gleason and Haas Automation. By contrast, eight are based in Japan, and six in Germany. And while its domestic machine tool sector remains nascent, China has emerged as a major machine tool customer. Machine tools laid the groundwork for the mobilization miracle of World War II, a fact understood by friends and foes alike, while America has allowed its machine tool sector to turn from a national asset into a national security vulnerability.

The second development was the end of the Cold War, which was seen by many to render obsolete the assumptions and requirements that drove a legacy defense industrial base aimed at defeating a peer competitor, the Soviet Union, i.e., producing weapons that would counteract the Soviet advantage in quantity in conventional arms. This included building a massive nuclear arsenal, and later innovations such as stealth, precision guided munitions, and the multiple independent re-entry vehicle (MIRV).

The collapse of the Soviet Union and the end of Cold War tensions and priorities should have brought an intense rethinking of the Department of Defense's needs, including fundamental changes to the structure of its industrial base. One change that did take place was the drastic consolidation of the largest defense contractors from fifteen to five, which, among other things, reduced competition for contracts, formerly a key driver behind controlling costs and spurring innovation.[3]

The War on Terrorism, with its focus on disrupting terrorist cells and havens, and counterinsurgency and stability operations delayed by a crucial decade and a half the adjustment to new geopolitical and military realities, including the steady rise of an aggressive and militant China, and an unreconciled Russia.

The third evolution has been the advent of high-tech and advanced digital technology, from personal computers, cell phones, and solid-state sensors to the internet and 5G wireless technology along with AI and quantum computing. These technologies are and will continue to be the driving forces of the U.S. and global economy, and will also determine the military balance of the future – while at the same time opening up critical security threats in peacetime, through cyber and intellectual property theft and information warfare, not to mention future scenarios involving quantum computer attacks on critical civilian and defense infrastructure.

Moreover, these technologies pose new problems for defense contractors and for the Pentagon in securing a trusted supply chain for critical items such as processed rare earth elements and microelectronics, where gaps and unanticipated interruptions can be triggered by the loss of a sole supplier for purely economic reasons, or by an embargo or military action by an adversary. Events of either type can jeopardize a sustainable industrial base.

Pentagon leaders recognized that this technological revolution would require a major shift in the military's basic requirements for warfighting, but also would demand building relations with an industrial base very different from the one that had supplied its equipment needs for decades, i.e., with newer companies such as Google, Oracle, and many other Silicon Valley firms. To facilitate this shift, the Department of Defense launched the Third Offset strategy, using, in the words of one thoughtful DoD official, "combinations of technology, operational concepts, and organizational constructs—different ways of organizing our forces, to maintain our ability to project combat power into any area at the time and place of our own choosing."[4]

However, the Pentagon's Third Offset did not evolve into a robust strategic doctrine. Meanwhile, the military services took an understandable and narrower approach, generally pursuing advanced technologies to fit their individual operational needs. This meant that the opportunity for a more extensive systematic rethinking and reordering of DoD's industrial base was missed or at a minimum delayed. Today's overseers of the defense industrial base have been busy making up for lost ground, as the Industrial Capabilities Report demonstrates.

The fourth evolution has been the rise of The People's Republic of China (PRC) as a dual threat, both military (the Chinese Navy is now the largest in the world with 350 vessels) and economic, which threatens critical supply chains, and also challenges our export control, foreign investment, and technology transfer policies.

China's spectacular rise as the world's second-largest economy is well known, with GDP growing at an average annual rate of 9.45 percent since 1978, and China is now poised to become the world's biggest economy by 2040. The rise of China's military spending has also been widely reported, with a nearly twenty-five-fold increase over the past two decades, jumping from over $10 billion in 1999, to over $250 billion in 2019. China currently spends more on defense than do

Japan, South Korea, the Philippines, and Vietnam combined, and is second only to the United States in its military budget. China's lower costs may mean that its defense spending has purchasing parity with ours.

China's defense spending is augmented by its policy of "military-civil fusion," which erases barriers between civilian and military sectors to ensure the latest technologies like AI and quantum computing are quickly integrated into security capabilities.

Though the exact amount of China's defense spending is opaque for the most part, the NATO definition of China's military expenditures captures the activities normally associated with defense spending and provides a reasonable benchmark. While China's defense budget is smaller than the U.S. defense budget, it is the vectors of that spending that are most alarming.

One is naval construction. The buildup of China's navy, including aircraft carriers, has been one of the most remarkable and strategically disruptive global defense spending trends in the past two

China's Defense Spending 1999-2018

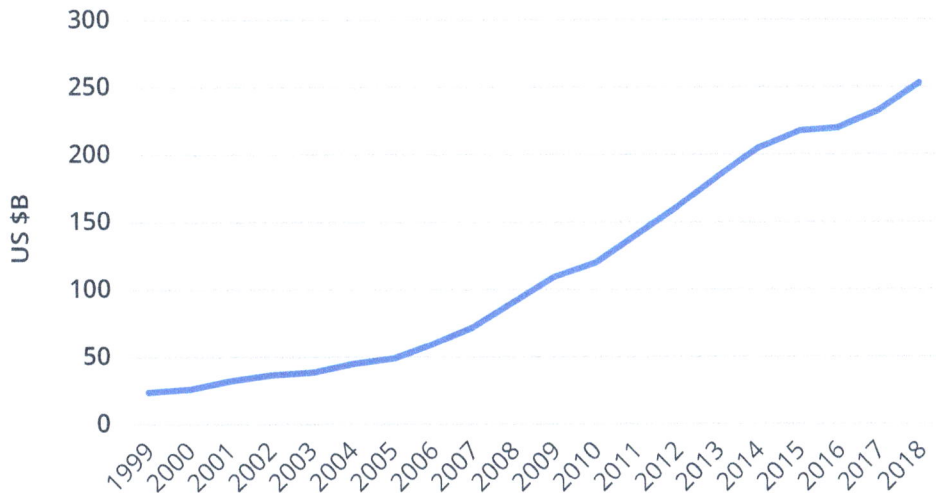

Data Source: World Bank
https://www.macrotrends.net/countries/CHN/china/military-spending-defense-budget

decades. By commissioning fourteen warships a year, Beijing has made clear that it intends to be a world-class maritime power in addition to having the world's largest military on land. While China's naval buildup has been able to piggyback on its rapidly expanding commercial shipbuilding industry, U.S. shipbuilding, by contrast, has become a key vulnerability in the U.S. defense manufacturing base, as we will see.

Two other critical components in China's growing military power have been a huge expansion in its ballistic and anti-ship missile inventory and its nuclear weapons arsenal. Its missile arsenal contains advanced capabilities such as maneuverable anti-ship ballistic missiles, MIRVs, and experimental hypersonic glide vehicles, all designed to target American aircraft carriers and forward air bases – the mainstays of U.S. military power projection in the Indo-Pacific region. In addition to the obvious cost in lives, replacing carriers or other ships, or repairing damaged vessels, would severely challenge the most robust shipbuilding base. Attempting to repair or replace forward bases in mid-conflict would be an even more complex challenge.

Nor should we ignore Beijing's on-going activities as the world's most egregious cyber threat and intellectual property (IP) thief. America loses nearly $450 billion on an annual basis to cyber hacking, which originates overwhelmingly from China. This behavior already has severely damaged the Department of Defense and its prime contractors, from stolen plans for major weapons systems such as the F-35, to identity theft from America's defense and security workforce.

The Department of Defense cannot, of course, reverse these global developments by itself. However, it is devising an industrial strategy that responds to this highly disruptive and rapidly changing environment, and is leading the way to turn these changes to America's advantage.

How will the Department accomplish this? By focusing that strategy on the four key categories outlined in the Industrial Capabilities Report: assessment, investment, protection, and promotion of our defense industrial base, both today and in the future.

****

Assessment. In September 2018, the Department of Defense released *Assessing and Strengthening the Manufacturing and Defense Industrial Base and Supply Chain Resiliency of the United States*, a report in fulfillment of Executive Order 13806. The "13806 report" isolated "five inter-related, but conceptually distinct, macro forces" affecting the U.S. industrial base. These included:

- The decline of the U.S. manufacturing base.
- Budget caps, sequestration, and inconsistent U.S. budgets that sharply reduced resources for the military across the board, particularly investment in the industrial base.
- "Deleterious U.S. government business and procurement practices," including contracting regulations and constant program changes that drive up cost without necessarily adding effectiveness.
- Industrial policies of nations such as China that provide an unfair comparative economic advantage and predatory trade policies that "degrade the viability, capabilities, and capacity of the U.S. national security innovation base."
- Diminishing U.S. science, technology, engineering, and mathematics (STEM) education and industrial jobs, both of which have a deleterious effect on the industrial base's ability to sustain itself and to innovate.

As a result, the study found examples by the dozens where "the vitality and resiliency of the industrial base" had been acutely affected, from aircraft design and cybersecurity to machine tools and materials.

Since then, the President and his Secretaries of Defense have taken significant steps to ameliorate vulnerabilities in the industrial base's critical sectors, as described in this report. But the number of cases, typically three to seven levels from the top of the supply chain, where there is just one – often fragile – supplier is staggering. This represents a significant deterioration from just a decade ago when three-to-five suppliers existed for the same component, let alone several decades ago, when the U.S. military generally enjoyed dozens of suppliers for each such item.

Many U.S. small and mid-size businesses exited the defense field over the last three decades not only because of reduced demand (we build a lot fewer platforms than we once did), but because doing business with the government proved too difficult, with margins too low. Rules that were designed to give good value to taxpayers did not necessarily provide good returns for these firms, often family-owned. They chose instead to employ their entrepreneurial talents and financial resources in the commercial market.

The 13806 report also identified sixteen key industrial sectors, whose risks and vulnerabilities are assessed in more detail below. The core of the department's industrial base includes government-owned government-operated (GOGO) and government-owned contractor operated (GOCO) shipyards, depots, arsenals, and ammunition plants. These have been at critical risk for many years thanks to the macro factors identified earlier: the decline of manufacturing and STEM education, the need to rely on single suppliers for many critical components, and a serious erosion of America's manufacturing workforce.

The National Security Strategy defines the National Security Innovation Base as the "American network of knowledge, capabilities, and people—including academia, National Laboratories, and the private sector—that turns ideas into innovations, transforms discoveries into successful commercial products and companies, and protects and enhances the American way of life." The strategy continues, the "genius of creative Americans, and the free system that enables them, is critical to American security and prosperity."[5] We would add, and to the future of our defense industrial resources and the ability of our military to arm itself effectively today and in the future.

Therefore, we have identified three steps to connect the defense industrial base to that U.S. national innovation base.

First is integrating new manufacturing technologies and processes, where a series of DoD programs across the military departments and Office of the Secretary of Defense are useful, indeed critical.

The second is a Department of Defense-wide focus on supporting an industrial base for peer conflict. After a decade and a half of equipping the military for operations in Iraq, Afghanistan, and elsewhere, and as directed by the National Defense Strategy, the Pentagon is recalibrating to face the challenges posed by China and Russia. While the Services never stopped planning and procuring for high-end combat, the threats posed by adversaries require increased investment and focus on the most advanced capabilities, and on the industrial base to support them.

The third and arguably most difficult is confronting difficult but necessary investment choices, including expanded funding for capital investment in facilities and training and maintaining the workforce. Without that serious and targeted investment – billions instead of millions – America's defense industrial base is simply unsustainable, let alone capable of supporting our deployed forces and legacy equipment while solving the complex warfighting challenges posed by advanced technologies in the 21st century, from AI and cyber to hypersonics and autonomous air and sea systems.

The Office of the Under Secretary for Acquisition & Sustainment works with the Military Departments to produce the analysis to drive actions to solve these problems. The Industrial Base Council (IBC) is the "executive-level forum established to ensure industrial base readiness and resilience" at the three- and four-star level. The Office of Industrial Policy and the Defense Contract Management Agency chair the IBC's Joint Industrial Base Working Group, which oversees the flow of information concerning the critical industry sectors identified under E.O. 13806 and emerging technology domains.

The Office of Industrial Policy assessed America's shipbuilding woes, both defense and commercial, which began more than five decades ago. Fourteen defense-related new ship-construction yards have shuttered, and three have exited the defense industry. Only one new-ship-construction yard has opened. Today, the Navy contracts primarily with seven private new-construction shipyards, owned by four prime contractors, to build its future Battle Force, representing significantly less capacity than the leading shipbuilding nations.

The Future Naval Force Study (FNFS), developed by the Department of Defense to ensure American naval supremacy, sets forth a multi-year program divided into five-year increments with careful attention to meeting base budgetary limitations to achieve the goal of a 355-ship navy. Yet that plan has to rely on a maritime industry, both naval and commercial, that has significantly less capacity than the world's other leading shipbuilding nations – South Korea, Japan, and, ominously, China.

So while today, the United States Navy's Battle Force consists of 297 ships, China has managed to build the world's biggest navy with 350 vessels. China's shipbuilders also enjoy the advantage of being part of the world's biggest national steel producer and user. The United States meanwhile is fourth, after China, India, and Japan.

How do we fill the shipbuilding gap? Start by building more ships. Not only will that expand the fleet, it will drive the analysis and decisions required to ensure a shipbuilding base that can produce and sustain an expanded Navy. That our shipbuilders delivered in 2020 no fewer than ten

ships (two Virginia-class submarines, one America-class amphibious assault ship, three littoral combat ships, two Spearhead-class expeditionary fast transports, one Arleigh Burke-class destroyer, and one Lewis B Puller-class expeditionary sea base) is a remarkable achievement. It is a harbinger of what can be done with even a modest expansion of that capacity.

Alexis de Tocqueville noted in 1832 that Americans "are born to rule the seas…." In the final analysis, reaching our nation's minimum naval goals will demand substantial investment in refurbishing old yards and establishing new ones, and partnering more with trusted allies who want to invest in the U.S. shipbuilding base. More broadly, a renewed commitment to reinforcing America's place as the world's leading maritime nation will, as it always has, lead to jobs, workers with skills that will be useful to a variety of other domains such as electric transportation, and next-generation energy storage and batteries that loom large in America's future.

Another area of concern, but also an example of recent progress, is software engineering. Software acquisition remains one of the most expensive and most complex sectors in the DoD. For example, the F-35 Joint Strike Fighter has required more than eight million lines of code, almost all of which had to be written by its prime contractor and sub-contractors, virtually from scratch and, then again, after Chinese cyber-theft. All software "blocks" – the systems designed to take the plane from testing to full production – experienced serious production and budgetary delays. These, in turn, contributed to expanding the Lightning II's total price tag.

One could argue that today's defense systems are no more or less than physical platforms for software, yet developing and buying that software had become a major bottleneck.

Standard Pentagon programming was not designed to deal with software, so crucial to operating systems large and small, including networked warfare. The Department of Defense has traditionally acquired IT and software-based systems in the way it bought aircraft carriers – as if they were physical items to be forged or welded or mass-produced. The standard acquisition cycle has been geared around multiyear milestones and intensive evaluation reviews that can take months or years. The modern software development cycle, by contrast, moves in weeks, days, and even hours and seconds – because software is a digital item, subject to real-time improvement and innovation, whose only limits are the human imagination and the speed of an electron. To take one example, given the unique iterative dynamic of software development, the Pentagon's traditional serial approach to "the color of money" – different budget accounts for development, production, and sustainment – was a major obstacle.

The Department of Defense Innovation Board and Defense Science Board dug into this problem and other challenges with software development and acquisition. Based on their findings, we issued in October 2020 a ground-breaking new direction: the Software Acquisition Pathway. We have been working with the Congress and the Services to pilot the creation of "software colored money" as an imperative.

Fixing software acquisition was part of a larger process of changing another key vulnerability, namely, how an outdated and sclerotic acquisition system, layered since the 1960s, has hampered the industrial sector.

Ultimately, the most important asset our defense industrial base possesses isn't machines or facilities, but people. America needs an ambitious effort, like the Eisenhower National Defense Education Act, to support education and training for manufacturing skills required to meet DoD and wider U.S. requirements. As the Industrial Capabilities Report notes, while China has four times the U.S. population, it has eight times as many STEM grads, while Russia has almost four times more engineers than the United States. We have lost ground also in many equally important touch labor industrial skills sets.

A skilled workforce is especially critical in a defense-focused industrial strategy, which requires innovative and bold solutions and production and integration of extremely complex systems. Here the OSD Industrial Base Analysis & Sustainment (IBAS) capability plays a crucial role. It is finding ways to close the gap, including programs for training and incentivizing a new manufacturing workforce. It is preparing the way for new affordable manufacturing of defense systems, and reducing the risk of over-extended supply chains and chronically low inventories.

Unfortunately, the budget allotted for IBAS, which has ranged from $10-104 million, is empirically inadequate for the job to be done. A budget of $1 billion would enable the program to expand, by a vast number, employment in the U.S. production sectors. The current mismatch between mission and means hampers the ability to focus solutions on the right problems across industrial sectors, and grow large numbers of highly-skilled, well-paying American jobs.

This issue is one that should be confronted more broadly, under the headings of:

1. Investment. The mismatch between what must be spent to support key programs and initiatives and the resources available must be addressed to avoid a series of catastrophic vulnerabilities in critical sectors of the defense industrial base. Fortunately, there are new paradigms available for public-private partnering to accomplish these ends, including creating a flexible manufacturing workforce that would be available for rapid mobilization of the defense industrial base in the event of a major conflict. Many of these are outlined in this report. We will take time here to point out two of them.

The first is in the critical area of semiconductors and microelectronics. Microelectronics are critical to producing and maintaining existing military systems, for advancing emerging technologies like AI, 5G, and quantum computing, and for sustaining critical infrastructure and indeed, our entire modern economy. Microelectronics are in nearly everything, including the most complex weapons the Department of Defense buys, such as Aegis warships, the F-35 joint strike fighter, soldier systems, and our nuclear weapons and their command-and-control – which together form the backbone of our national defense.

Thirty years ago, more than one-third of all microchips produced worldwide came out of the American companies that gave Silicon Valley its name (silicon being the key ingredient in manufacturing microchips containing millions of microscopic transistors). Today that number has slipped to only 12 percent, with most production in Asia. China is projected to dominate global semiconductor production by 2030, and in the meantime, current suppliers in Taiwan, South Korea, Malaysia, and elsewhere are in easy range of Chinese missiles, subversion, or air or maritime interference.

Thus in addition to its growing dominance in the area of production, Beijing is already in a position, through its geographic and political position, to threaten virtually our entire supply chain through theft, corruption of microelectronic products, disruption of supply, coercion, and other measures even short of military action. This leaves American deterrence and critical warfighting capabilities at the mercy of our main strategic competitor.

The Boston Consulting Group and the Semiconductor Industry Association recently issued a report calling for public-private funding of up to nineteen new semiconductor manufacturing facilities (or fabs) in the continental United States over the next decade.[6] The report estimates that this will require at least a $50 billion federal investment in addition to industry's share. However, it also forecast that initiative will create more than 70,000 high-paying jobs, and would position the United States to capture a quarter of the world's growing chip production.

The cost of a new fab today is roughly $10-30 billion, which is far more capital investment than even America's biggest semiconductor companies

can afford if they are to produce chips that are price-competitive – that is, that Americans and other customers will buy. Chip manufacturing equipment is hugely expensive and has to be replaced with each new wave of innovation.

Outside of the United States, foreign governments and their citizens pay the lion's share, one way or another, of the cost of building the fab. The companies do not. They take on the other massive set of costs: running the fab. The hard truth is that if the United States does not start doing the same, our nation will continue to see its historically low share of chip production continue to decline to irrelevance. We will have few new fabs. We will have fewer semiconductor production jobs. We will have frightening vulnerability to foreign cut-offs whose impact would make our COVID-related shortages look miniscule.

A recent success story is the recent ribbon-cutting for the new Skywater Technology Foundry in Bloomington, Minnesota – the first new semiconductor fab to open in the United States in a generation. A combination of Defense Department investment in facilities and research and development and private equity capital to streamline operations is producing integrated circuits for the automotive, computing and cloud, consumer, industrial, and medical sectors, and radiation-hardened microelectronics that are vital for the military's use of outer-space.

Congress's recent bipartisan passage of the landmark semiconductors legislation opens vistas for future creative pooling of federal and private capital to fund fabs in the United States. A cost-effective and hugely successful model worthy of intense American study is the Taiwanese approach, which catapulted the island in just several decades into the leading producer of microelectronics in the world.

Hypersonics development and nuclear weapons sustainment are other areas quickly approaching a tipping point in terms of investment. Facilities – including unique production equipment and in many cases the necessary workforce – require reconstitution, major modernization, and increases in capacity. Test ranges and instrumentation need significant capacity increases and modernization. Investment in both industry and Defense Department facilities is necessary to achieve the required capability and capacity.

Finally, it is also worthwhile to take a hard look at the overall research and development (R&D) picture. The United States continues to lead the world in gross domestic spending on R&D in 2019, although China is rapidly and consistently closing the gap. Nonetheless, aerospace and defense companies are among the lowest R&D spenders compared to other critical sectors. America's six biggest defense contractors have spent on average 2.5 percent of their sales on R&D each year. This compares to 10 percent of sales for "big tech" firms like Facebook, Amazon, and Google. So, while defense companies' R&D spending has increased from 2014 to 2019, and while aerospace firms in general spend more than pure defense firms, R&D spending per firm would have to increase by 50-60 percent to keep pace with other domestic technology leaders. It remains for lawmakers and the Department to find ways to incentivize internal research and development (IRAD) so that our leading defense companies expand their engines of innovation and technological breakthroughs.

The bottom line is: if we are going to secure the future versus China, then far more investment is going to be required both by Federal authorities and the private sector. That includes funding to ensure that research, development, and resulting products are safe and secure from adversary influence and manipulation.

2. Protection. One of the most important developments in the past four years has been how the White House, the Defense and other Cabinet departments, and Congress have worked together to limit adversarial foreign investment into and technology transfer out of our defense industrial base – especially from and to China.

A landmark achievement was the bipartisan passage of the Cornyn-Feinstein sponsored Foreign Investment Risk Review Modernization Act (FIRRMA), which President Trump welcomed and executed with vigor. It updated the interagency Committee on Foreign Investment in the United States (CFIUS) to further restrict investment by adversaries, including China, in U.S. companies and the economy. New rules were also put in place to limit allies' reliance on Chinese technology and industry when purchasing American defense-related goods.

The DoD Directorate for Foreign Investment Review is marshalling the information and insight of more than thirty Department of Defense components to contribute to the effort by U.S. national security and financial authorities to halt dangerous Chinese acquisition of hard-earned American economic crown jewels and the private personal data of ordinary Americans.

Foreign investment is welcome, especially from allies and friends. That is why the Pentagon has encouraged participation in the National Technology and Industrial Base (NTIB) by allies such the U.K., Australia, and Canada, and why steps should be considered to expand our base of trusted partners, when they are willing to take the steps necessary to strengthen their foreign investment screening and defense industrial security rules.

Of course, and as evidenced by extensive reporting on Chinese and Russian cyberattacks, the same protections need to be implemented within the Department of Defense and its contractor base to protect our industrial assets from foreign cyberattacks and cyber theft. Preserving the U.S. overmatch in defense technology inside cyberspace is an explicit objective of the National Cyber Strategy, including ramping up offensive, defensive, and cybersecurity capabilities. The on-going effort to protect the industrial base also meshes with the recently established DoD Cybersecurity Maturity Model Certification (CMMC) program, with its five levels of new cybersecurity standards for all DoD contractors.

But there are also important vulnerabilities concerning major defense platforms that deserve to be addressed as part of progress on industrial base reform.

3. Promotion. The hard truth is, in a globalized economy, America cannot solve its defense industrial problems (or indeed many of our other industrial challenges) solely by itself. The days when our military could arm itself effectively by relying entirely on its domestic manufacturing base, as it did during World War II and the Cold War, are long gone. Instead, a long-term strategy of reshoring defense manufacturing must balance and mitigate the risks of relying on other countries as supply chain partners, in particular, countries that are allied or friendly with the United States but also have economic and/or technological ties to China, or are simply vulnerable to Chinese coercion, disruption, pressure or military action. Another side of the reshoring imperative is crafting an effective export policy for the U.S. and its allies that protects national security while not hampering innovation or key scientific advances – while also promoting the idea that the safest course always is having American companies manufacturing defense goods, right here in America.

With both these points in mind, we have been constantly looking for ways to draw in reliable international partners to become part of a trusted industrial base and supply chain. This effort might be dubbed "strategic reshoring," which includes expanding the reach of mechanisms like the NTIB and the U.S.-India Defense Technology & Trade Initiative (DTTI), as well as the new DoD Trusted Capital Program to facilitate capital investment into the industrial base from safe foreign and domestic sources.

The promotion of partnerships is not just limited to foreign partners. For example, the OSD Office of Small Business Programs has been expanding the opportunities for small and medium-sized firms across the fifty states to participate in creating a new reshored American industrial base.

It would also be a mistake to overlook how the Department of Defense can be a leader in promoting innovation in America's industrial and manufacturing base. Here a flagship program can emerge from the Manufacturing Technology program in the Office of the Secretary of Defense, whose nine institutes showcase how the Pentagon's own manufacturing techniques and innovations can lead not just its own industrial base but American industry as a whole.

Created in 1956, Manufacturing Technology is comprised of component investment programs operated out of the Office of the Secretary of Defense, Army, Navy, Air Force, Defense Logistics Agency, and Missile Defense Agency. Its nine manufacturing innovation institutes are public-private partnerships designed to overcome the challenges faced by manufacturing innovators in various technology areas, from light manufacturing to composite materials and biotechnology. To date, the DoD has invested $1.2 billion in the Manufacturing Technology Institutes, with $1.93 billion in matching funds from industry, state governments, and academia. To become a truly global leader in manufacturing innovation, a two to three-fold increase in the innovation budget by the Congress is needed.

Finally, officials need to demonstrate how advancing and modernizing the defense industrial base is vital to keeping costs down and innovation up for present and future military readiness as the U.S. prepares its armed forces in the 21st century. This will be especially true of naval and maritime forces, where reviving U.S. shipyards and launching new initiatives for manufacturing advanced systems for sea control, such as unmanned and robotic systems, will be a hinge for strategic success. But the same applies to air and land defense assets, where making acquisition cost-effective as well as timely will depend on the strength and health of our defense industrial base.

In short, following through on promoting a strong and resilient industrial base can point the way to streamlining the Department of Defense's acquisition process and defense systems' life cycle, which not only saves money but makes our men and women in uniform safer and more effective – while securing our national security future.

****

In conclusion, our defense industrial base has reached an inflection point in its history regarding the balance between its vulnerabilities and its opportunities for modernization and reform. Some might say restoring our defense industrial and manufacturing base dominance will require nothing less than a miracle. The truth is, the United States and its military organizations have performed similar "miracles" before: the resolve to see that miracle through is deeply steeped in our history as a nation. Ambitious policies like these require an ability and willingness to make strategic decisions, for example, recognizing that what may have worked in the past is no longer working and will not work in the future. The consensus is growing, across political lines, on the need to reshore critical industries, create American jobs, and counter the challenges of China.

In fact, the requirement that the federal government guide and direct the Nation's industrial future, including its defense needs, is part and parcel of the American tradition. In his ground-breaking *Report on Manufactures* published in 1791, Secretary of the Treasury Alexander Hamilton urged Congress to promote what we would call America's industrial base so that the United States could be "independent on foreign nations for military and other essential supplies." In addition to protecting national independence, support for manufacturing incentives for emerging industries would level the playing field in the global markets of the day.

Virtually every U.S. president from Hamilton's day until the dawn of the twentieth century understood that sensible and targeted trade measures – anti-dumping fees, countervailing duties, and even modest tariffs to level an unfair playing field – formed the principal tool by which America fostered its industrial base. The 1990s saw an experiment in radical trade policies – dropping reciprocity – that made earlier presidents, such as FDR, Eisenhower, and JFK, all advocates of free trade, look, with their prudent tariffs, like protectionists.

The industrial base enabled our War and Navy Departments to execute the first of these defense production miracles during World War II when our military had to move from a virtual standing start (the U.S. Army ranked nineteenth in the world in 1939) to becoming the most powerful military and industrial base in the world in less than three years.

A similar pivot took place during the Eisenhower administration in the 1950s, when the Cold War forced the Department of Defense to re-engineer its concept of how to achieve victory over a conventionally-armed Soviet Union, with a bold shift of resources from World War II-era strategic doctrines to nuclear deterrence and ballistic missiles. This strategic rebalance resulted in a corresponding shift in America's defense industrial and scientific-technological base, the First Offset.

With the Second Offset in the 1970s and 1980s, the Department of Defense learned how to incorporate new technologies including GPS, networked computers, and stealth technology into a bold strategic vision and capabilities that made our warfighters more powerful and lethal, yet also safer and more secure. That transformation also led to a corresponding shift in supply chains, especially a new reliance on emerging commercial off-the-shelf technologies and companies as well as the traditional defense contractor base.

Later came the Third Offset as a way to integrate the latest advanced technologies, including cyber and autonomous systems and artificial intelligence, into a military that would have to be ready to deal with rising Russian and Chinese challenges. What we have learned in the past four years is that such an offset will not take place without conscious, difficult decisions and investments to repair and modernize our defense industrial base, including the need for a larger reshoring of American manufacturing as a whole.

Fortunately, as noted above, a broad consensus is emerging in our political leadership and the American public as a whole on the need both to reshore our manufacturing and to deal boldly with the global threat of China.

The reshoring imperative has received an additional impetus from the coronavirus pandemic, which demonstrated the hazards of relying on other, especially adversarial nations for critical materials and medical equipment. The U.S. Government successfully ramped up production of vital medical supplies, most notably vaccines, as well as ventilators, personal protection equipment (PPE's), and other products under Title III of the Defense Production Act and the Coronavirus Aid, Relief, & Economic Security (CARES) Act. This initiative relied on the World War II industrial mobilization model described in Arthur Herman's *Freedom's Forge: How American Business Produced Victory in World War II and James Lacey's The Washington War: FDR's Inner Circle and the Politics of Power That Won World War II.* The same model in Operation Warp Speed has produced coronavirus vaccines – in what can only be described as a medical research, development, and manufacturing miracle.

All these examples prove that federal resources and direction combined with the private sector's unique manufacturing and industrial ingenuity can respond to a national crisis, especially when the objectives are well-defined and funds effectively deployed. The Department of Defense, the President, and the Congress can – and must – join to reduce America's vulnerabilities, increase its security, and provide the resources for an industrial renaissance that will lift up the economic prospects and dignity of millions of ordinary Americans.

Today we see more clearly than ever what America must do to restore and sustain its vital defense industrial base. The elements for a comprehensive defense industrial strategy are all in place. Now must come the hard work of making that "robust, resilient, and innovative industrial base" a reality – for our women and men in uniform in the 21st century and for all Americans.

Ellen M. Lord, Under Secretary of Defense

Jeffrey (Jeb) Nadaner,
Deputy Assistant Secretary of Defense

SECTION 2

CONGRESSIONAL REQUIREMENT

CONGRESSIONAL REQUIREMENT

Section 2504 of title 10, U.S. Code requires the Secretary of Defense to submit an annual report to the Committee on Armed Services of the Senate and to the Committee on Armed Services of the House of Representatives by March of each year. The report is to include:

1. A description of the departmental guidance prepared pursuant to section 2506 of this title.

2. A description of the assessments prepared pursuant to section 2505 of this title and other analyses used in developing the budget submission of the Department of Defense (DoD) for the next fiscal year.

3. Based on the strategy required by section 2501 of this title and on the assessments prepared pursuant to Executive order or section 2505 of this title—

a. A map of the industrial base;

b. A prioritized list of gaps or vulnerabilities in the national technology and industrial base, including—

c. A description of mitigation strategies necessary to address such gaps or vulnerabilities;

   i. The identification of the Secretary concerned or the head of the Defense Agency responsible for addressing such gaps or vulnerabilities; and

   ii. A proposed timeline for action to address such gaps or vulnerabilities; and

   iii. Any other steps necessary to foster and safeguard the national technology and industrial base.

4. Identification of each program designed to sustain specific essential technological and industrial capabilities and processes of the national technology and industrial base.

This Industrial Capabilities Report for Fiscal Year (FY) 2020 satisfies the requirements pursuant to section 2504, title 10, U.S. Code. It does not respond to section 2504a, title 10, U.S. Code, which will be delivered as a separate report.

House Report 116-442, accompanying the FY2021 National Defense Authorization Act (NDAA), directs the Secretary of Defense to include a supply chain and vulnerability assessment for rare earth elements, tungsten, neodymium-iron-boron magnets, niobium, indium, gallium, germanium, and tin in the annual Industrial Capabilities Report, along with recommendations for stockpiling actions for those materials and any other relevant materials. The Department will satisfy this reporting requirement with the submission of the *Strategic and Critical Materials 2021 Report on Stockpile Requirements,* in accordance with 50 U.S.C. 98h–5.

SECTION 3

INTRODUCTION

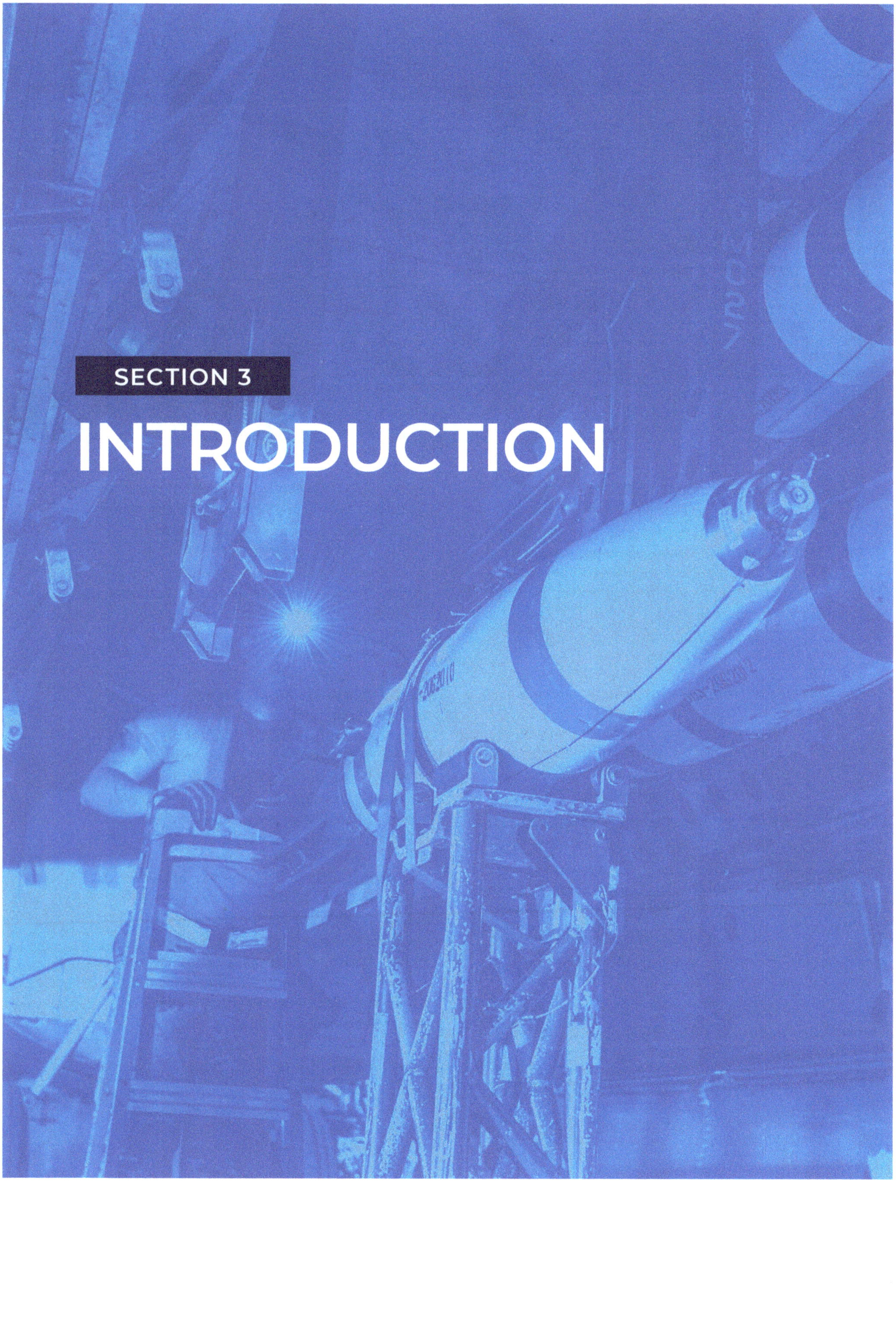

INTRODUCTION

By law, the Secretary of Defense must submit an annual report to the congressional armed services committees on the actions, investments, and assessments conducted in support of the U.S. defense industrial base (DIB). The FY 2020 Industrial Capabilities Report satisfies the requirements pursuant to title 10, U.S. Code., Section 2504, and provides context to the challenges facing the U.S. DIB.

This report includes the following components:

- A description of the Department's primary lines of effort (assess, invest, protect, and promote) to build resiliency in the DIB and implement the National Defense Strategy (NDS);
- A summary of the Department's response to the coronavirus pandemic and its impacts on the DIB;
- An overview of the U.S. defense industry and its outlook relative to the global defense market;
- Assessments of each of the 16 industrial base sectors, including priority gaps and vulnerabilities, and FY2020 developments;
- Assessments of emerging technology sectors;
- Overviews of the primary DIB authorities and investment mechanisms; and

- An appendix including a map of U.S. industrial base COVID-related 'hotspots' and summaries of the industrial capabilities studies and assessments completed in FY2020. This appendix contains controlled unclassified information (CUI) and will not be included in the public report.

The Office of Industrial Policy within the Office of the Under Secretary of Defense for Acquisition and Sustainment (OUSD(A&S)) is tasked with compiling this report. However, there is an extensive list of stakeholders across the Office of the Secretary of Defense (OSD), Military Departments, and other federal agencies, whose assessments and knowledge provide critical contributions to the Industrial Capabilities Report and the ongoing work of building resilience in the DIB.

The coronavirus pandemic created new risks within the industrial base, and exacerbated existing vulnerabilities. The Department's response to coronavirus pandemic drove industrial base actions and investments in FY2020. Collectively, U.S. government and industry stakeholders strove to navigate the challenges brought about by the pandemic, and continue to ensure a robust, secure, resilient, and innovative industrial base. The Office of Industrial Policy will continue to champion the DIB and implement the NDS through four primary lines of effort: assess, invest, protect, and promote.

Assess

The first step in ensuring a robust, secure, resilient, and innovative industrial base is understanding its components and current and future requirements, as well as constantly evolving threats, vulnerabilities, and opportunities. U.S. government and industry stakeholders contribute to detailed industrial sector summaries, fragility and criticality assessments, and capacity analyses, to inform the Department's budgetary, programmatic, and legislative policies in support of a strong and resilient industrial base.

Industrial Policy, Assessments
Subject matter experts within Industrial Policy's Assessments Team coordinate with program offices and other OSD and industry partners to identify, mitigate, and monitor risks, issues, and vulnerabilities across the industrial base.

Emerging Technology Assessments
The Technology, Manufacturing, and Industrial Base (TMIB) Office acts as Industrial Policy's counterpart within the Office of the Under Secretary of Defense for Research and Engineering (OUSD(R&E)). The Emerging Technology Assessments team is responsible for translating technology requirements into manufacturing and industrial base requirements. The results of these assessments are used to create technology and industrial base protection and promotion strategies.

Industrial Policy continues to identify and assess risks based on the sectors and risk frameworks developed in the Executive Order (EO) 13806 report, "Assessing and Strengthening the Manufacturing and Defense Industrial Base and Supply Chain Resiliency of the United States".

As part of the interagency response to EO 13806, the Department identified 16 industrial base sectors which continue to serve as a framework for identifying and assessing industrial base risk. Sector leads support various interagency working groups (WGs) and track specific (though frequently overlapping) gaps and vulnerabilities within the sector. These working groups are organized based on DIB sectors and emerging technologies, or are further broken down into program or issue-specific working groups and integrated product teams (IPTs).

The Joint Industrial Base Working Group (JIBWG), chaired by the OUSD (IP) and the Defense Contract Management Agency (DCMA), serves as a central hub for U.S. government stakeholders to share information, identify and prioritize risks, and accelerate the implementation of risk mitigation strategies. Dozens of offices and working groups focused on specific sectors programs, and risks, feed into the JIBWG to ensure thorough representation of DIB equities.

Invest

The *Invest* line of effort supports the Department to leverage investment opportunities to address risks, priority gaps, and vulnerabilities across the DIB. The DoD plans for sustainment activities as part of the annual budgeting process. However, business closures, changing requirements, obsolescence, and other issues can result in unforeseen funding requirements.

The following authorities and investment mechanisms enable the Department to target investments toward DIB gaps and vulnerabilities, and bring attention to funding requirements that are not addressed through traditional appropriations.

The Industrial Base Analysis & Sustainment (IBAS) Program
The IBAS Program advances and sustains traditional defense manufacturing sectors, plans for next generation and emerging manufacturing and technology sectors, and leverages global manufacturing innovation.

Defense Production Act (DPA) Title III

The Title III Program leverages authorities provided under the DPA to "create, maintain, protect, expand, or restore domestic industrial base capabilities essential to national defense."[7] The program plays a leading role in strengthening the health and resilience of domestic supply chains of strategic importance. This role includes supporting the national response to the coronavirus pandemic and addressing supply chain risks identified in the EO 13806 report, such as microelectronics and the rare earths supply chain.

To support national security requirements, DPA Title III actions stimulate private investment for critical components, technology items, materials, and industrial resources. Additionally, on May 14, 2020, EO 13922 delegated authority under section 302 of the DPA to the U.S. International Development Finance Corporation (DFC) to make loans supporting the national response and recovery from the coronavirus pandemic or the resiliency of any relevant domestic supply chains. On June 22, 2020, Under Secretary of Defense Ellen Lord and DFC Chief Executive Officer Adam S. Boehler signed a Memorandum of Agreement (MOA) to implement EO 13922.

The Manufacturing Technology (ManTech) Program

The ManTech Program and National Manufacturing Innovation Institutes (MII) are designed to help anticipate and close gaps in manufacturing capabilities for affordable, timely, and low-risk development, production, and sustainment of defense systems.

The Warstopper Program

The Defense Logistics Agency's (DLA) Warstopper Program is the Department's primary industrial readiness program for consumable items in sustainment. The program is designed to incentivize industry to meet consumable sustainment requirements for which business would otherwise not support. The program had a proactive strategy for medical Personal Protective Equipment (PPE) items prior to the coronavirus pandemic; in 2014, the Warstopper Program made a significant readiness investment in N95 respirators, coordinated for 3M to rotate six million masks for DoD after the H1N1 virus. In the midst of the coronavirus pandemic, this strategy has proven to be a successful best practice, as DLA supported the production of ventilators, and worked with other federal organizations to mirror their strategy.

Protect

The *Protect* line of effort includes actions to protect the industrial base and to mitigate risks associated with counterfeit parts, supply chain security, cybersecurity, foreign dependence, predatory investment, industry consolidation, and a number of other factors that introduce risk to the DIB.

Foreign Investment Review

Within Industrial Policy, the *Protect* function is predominately carried out by the Office's Foreign Investment Review (FIR) team. FIR leads the Committee on Foreign Investment in the United States (CFIUS) reviews for DoD and acts as the principal advisor to the USD(A&S) on foreign investment in the U.S. This involves coordination across more than 30 DoD component organizations to identify, review, investigate, mitigate, and monitor foreign direct investment in the United States. FIR relies on DoD stakeholders for the technical expertise needed to analyze the threats, vulnerabilities, and consequences associated with foreign investment.

Predatory and adversarial investments can result in diminishing U.S. sources and expertise, and increasing foreign dependence and illegitimate technology transfer, thereby threatening U.S. military superiority. To address these risks, Congress passed the Foreign Investment Risk Review Modernization Act (FIRRMA), which updated the scope of CFIUS authority. Effective February 2020, FIRRMA provides the Committee with expanded authorities to review transactions related to critical technologies and infrastructure (including the DIB), sensitive personal data, real estate transactions, and joint ventures. A "non-notify" team, also part of FIR, is responsible for identifying transactions that were not voluntarily brought before the CFIUS process.

The statute also strengthens bilateral cooperation through "excepted foreign states", including the participating nations of the multilateral National Technology and Industrial Base (NTIB). Citizens from NTIB countries (Australia, Canada and the United Kingdom) do not need to file for minority investments or real estate transactions.

The Department also conducts Mergers & Acquisitions (M&A) activities, which review consolidations in the U.S. defense industrial base to assess related risks and impacts.

Technology Industrial Base Protection, Promotion, and Monitoring

Within TMIB, the Technology Industrial Base Protection, Promotion, and Monitoring team facilitates the creation of strategies to protect and promote the industrial base by mitigating risks and exploiting opportunities identified in *emergent technology assessments*. TMIB aims to establish balance between the protection of technology and promotion of the industrial base providing it. This balance aids the Department's advancement of critical and emergent technologies, while sustaining a healthy, resilient, and competitive industrial base.

Promote

To cultivate a robust, resilient, and innovative industrial base, the Department must maintain the current DIB and identify new participants and opportunities from domestic and international partners. As the lead for industry engagement for the USD(A&S), Industrial Policy facilitates dialogue and drives collaboration and communication between the DoD and global industrial bases. OUSD(IP) encourages increased international participation in the DIB, and facilitates government-to-government discussions on industrial policy with partners and allies.

Office of Small Business Programs (OSBP)

The OSBP promotes small business involvement in the DIB by maximizing prime and subcontracting opportunities that ensure our nation's small businesses remain responsive, resilient, secure, and diversified to directly support the DIB, the NDS, and a robust economy. For more information, see the Office of Small Business Programs section of this report.

International Outreach

OUSD (IP) and the Office of International Cooperation (IC) work closely with our international allies and partners to strengthen and diversify our DIB. Outreach efforts directly support the NDS, which aims to strengthen alliances and partnerships around the globe in support of our national security. OUSD (IP) routinely coordinates government-to-government dialogue with allies and partners on joint industrial base concerns and areas for potential collaboration. Two key areas of government-to-government outreach in FY2020 focused on enhancing key partnerships, including:

- The NTIB: OUSD (IP) efforts to seamlessly integrate the United States DIB with those of Australia, Canada, and the United Kingdom are ongoing. In FY2020, NTIB initiatives focused on maintaining the continuity of medical and defense supply chains.

- The United States-India Defense Technology and Trade Initiative (DTTI): In December 2019, Under Secretary Ellen Lord and Indian Secretary for Defense Production Subhash Chandra signed the DTTI Industry Collaboration Forum agreement to provide a mechanism for developing and sustaining an Indian-United States industry dialogue on defense technological and industrial cooperation.

Trusted Capital

The Trusted Capital program is an unfunded initiative that connects companies critical to the defense industrial base with vetted trusted capital providers. The Trusted Capital Marketplace is a forum to convene trusted sources of private capital with innovative domestic companies that have been previously down-selected by the military services and operate in emerging technology sectors critical to the U.S. defense industrial base. This serves to strengthen domestic manufacturing by increasing access to critical technology while simultaneously limiting foreign access. For more information, see the Trusted Capital Program section of this report.

SECTION 4

INDUSTRIAL BASE COUNCIL

INDUSTRIAL BASE COUNCIL

The Industrial Base Council (IBC) is an executive-level forum, composed of senior three- and four-star level leaders, established to ensure industrial base readiness and resilience across the DoD. The IBC works to assess industrial base risk, leverage DoD-wide mitigation efforts, and develop policy to address and prevent critical risks. The IBC was created with four main goals:

1. Provide an aggregated assessment to Congress on DIB risk

2. Prioritize / align industrial base (IB) efforts to DoD's Strategic priorities

3. Leverage the full authorities of the DoD to act decisively to mitigate DIB risks

4. Develop policy and inform planning, programming, budgeting, and execution (PPBE) processes to address DIB vulnerabilities

The IBC is informed by the working-level Joint Industrial Base Working Group (JIBWG), comprised of subject matter experts in each industrial base sector (Figure 4.1). Interagency working groups and task forces bring emerging industrial base

Industrial Base Council Construct

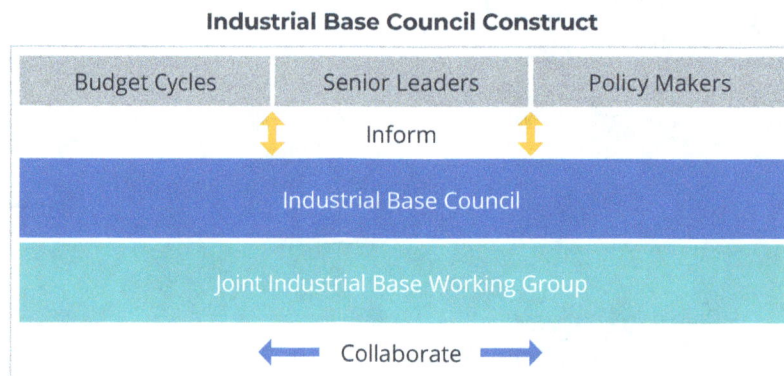

Figure 4.1

risks to the JIBWG for discussion and action. Risks and issues that require senior-level intervention are elevated to the IBC. The Council has leveraged the JIBWG's subject matter expertise and sector-based approach to mitigate and prevent systemic industrial base risk.

The IBC and COVID-19

To respond to the impact of the coronavirus pandemic on the U.S. industrial base and global defense supply chains, the IBC became a key decision-making body, working to manage DPA investments in response to the pandemic. In March 2020, the U.S. Congress passed the Coronavirus Aid, Relief, and Economic Security (CARES) Act, which appropriated $1 billion to the DPA Purchases account to prevent, prepare for, and respond to COVID-19. CARES Act funding decisions were all approved by the IBC after analysis and recommendation from the JIBWG.

SECTION 5

COVID-19 RESPONSE HIGHLIGHT

COVID-19 RESPONSE HIGHLIGHT

Introduction

The coronavirus pandemic poses a severe threat to essential industrial base capabilities, sources, and workforce skills. On March 2020, the President declared a national emergency and issued a series of Executive Orders covering nearly every DPA authority, including priority ratings and allocations (Title I), domestic production expansion and loans (Title III), and the formation of voluntary agreements among industry (Title VII).

In March 13, 2020, Congress appropriated $1 billion to the DPA Purchases account through the CARES Act; a two-fold increase from the combined total of the past decade. The program executed 46 awards in less than six months, compared to a historic program baseline of less than five new-start actions per year. The Department made a series of initial investments to improve supply chains and increase domestic production of health resources, such as N95 respirators and testing consumables.

The CARES Act also provided the Department of Health & Human Services (HHS) with authority and funding to increase domestic production of personal protective equipment (PPE) and other health resources. HHS focused its resources on healthcare investments, while the DoD allocated remaining Title III funds to mitigate COVID-19 impacts on the defense industrial base.

The DPA Title III program also provided critical support to HHS and the Department's Joint Acquisition Task Force (JATF) by right-sizing investments against COVID-19 requirements and overcoming obstacles to successful execution by the industrial base. The JATF and DLA also provided substantial assistance to HHS by increasing domestic production capacity and replenishing HHS's Strategic National Stockpile.

Spending Plans

In May 2020, the DPA Title III program submitted a spend plan for CARES Act investments to Congress and has provided subsequent weekly briefings on the plan's implementation. Of the $1 billion appropriated to the DPA Purchases account, the Department allocated approximately $676 million to defense industrial base risk mitigation, $213 million to healthcare sector investments, and $100 million to a Federal Credit Loan program in cooperation with the DFC.

The IBC reviewed subject matter input from across the Department and issued DIB investment decisions for Title III CARES Act funds. For healthcare investments, the Title III program forged partnerships with HHS and the Federal Emergency Management Agency (FEMA), quickly responding to both agencies' requests for assistance. As the Department's COVID-19 response activities became more complex, the Title III program also joined the JATF in supporting industrial base expansion and other interagency functions.

Although the Department did not issue any loans through the DFC loan program in FY2020, it expects to conclude several loan agreements in FY2021 and continue the program in FY2022.

Medical Industrial Base Case Study – Puritan Medical Product Company

Swabs are a key node in the logistics "chain" for COVID-19 testing, which stretches from swabs and PPE at the collection site to chemical reagents and test batteries at a laboratory facility.

In late April 2020, DoD entered into a $75.5 million (not-to-exceed) agreement with Puritan Medical Product Company ("Puritan") under DPA Title III. Pursuant to this agreement, Puritan will increase its aggregate production capacity for foam swabs by at least 20 million units per month, thereby doubling its production capacity.

With this award, Puritan Medical Products established a new swab manufacturing facility in Pittsfield, Maine, where it renovated 95,000 square feet of unused factory space and added more than 100 people to its workforce. Puritan realized initial production gains by June 2020, and exceeded production rate targets, established in their agreement with the Title III program, by the end of September 2020.

The U.S. government and Puritan accomplished this rapid production increase by coordinating supply chain activities on a nearly daily basis. Puritan, the Title III program, and the JATF engaged the Department of Commerce to apply priority ratings to industrial resources necessary for Puritan's production scale-up. When incumbent suppliers could not meet the need, DoD assisted Puritan with identifying alternative suppliers. The Title III program and the Department of State also assisted Puritan personnel and its subcontractors with overseas travel, so they could debug and accept automated production equipment.

Defense Industrial Base Case Study – eMagin Corporation

eMagin Corporation ("eMagin") is the leading domestic technology supplier of high brightness organic light emitting diode (OLED) microdisplays. eMagin's OLED microdisplays support DoD programs of record and ongoing requirements.

As the COVID-19 epidemic spread through the state of New York, eMagin and several of its suppliers were compelled to shut down operations for multiple weeks. The shutdown resulted in reductions in production and revenue, increases in the costs of goods sold, and cancellation of or delays in many of eMagin's customer opportunities into 2021.

DPA Title III investment at eMagin prevented the immediate loss of a critical DoD supplier, which would have been costly and difficult to reconstitute in a post-COVID-19 environment. eMagin will use DPA Title III funds to refurbish existing production equipment and purchase new equipment that will increase product yields, debottleneck production, and increase aggregate capacity.

This effort will enable the recipient to retain current staff put at risk by COVID-19 and will create 14 new jobs made up of engineers, maintenance technicians, and manufacturing personnel. It will also ensure the U.S. government maintains access to this critical domestic capability.

Defense Industrial Base Case Study – General Electric-Aviation

General Electric (GE) Aviation is one of two U.S. suppliers capable of producing large advanced combat engines. As part of the national response to the coronavirus pandemic, in support of the Propulsion defense industrial base, the DoD entered into a $20 million contract with GE Aviation to sustain critical industrial base capability for highly-specialized engineering resources.

GE Aviation will retain more than 100 highly-skilled and experienced design and mechanical engineers, preserving critical engineering skillsets and subject matter expertise. GE Aviation will accomplish this by expanding development in advanced manufacturing techniques (including additive manufacturing), promoting advanced material development, and improving digital engineering proficiencies. This will enable GE Aviation to retain critical workforce capabilities and sustain engineering positions put at risk by commercial aviation contraction during the pandemic.

DEFENSE INDUSTRY OUTLOOK

DEFENSE INDUSTRY OUTLOOK

Characteristics of the Market/Overview

The Aerospace and Defense (A&D) sector declined in performance compared to the previous year. The decline in performance is due, in large part, to a downturn in the commercial aircraft sector, preceded by the following events of early 2020:

- Boeing's 737 MAX, formerly the largest commercial aircraft program in the industry by value, was decertified after two fatal crashes, which led to a production halt in January 2020. The production freeze disrupted the production and deliveries of 737 MAX parts from the suppliers, dramatically reducing revenue and production throughout the industry. These events eventually resulted in liquidity issues among suppliers due to work stoppages and restricted cash flow. Over 100 suppliers for the 737 MAX also provide parts and services for the DoD.

- The coronavirus pandemic further aggravated supply chain issues in the aircraft sector. The sector experienced significant challenges in maintaining and sustaining the health of the DIB, as a large number of defense suppliers experienced facility shutdowns,

high absenteeism, furloughs, and financial instability. The decline in global air passenger traffic due to the coronavirus pandemic also threatens the viability of commercial airlines, aircraft manufacturers and their suppliers, and puts many jobs at stake.

The health of the aircraft defense industrial base will be inextricably linked to the recovery of the commercial aircraft industry, which could take three to five years to return to pre-COVID global passenger traffic. The U.S. A&D sector did not outperform the broader U.S. equity market in 2020, suggesting that investors are pessimistic about the overall health, profitability, and long-term prospects of the sector (Figure 6.1). The A&D sector averaged 2.2 percent of total Market Capitalization of the Dow Jones for the last six years.

The Big 6 Defense Suppliers

The largest six prime defense suppliers (Lockheed Martin, Boeing, Northrop Grumman, Raytheon, General Dynamics, and BAE Systems) are known collectively as the "Big Six" and represented 32 percent of all DoD prime obligations in 2019. They are also the largest companies globally by defense revenue. The Big Six thus provide a useful view with which to judge the overall health of the defense sector. The Big Six are financially healthy, continue to expand in market share, and have seen a general increase in revenue with a Market Capitalization Weighted Average Combined Annual Growth Rate (CAGR) of 5.6 percent from 2014-2019 (Figure 6.2).

Continued growth across the defense sector is further exemplified by the Market Capitalization Weighted Average of Revenue for the 25 Mid-Tier U.S. Defense Suppliers.[8] These 25 companies

are a combination of U.S. and Foreign based suppliers to the DoD, based on prime obligations, as well as inclusion on the Defense News Top 100 list for 2020. These 25 companies represented nine percent of all DoD prime obligations in 2019. Average revenues for these companies reached approximately a quarter of the Big Six average revenues each year and generally increased with a Market Capitalization Weighted Average CAGR of 5.9 percent from 2014-2019 (Figure 6.2).

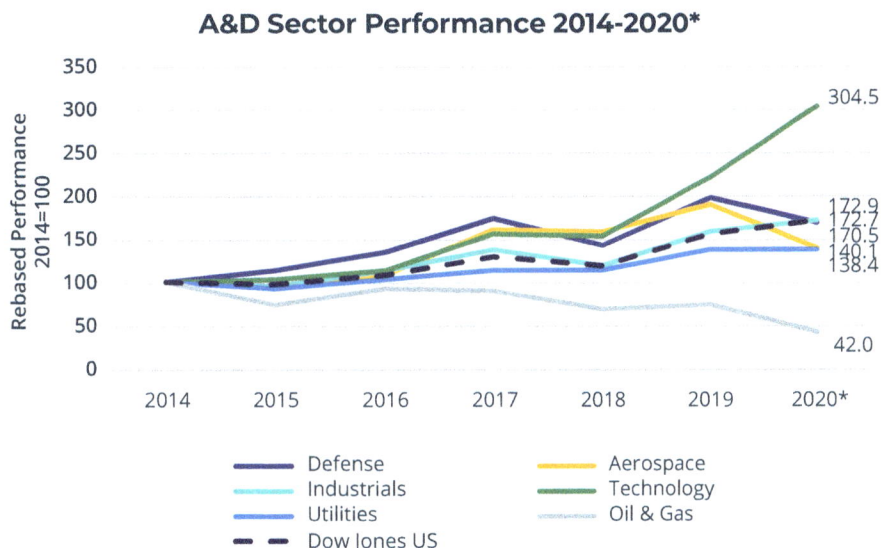

A&D Sector Performance 2014-2020*

Figure 6.1: Stock Performance Trend by Market Sector [CY2014-CY2020*] (2014 Rebase) *2020 Performance as of November 16th 2020. Source: Refinitiv Eikon

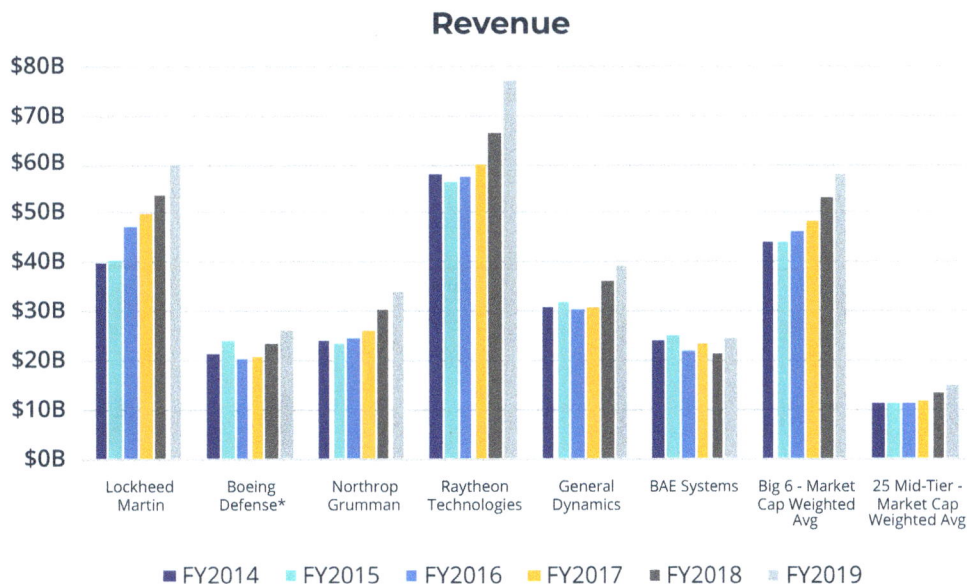

Revenue

Figure 6.2: Big 6 DoD Primes Annual Revenue & 25 Mid-Tier Market Cap Weighted Avg Revenue [FY2014-FY2019] Source: Refinitiv Eikon
*Only Revenue for Boeing Defense Business Segment Displayed. The large increase in Raytheon revenues compared to prior years' reports is due to the merger between Raytheon and UTC. Historic revenues were compiled for the entities taking into account any divestitures by Refinitiv Eikon.

The Big Six are also profitable, showing positive Earnings Before Interest, Tax, Depreciation, and Amortization (EBITDA), though margins have varied by company over the last five years (Figure 6.3). Major defense suppliers saw, on average, a growing demand for their products and services within the last year, driving higher sales and greater scale and helping to reduce costs and boost competitiveness. The Boeing Defense Business Segment also helped to offset significant profit losses for the company in 2019 resulting from the Boeing 737-Max grounding. The 25 Mid-Tier Defense Suppliers also show consistent profitability, though at a lower Margin than the Big Six. The 25 Mid-Tier EBITDA Market Cap Weighted Average CAGR from 2014-2019 was 1.9 percent.

However, to maintain top line growth and mitigate the cyclicality of U.S. defense spending, some firms will continue to diversify their customer base by pursuing international and non-defense customers. Over the last several years, the Big Six maintained a relatively stable share of sales coming from outside the United States (Figure 6.4.a). Despite minimal change as a percent of total revenue, Big Six international sales increased at an annualized

EBITDA Margin (%)

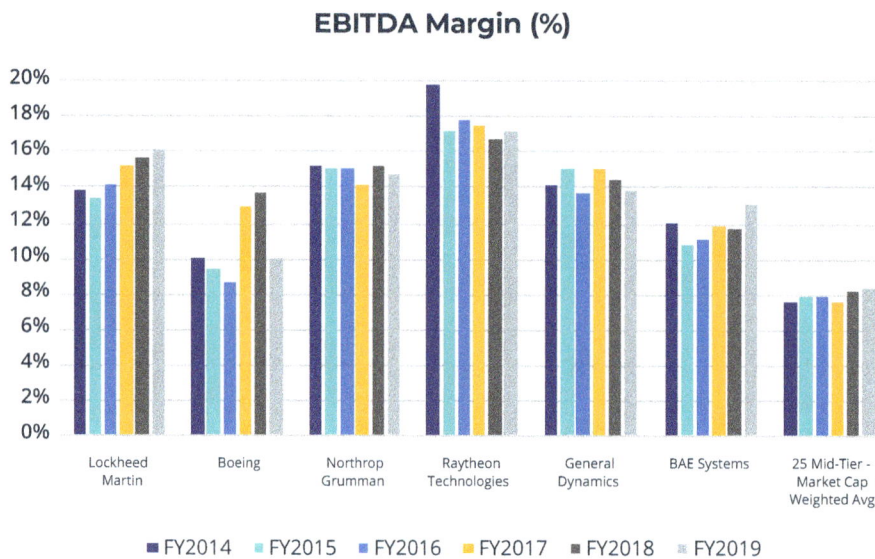

Figure 6.3: Big 6 DoD Prime & 25 Mid-Tier Market Cap Weighted Average EBITDA Margin [FY2014-FY2019] Source: Refinitiv Eikon

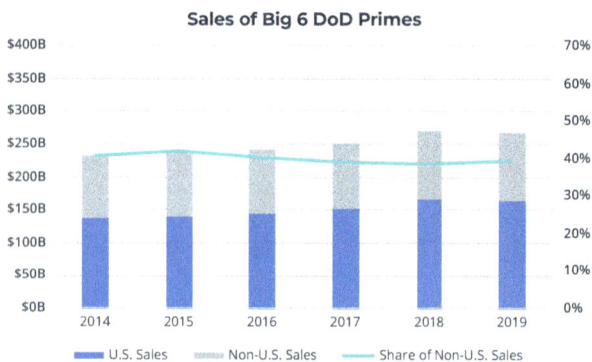

Figure 6.4.a Defense vs. Non-Defense Revenue for Big 6 Primes [FY2014-FY2019] Source: Refinitiv Eikon & Defense News Top 100

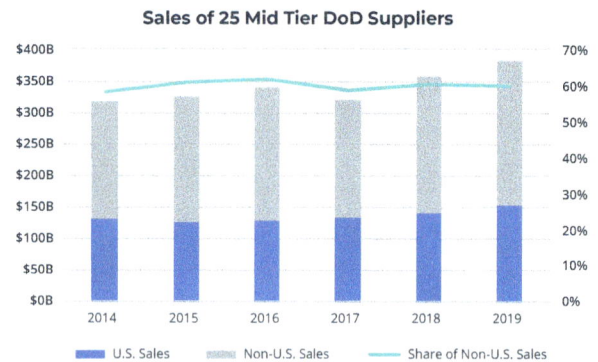

Figure 6.4.b Defense vs. Non-Defense Revenue for 25 Mid-Tier DoD Suppliers [FY2014-FY2019] Source: Refinitiv Eikon & Defense News Top 100

rate of 2.3 percent over the last six years. Non-U.S. Sales maintained a higher percentage of total sales for the 25 Mid-Tier Defense Suppliers, attributable largely to the inclusion of 12 foreign based defense suppliers in the list of 25 (Figure 6.4.b). Big Six and 25 Mid-Tier Defense Supplier sales in the U.S. increased at a similar annualized rate of approximately three percent since 2014. Non-U.S. Sales for the 25 Mid-Tier Suppliers were not as constant, but saw an annualized increase of 4.3 percent from 2014-2019.

Historically, the Big Six trended toward a rise in non-defense revenue. In 2019 the share of non-defense business revenue decreased for the Big Six, primarily due to Boeing's commercial sales losses resulting from the 737-Max grounding and historic business segment realignment following the merger of United Technologies and Raytheon (Figure 6.5).

Revenue Breakdown

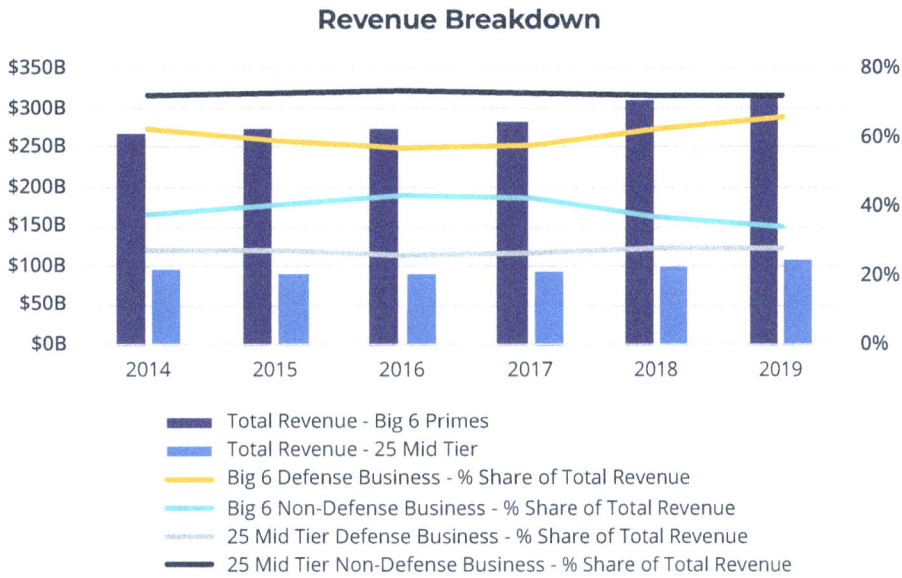

- Total Revenue - Big 6 Primes
- Total Revenue - 25 Mid Tier
- Big 6 Defense Business - % Share of Total Revenue
- Big 6 Non-Defense Business - % Share of Total Revenue
- 25 Mid Tier Defense Business - % Share of Total Revenue
- 25 Mid Tier Non-Defense Business - % Share of Total Revenue

Figure 6.5: Defense vs. Non-Defense Revenue for Big 6 & 25 Mid-Tier Defense Suppliers [FY2014-FY2019] Source: Refinitiv Eikon & Defense News Top 100

Big 6 Capital Deployment

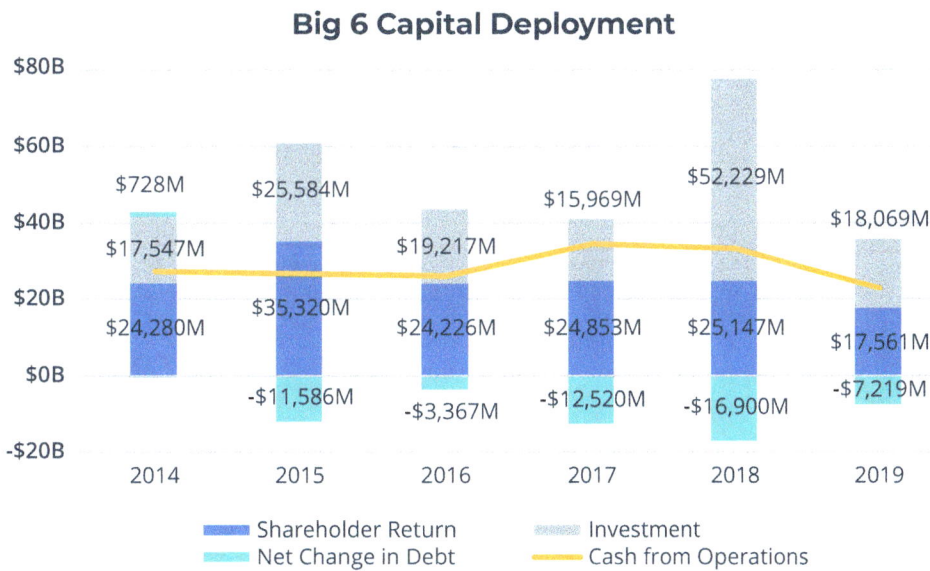

- Shareholder Return
- Net Change in Debt
- Investment
- Cash from Operations

Figure 6.6: Capital Deployment of Big 6 Primes [FY2014-FY2019] Investment: Cash for Acquisition of Subsidiaries, R&D Expense, and CAPEX Shareholder Return: Dividends Paid, Decrease in Capital Stocks Net Change in Debt: Proceeds from Repayment of Borrowings Source: Bloomberg & Refinitiv Eikon

The Big Six continue to focus their capital deployment on Shareholder Return (Five Year CAGR: -6.3 percent) and Investment (Five Year CAGR: 0.6 percent). Investments hit a six year high in 2018 at $52.2 billion with firms investing largely in acquisition of subsidiaries, research and development, and capital expenditures. Investments in 2019 declined steeply to just over $18 billion following the finalization of several mergers (Figure 6.6).

Research & Development Spending

Globally, A&D companies are among the lowest R&D spenders compared to other critical sectors. The Big Six have spent on average 2.5 percent of their sales on R&D each year. The 25 Mid-Tier Defense Suppliers spent on average about half as much each year on R&D compared to the Big Six; although as a percentage of sales, they averaged slightly higher than the Big Six at around four percent of sales spent on R&D. A rebased trend plot shows that expenditures on R&D by the Big Six closely track DoD Research, Development, Testing, and Engineering (RDT&E) spending, while having little effect on the average R&D spending of the 25 Mid-Tier Defense Suppliers (Figure 6.7). This implies that the largest defense suppliers rely on the guidance provided by DoD to drive development of newer technologies and capabilities, while the Mid-Tier suppliers generally spend more of their revenues on further product development internally.

DoD RDT&E and DoD Supplier Avg Change in R&D Spend

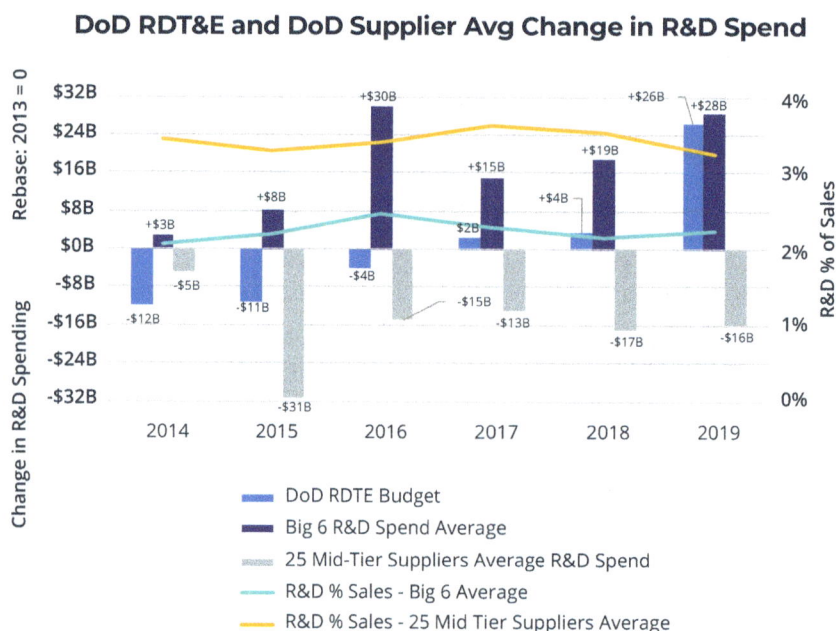

Figure 6.7: DoD RDT&E Budget Allocations; Big 6 Avg. R&D Spending; & 25 Mid-Tier Avg. R&D Spending (Rebased 2013) [FY2014-FY2019] Source: Refinitiv Eikon & DoD Budget

R&D by Country

The United States continued to lead the world in Gross Domestic Spending on R&D in 2019, although China is rapidly and consistently closing the gap with the United States. Meanwhile, the National Technology and Industrial Base, consisting of the United States, United Kingdom, Canada, and Australia, averaged just below $100 billion over the last nine years in combined GDS on R&D (Figure 6.8).

Top Three Countries by R&D Spending; NTIB; & Russia

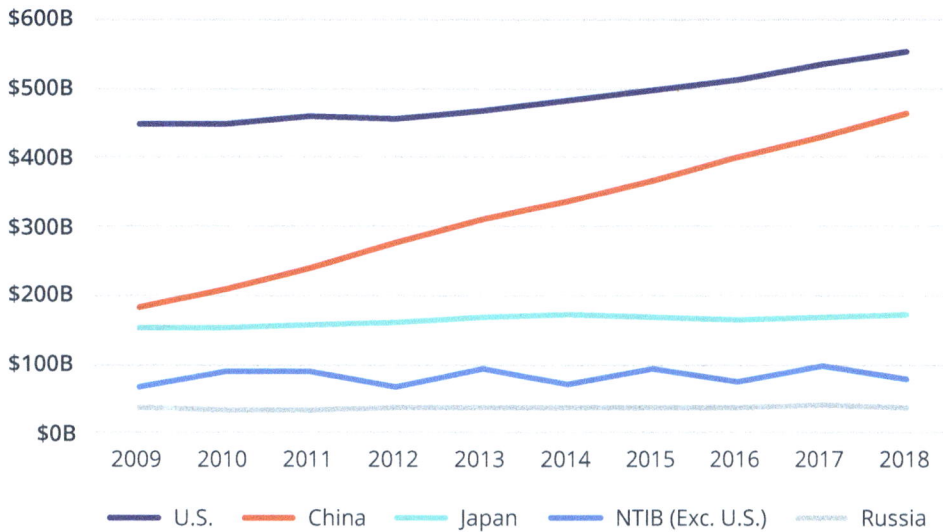

Figure 6.8: Top Three Countries, NTIB, and Russia by Gross Domestic Spending on R&D [CY2009-CY2018]
Source: OECD (R&D Data is Released on a 2-Year Lag)

R&D by Industry

The Technology sector primes known as the FAANG companies (Facebook, Amazon, Apple, Netflix, and Google) spend, on average, ten percent of their sales on R&D each year. Comparable to the characteristics of the markets (Figure 6.9), the average R&D spending by the Technology sector continues to outpace all other industries. Meanwhile the Aerospace sector decreased average R&D from 2016-2018. R&D spending appears to be trending up once again for the Aerospace sector in 2019 and consistently increased in the Defense sector from 2014-2019 (CAGR: 9.96 percent). The Dow Jones average spending on R&D continues to outperform the U.S. Aerospace and Defense sectors when compared as whole number averages.

Average R&D Spending by Industry

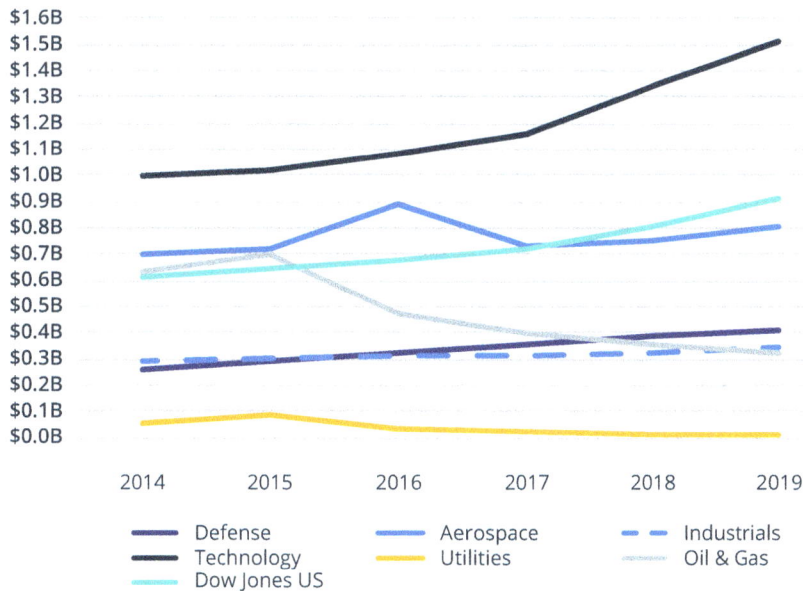

Figure 6.9: Average R&D Spending by Industry Utilizing Averages of Total Reported R&D Spending by Companies in Each Market Sector Source: Refinitiv Eikon

Global Military Spending

Global military spending continues to grow, expanding from $1.81 trillion in 2018 to $1.87 trillion in 2019 (in constant 2018 U.S. dollar value). The United States maintains its position as the largest purchaser of military goods and services in the world. Over the last decade, China established itself as the second largest purchaser of military goods and services, spending just over $266 billion in 2019. Combined, the NTIB countries, excluding the U.S., spent on average $96 billion each year from 2009-2019 on their militaries and defense related goods and services. Military spending grew in the rest of the world from $639 billion in 2008 to $793 billion in 2019, led by India, Saudi Arabia, France, Germany, Japan, and South Korea. Russia continued to maintain an average of $62 billion over the last ten years on their military spending (Figure 6.10).

U.S. Position in the Global Military Market

U.S. defense spending fluctuated over the last decade, seeing a 19.9 percent decrease from 2011-2017 and then rising 8.5 percent to its 2019 level of $718.7 billion. By contrast, China steadily increased its defense spending at an annualized rate of 14.3 percent over the past decade. The Chinese share of global military spending rose from 7.8 percent in 2009 to 14.2 percent in 2019, while the United States share of global military spending fell from 47.2 percent in 2009 to 38.4 percent in 2019 (Figure 6.11).

Global Trade in Arms

The United States and Russia remain the two largest exporters of arms in the world (Figure 6.12). The United States and Russia remain the two largest exporters of arms in the world (Figure 6.12).

Global Military Spending 2009-2019

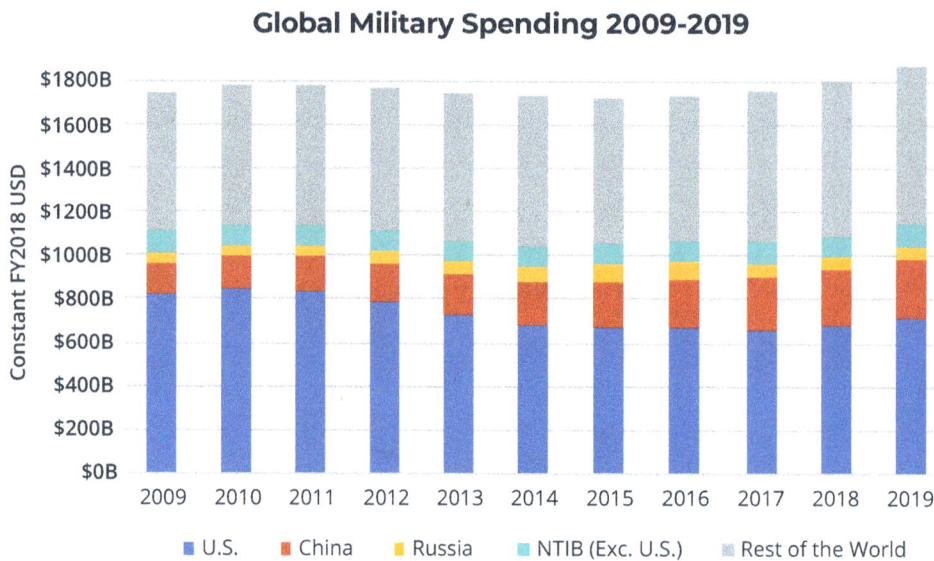

Figure 6.10: Global Military Spending (2018 Dollars) [CY2009-CY2019]
Source: SIPRI Military Expenditure Database

The United States increased its market share of Global Arms Exports from 28.3 percent in 2009 to 39.5 percent in 2019 (10 Year CAGR: 4.6 percent). Russian arms exports continue to trend downward contracting from 20.9 percent in 2009 to 17.3 percent in 2019 (ten Year CAGR: -0.7 percent). Finally, China's global arms exports market share remains relatively small despite its significant increase in defense spending, growing slightly from 4.7 percent in 2009 to 5.2 percent in 2019.

Saudi Arabia and India remain the two largest importers of arms in the world. Saudi Arabia, India, Australia, and the United Arab Emirates (U.A.E.) all increased market share of Global Arms Imported from 2009-2019, while China and Pakistan both decreased their market share for the same period (Figure 6.13).

US & China Defense Spending

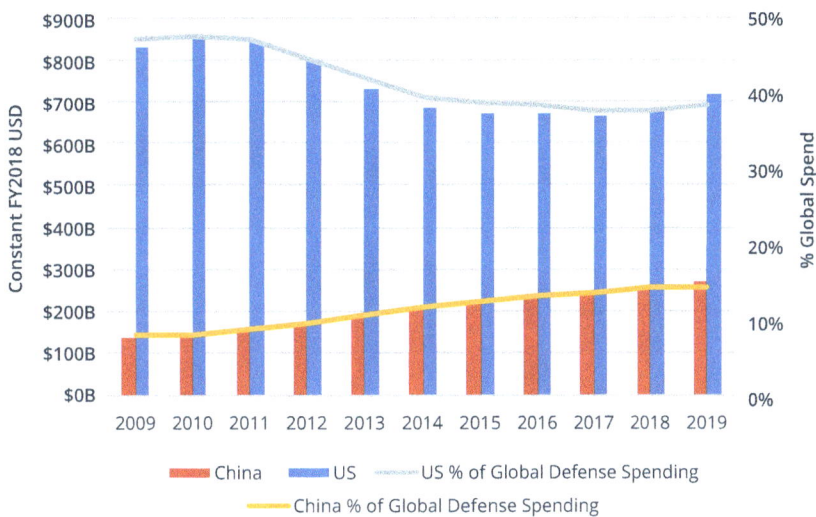

Figure 6.11: U.S. & China Defense Spending and % of Global Defense Spending (2018 Dollars) [CY2009-CY2019] Source: SIPRI Military Expenditure Database

Global Arms Exports

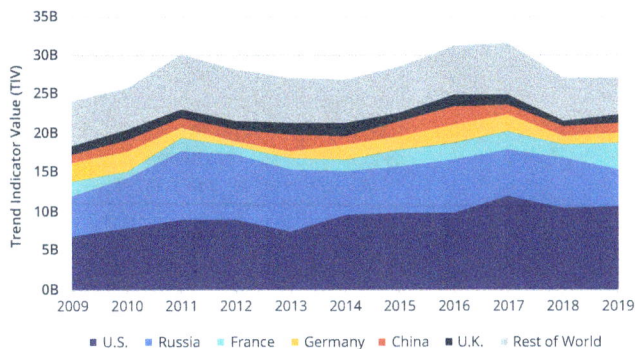

Figure 6.12: Global Arms Exports in Trend Indicator Value (Top 5 Countries) [CY2009-CY2019] Source: SIPRI Arms Transfers Database

Global Arms Imports

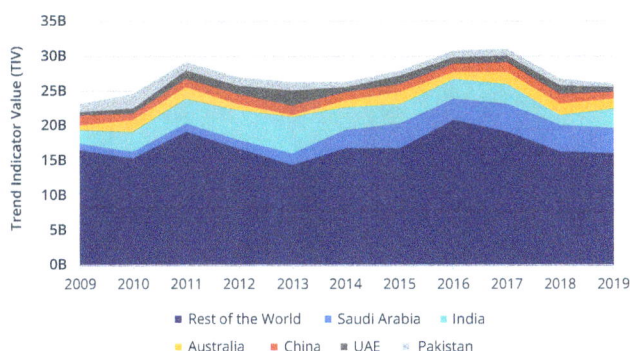

Figure 6.13: Global Arms Imports in Trend Indicator Value (Top 6 Countries) [CY2009-CY2019] Source: SIPRI Arms Transfers Database

U.S. Foreign Military Sales

U.S. Foreign Military Sales (FMS) remain inconsistent year to year, requiring the approval of military sales by Congress to foreign entities and the varying requests for military equipment from those entities. The U.A.E. and Australia purchased military equipment from the United States every year since 2011. Year to date (YTD) sales in 2020 were made to Japan, Australia, the U.A.E., Kuwait, and South Korea. Saudi Arabia in total value purchased the most military equipment from the United States over the last ten years totaling $139.1 billion (Figure 6.14).

Products from Lockheed Martin Corporation and Raytheon Technologies Corporation made up the largest share of U.S. FMS over the last several years. FMS in YTD 2020, however, saw a decrease for these two companies' products (Figure 6.15).

U.S. Foreign Military Sales (FMS) by Country

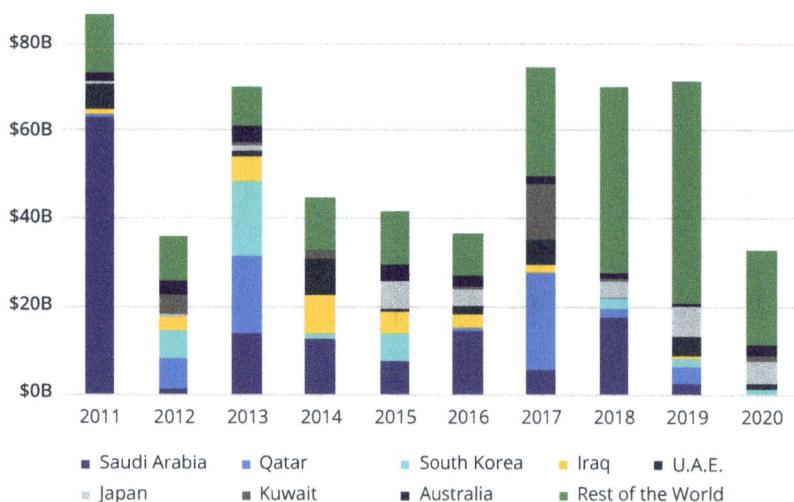

Figure 6.14: U.S. Foreign Military Sales (FMS) by Country (Top 8). [CY2011-CY2020YTD] Source: Bloomberg

U.S. Foreign Military Sales (FMS) by Company

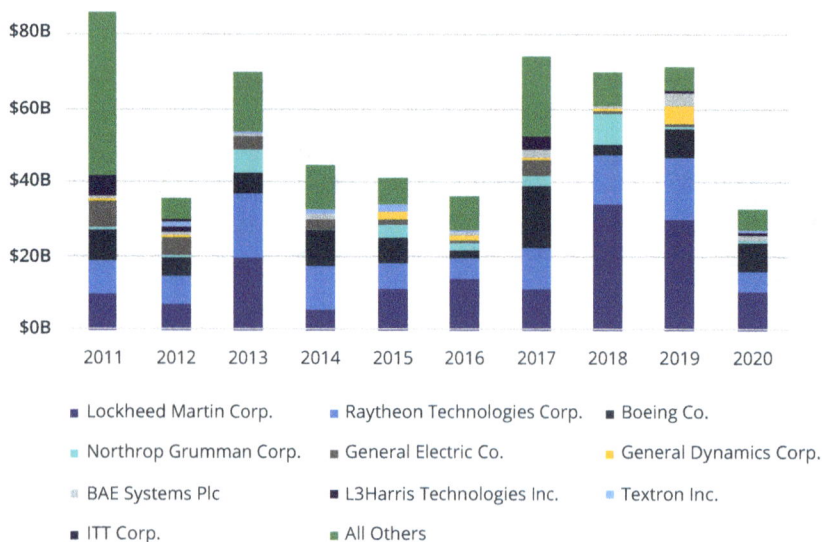

Figure 6.15: U.S. Foreign Military Sales (FMS) by Company (Top 10) [CY2011-CY2020YTD] Source: Bloomberg
* FMS sales reflect the historic combination of UTC and Raytheon for 2011-2019 and the actual reported FMS for the new entity Raytheon Technologies.

SECTION 7

SECTOR ASSESSMENTS

SECTOR ASSESSMENTS

Introduction

On July 21, 2017, President Donald J. Trump signed EO 13806 on "Assessing and Strengthening the Manufacturing and Defense Industrial Base and Supply Chain Resiliency of the United States." The EO directed the Secretary of Defense to conduct a whole-of-government effort to assess risks, identify impacts, and propose recommendations in support of a healthy manufacturing and defense industrial base. The findings were published in September 2018.

Since 2018, OUSD (IP) has continued to use the EO 13806 framework as a basis for identification and categorization of industrial base risks. However, the industrial base and supply chains are constantly evolving with new requirements, business entrants, and competitors in the defense sphere. As the DIB evolves, so do related risks.

The following section provides an assessment of industrial base gaps, vulnerabilities, and major developments within each of the traditional and cross-cutting sectors defined in the EO 13806

Report (see Table 7.1). The FY2020 DIB sector assessments identify both ongoing and short-term risks resulting from the coronavirus pandemic.

Priority gaps and vulnerabilities are also outlined in the Department's annual Unfunded Priorities List, which describes investment priorities identified across the traditional, cross-cutting, and emerging industrial base sectors, not included in the President's budget. Where the Department has identified concrete steps to address specific risks, this report provides recommended actions and investments. However, specific timelines for action depend on a variety of factors including; availability of funding, competing impacts from COVID-19 and other emerging requirements, and the extent of industry and international participation. Industrial base issues can rarely be addressed unilaterally, if ever, and must take into account both defense and economic considerations.

The sector assessments also include a sector outlook, which discusses emerging technologies and strategic competition within each sector. As OUSD (IP) and its interagency partners work to

Traditional Sectors	Cross-Cutting Sectors
• Aircraft • Chemical, Biological, Radiological, Nuclear • Ground Systems • Missiles and Munitions • Nuclear Matter Warheads • Radar and Electronic Warfare • Shipbuilding • Soldier Systems • Space	• Materials • Cybersecurity for Manufacturing • Electronics • Machine Tools • Organic Defense industrial base • Software Engineering • Workforce

Table 7.1 Traditional and Cross Cutting Industrial Base Sectors

correct existing vulnerabilities, the Department continues to identify emerging industries and technologies to provide for the needs of U.S. national defense now and in the future.

Aircraft

Sector Overview

The aircraft sector is categorized into three subsectors: fixed-wing aircraft, rotary-wing aircraft and unmanned aircraft systems (UAS) (Figure 7.2).

Fixed-Wing Aircraft	Includes fighters, bombers, cargo, transportation, and any manned aircraft that uses a set of stationary wings to generate lift and fly.
Rotary-Wing Aircraft	Includes those that use lift generated by rotor blades revolving around a mast. These aircraft are designed to operate in harsh battlefield environments, requiring robust, advanced capabilities and systems.
Unmanned Aircraft Systems (UAS)	Includes the necessary components, equipment, network, and system to control an unmanned aircraft. The unmanned aircraft systems' industry ranges from bird-size to 100+ foot wingspans. Unmanned aerial vehicles (UAVs) typically fall into one of six functional categories: target and decoy, reconnaissance, combat, logistics, R&D, and civil/commercial. The growing demand for increasingly sophisticated and versatile unmanned systems reflects the warfighter's need for intelligence, surveillance, and reconnaissance support that can reduce risk to combat forces and associated deployment costs.

Figure 7.2

Aircraft prime contractors and suppliers often rely on revenues from both defense and commercial customers. For example, Boeing's share of revenue from the U.S. government was around 24 percent between 2016 and 2018 and it sharply increased to 30.5 percent and 33.9 percent in 2019 and 2020, respectively.[9] A list of U.S. military aircraft by prime contractor (fixed-wing, rotary, and UAS) are listed in Figure 7.3.

Commercial aviation customers typically bring in large-volume orders and stable demand forecasts over longer terms than the government's future year defense program (FYDP) planning process. The suppliers often share their internal resources such as equipment, buildings, and human resources between commercial and defense work to optimize overhead cost and production efficiency. As such, demand from commercial customers is essential to support and sustain manufacturers and suppliers within the defense industrial base.

Subsector	Prime Contractor	Aircraft Type by Service		
		Army	Navy & USMC	Air Force
Fixed-Wing	Boeing		F/A-18 Hornet/Super Hornet P-8 Poseidon EA-18G Growler E-6 Mercury AV-8B Harrier II	A-10 Thunderbolt II B-52 Stratofortress B-1 Lancer C-17 Globemaster III E-3 Sentry Command Post F-15 Eagle KC-46 Pegasus VC-25 T-7A Red Hawk
	Lockheed Martin		F-35B/C Lightning II P-3 Orion/ARIES	C-130 Hercules / Compass Call F-16 Fighting Falcon F-22 Raptor U-2 Dragon Lady F-35A Lightning II C-5 Galaxy
	Northrop Grumman		E-2D Advanced Hawkeye	B-2 Spirit B-21 Raider E-8 Joint STARS
	Various	C-12 Huron		

Subsector	Prime Contractor	Aircraft Type by Service		
		Army	Navy & USMC	Air Force
Rotary-Wing	Airbus	UH-72A Lakota	UH-72A Lakota	
	Bell Boeing		CMV/MV-22B Osprey	CV-22B Osprey
	Bell Textron		AH-1Z Viper UH-1Y Venom	
	Boeing	AH-64 Apache CH-47 Chinook		MH-139 Grey Wolf
	LM-Sikorsky	UH-60 Black Hawk VH-60N White Hawk,	MH-53E, CH-53D/E/K H-60 Seahawk / Knighthawk VH-92 VH-3D Sea King	HH-60 Pave Hawk

Subsector	Prime Contractor	Aircraft Type by Service		
		Army	Navy & USMC	Air Force
UAS	Aerovironment	RQ-11 Raven	RQ-12A WASP	RQ-20 Puma
	Boeing		RQ-21 Blackjack MQ-25 Stingray	
	FLIR	Black Hornet 3		
	General Atomics	MQ-1C Gray Eagle		MQ-9 Reaper
	Lockheed Martin			RQ-170 Sentinel
	Northrop Grumman		MQ-4C Triton MQ-8B/C Fire Scout	
	Textron	RQ-7B Shadow		

Figure 7.3

Major Risks & Issues

Risk Archetypes

- Foreign Dependency
- Fragile Supplier
- Product Security

Downturn of Commercial Aviation

In FY2019, the aircraft sector was considered one of the strongest and most stable sectors; the sector exhibited growing demand in the commercial aircraft sector and stable defense demands until two significant events occurred consecutively in early 2020.

- Boeing's 737 MAX, formerly the largest commercial aircraft program in the industry by value, was decertified after two fatal crashes, which led to a production halt in January 2020. The production freeze disrupted the production and deliveries of 737 MAX parts from the suppliers, dramatically reducing revenue and production throughout the industry. These events eventually resulted in liquidity issues among suppliers due to work stoppages and restricted cash flow. Over 100 suppliers for the 737 MAX also provide parts and services for the DoD.

- The COVID-19 outbreak further aggravated supply chain issues in the aircraft sector. All three aircraft sub-sectors faced significant challenges in maintaining and sustaining the health of the DIB due to a large number of defense suppliers experiencing facility shutdowns, high absenteeism, furloughs, and financial instabilities.

Small Unmanned Aircraft Systems (sUAS)

The small UAS class applies to UAS that have maximum gross takeoff weight of less than 20lbs with normal operating altitude less than 1,200ft above ground level and airspeed less than 100 knots. As of early 2020, there were five U.S. companies in the top ten of U.S. sUAS market share holders. However, the combined market share of the five companies was only eight percent, while a single foreign company held 77 percent of the U.S. sUAS market share.[10] In recent years, many sUAS manufacturers in the U.S have either exited the consumer market or been consolidated into a fewer number of entities.

In the FY2020 DoD budget, both procurement and RDT&E budgets for UAS programs were approximately $3.2 billion in total. Approximately $153 million was allocated to sUAS programs. The DoD's annual budget for sUAS was less than four percent of the U.S. small drone market size of $4.2 billion in 2020, indicating that the U.S. small drone market is predominantly driven by commercial interests. As such, it is critical that the DoD work with the commercial sUAS industry to develop new and advanced UAS that could benefit both commercial and defense sectors and to quickly adopt commercially available systems that meet DoD requirements.

Approximately $13.4 million was awarded to sUAS suppliers under Defense Innovation Unit's (DIU's) Commercial Solutions Opening using the funds authorized and appropriated under the CARES Act. The DPA Title III efforts will allow five domestic sUAS suppliers to build sUAS components and software to keep the domestic sUAS industrial base healthy and competitive with foreign sUAS producers. The DIU specializes in accelerating adoption of leading commercial technology throughout the military and growing the national security innovation base.

The DIU has also awarded contracts totaling $11 million to six sUAS companies in 2019 and hosted an event called Blue sUAS Demonstration Day in August 2020, where five of the six companies presented cybersecure sUAS products. The Blue sUAS platforms were approved through a cyber-security vetting process and made available for purchase by any government agencies through the GSA schedule in September 2020. Although there are sUAS options that the DoD can safely procure and operate, there are still supply chain risks to be mitigated. An analysis of the bill of materials from four randomly selected U.S. sUAS platforms that meet the DoD requirements revealed that certain components rely heavily on Chinese suppliers.

Fuselage structures (e.g. carbon fiber or plastic frames), electric motors (e.g. Neodymium Iron Boron magnets) and printed circuit board (PCB) were the top three component categories that had the most reliance on parts from China (Figure 7.4). The DoD is continuously working on efforts to identify and mitigate supply chain risks within the sUAS industrial base.

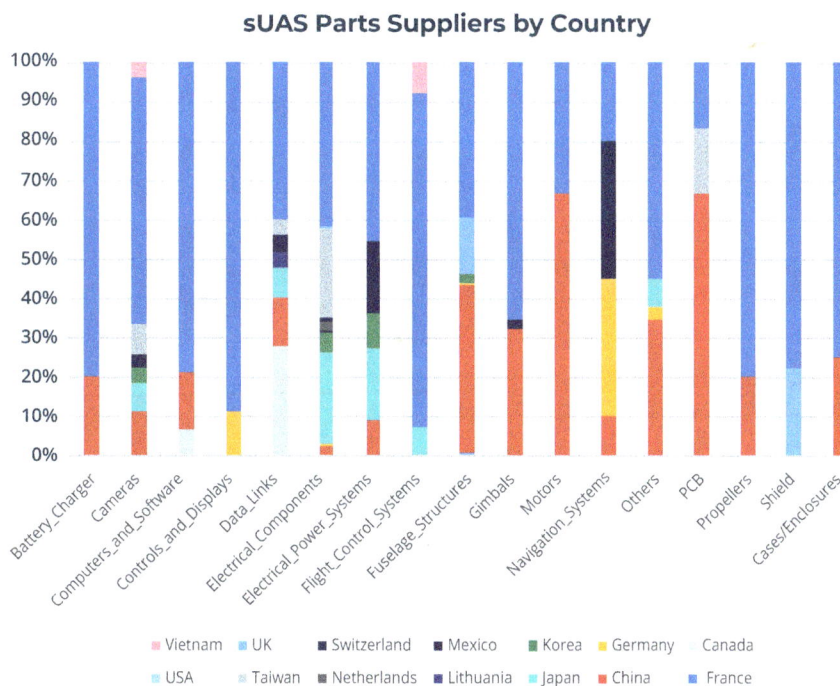

Figure 7.4: sUAS Parts Suppliers by Country

FY2020 Developments

Budgetary Impacts

Overall, the DoD aircraft procurement budget for FY2020 - FY2024 is stable (Figure 7.5).

A surge of funding is anticipated in FY2025-2027 due to the likelihood of the B-21 and the Future Vertical Lift programs entering production and the F-35 and the T-7A programs in peak procurement.

A decline in procurement funding is anticipated after FY2029 due to a scheduled decline in aircraft production and likely transition to the development of 6th generation aircraft, cargo aircraft, and fighter drones.

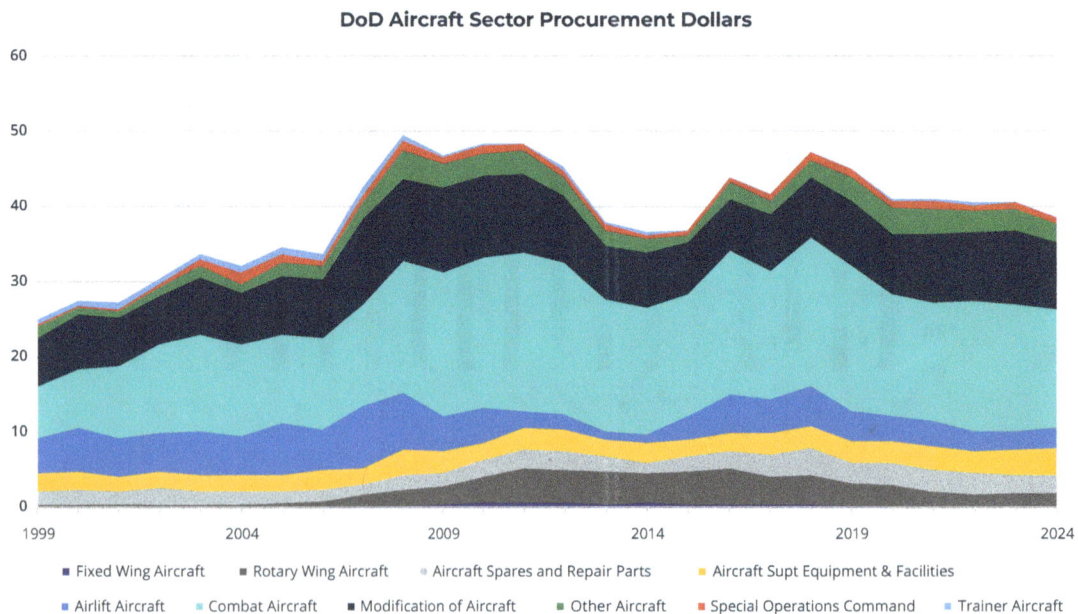

DoD Aircraft Sector Procurement Dollars

Figure 7.5: DoD Aircraft Sector Procurement Budget by Year

The RDT&E investment from FY2019 to FY2024 will decrease by approximately 45 percent due to aircraft funding moving from development to production (Figure 7.6). In FY2025, the RDT&E budget is forecasted to increase slightly above the 1999 level for programs such as 6th generation tactical aircraft, unmanned fighter, and new cargo aircraft.

The UAS sector will experience an anticipated 64 percent decrease in the RDT&E budget from FY2019 to FY2024 (Figure 7.7). However, the budgets for Counter Unmanned Aircraft Systems programs are likely to grow in the next several years.

DoD Aircraft Sector RDT&E Budget by Year

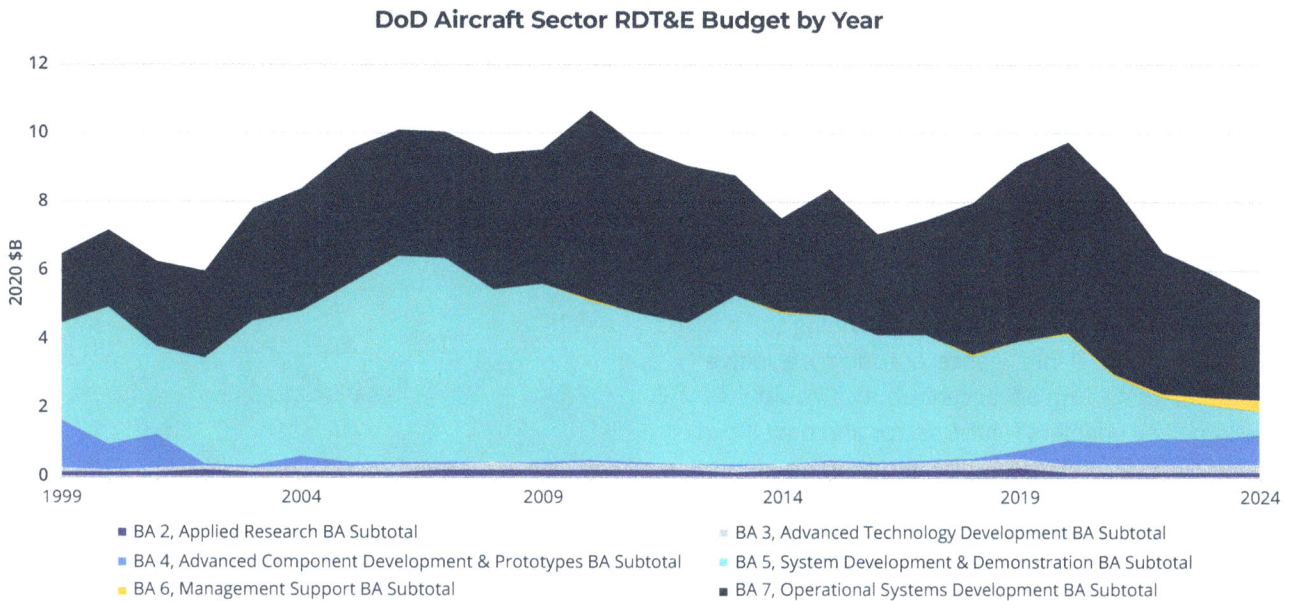

- BA 2, Applied Research BA Subtotal
- BA 3, Advanced Technology Development BA Subtotal
- BA 4, Advanced Component Development & Prototypes BA Subtotal
- BA 5, System Development & Demonstration BA Subtotal
- BA 6, Management Support BA Subtotal
- BA 7, Operational Systems Development BA Subtotal

Figure 7.6: DoD Aircraft Sector RDT&E Budget by Year

DoD UAS Procurement & RDT&E Budget by Year

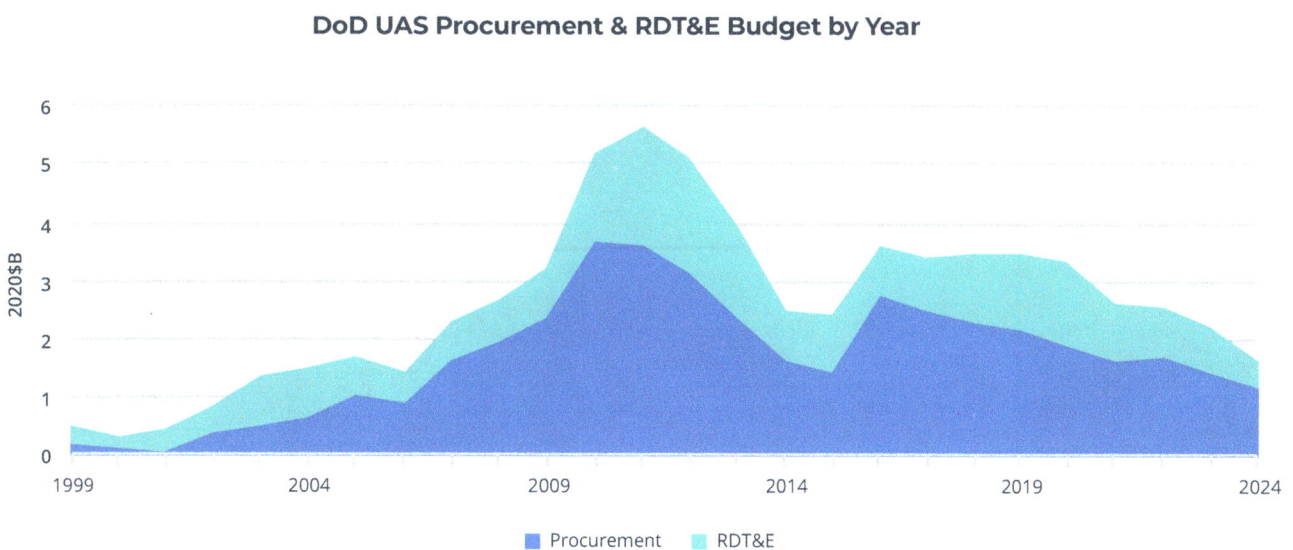

- Procurement
- RDT&E

Figure 7.7: DoD UAS Procurement & RDT&E Budget by Year

Mergers and Acquisitions (M&A)

The Aerospace and Defense sector experienced a significant decline in deals, volume, and, value in FY2020. Three of the four biggest M&A transactions in FY2020 (i.e. Raytheon/United Technologies Corporation: $33.17 billion, Cobham/Advent International: $5.23 billion, and Collins/BAE: $1.9 billion) were carry-overs from FY2019, and an additional deal between Hexcel and Woodward ($7.74 billion) was mutually terminated after the COVID-19 outbreak.

Sector Outlook

Emerging Technologies

The DoD continues to track emerging threats and opportunities within the sector. Some of the fastest growing, game-changing technologies, including artificial intelligence, autonomy, additive manufacturing, and advanced robotics, could become key enablers for the sector and next generation of fighters, including both manned and unmanned systems. The U.S. Air Force has launched programs such as Skyborg, to build an artificial intelligence-enabled drone wingman, and Agility Prime, to accelerate the commercial market for advanced air mobility vehicles (i.e., flying cars). The DoD also has on-going efforts to increase its organic industrial base capabilities by integrating additive manufacturing, automation, and advanced robotics into depots.

Aviation's Recovery

The health of the aircraft defense industrial base will be inextricably linked to the recovery of the commercial aircraft industry. Many industry experts anticipate it will take at least three to five years for the airline industry to return to pre-COVID global passenger traffic.[12] Due to the downturn of the commercial aviation industry, suppliers may choose to downsize their production capacity by closing facilities or not operating equipment and machines. This in turn can potentially create supply chain bottlenecks, especially when airline passenger traffic numbers improve and the aircraft original equipment manufacturers start increasing order quantities again.

Chemical, Biological, Radiological, Nuclear Defense (CBRND)

Sector Overview

The CBRND sector of the DIB integrates science, engineering, testing, and logistics to field products that provide protection from chemical, biological, radiological, and nuclear (CBRN) threats and attacks. The 2017 NSS emphasized the importance of this sector in implementing critical capabilities to counter hostile states and terrorist groups increasingly trying to acquire CBRN weapons.

The Department of Defense Chemical and Biological Defense Program's (CBDP) mission is to enable the Warfighter and first responders to deter, prevent, protect, mitigate, respond, and recover from CBRN threats and attacks as part of a layered, integrated defense. To support this mission, the CBDP industrial base sustains the capabilities needed to support the three strategic readiness goals:

1. Equip the force to successfully conduct military operations to prevent, protect, and respond to CBRN threats.

2. Develop new capabilities to counter emerging CBRN threats.

3. Maintain industrial capabilities to achieve NSS requirements.

The sector is composed of commercial and organic industries that support a niche market heavily dependent upon DoD procurements for sustainability and new technology development. The sector is an aggregate of capabilities that are required to provide technical products in the areas of:

- Medical countermeasures to address CBRN and emerging infectious diseases,

- Protection for the Warfighter through respirators, masks, decontamination kits, etc.,

- Contamination avoidance through development and use of sensors, monitors, and detectors,

- Information systems that consist of integrated early warning, hazard prediction models, consequence management, and decision support tools,

- Rapid development and acquisition of crucial CBRND technology for the survival and unimpeded employment of special operations forces in toxic environments.

Major Risks and Issues

Risk Archetypes

- Erosion of U.S.-based infrastructure
- Capacity-constrained supply market
- Single source

The case studies below, covering a subset of CBRND products and organic industrial capabilities, illustrate how a capacity-constrained supply market and the erosion of U.S.-based infrastructure can potentially result in gaps within the sector. These gaps may lead to limited or non-existent domestic industrial capabilities necessary to protect the Warfighter and achieve NSS requirements. The case study summaries are based on analyses conducted during FY2020.

Joint General Purpose Decontaminant for Hardened Military Equipment (JGPD-HME)

JGPD-HME is an Acquisition Category III Joint Services program military decontaminant kit. JGPD-HME consists of three powdered components packaged in individual pouches. There is currently one single qualified commercial source of supply for JGPD-HME capable of producing all three components of the kit. Supply chain or manufacturing issues at the contractor level can lead to a single point of failure for JGPD-HME procurement.

The U.S. government has full technical data package rights and is standing up production capability at Pine Bluff Arsenal (PBA). First article samples for two of the three powdered components are being tested in quarter one of FY2021. PBA does not currently possess the capability to produce the third component, and has entered into a contract with the current manufacturer for a two-year supply, with the potential for additional sales beyond that timeframe. PBA is developing a pilot scale production process for the component, and anticipates their production process to be qualified within the two-year timeframe. Until PBA's production methods for all three components have been fully qualified, there will continue to be a dependency on a single source of supply for part of the kit.

Organic Industrial Base: Pine Bluff Arsenal CBRND Center of Industrial and Technical Excellence (CITE)

The PBA Arsenal directly supports numerous Joint Force readiness requirements by providing manufacturing, depot repair, and stock management of CBRND equipment and materials. Fluctuations and inconsistencies in CBRND workload and demand projections degrade the ability to sustain current capabilities and capacities, and develop capabilities for future requirements. Fluctuating demand is caused by various factors, including infrequent or inconsistent government purchases, which can cause production lines to shut down or require supplemental backing between orders. An example of this is a nerve agent antidote maintained with the DLA Warstopper program. The Department cannot afford to lose the capability, even if there are no orders at this point in time. These fluctuating demands limit the ability to surge or respond quickly to CBRND requirements. In response to these fluctuating demands, PBA is in the process of restoring metalworking and welding capabilities, as well as entering into a Public Private Partnership (PPP) with a contractor to strengthen the production of the defense industrial base.

Organic Industrial Base: DEVCOM Chemical Biological Center (CBC) Edgewood Engineering Directorate Test Laboratories

DEVCOM CBC Edgewood Engineering Directorate Test Laboratories test chemical and biological defense products against a variety of dangerous chemical and biological agents and toxic compounds. The Center performs testing on systems and products, such as individual and collective protection, contamination avoidance, decontamination materials, and component and systems testing. After an initial shutdown period in March 2020 due to COVID-19, the majority of the Engineering Directorate Laboratories developed and implemented procedures allowing a return to work with no lost test capabilities. For these capabilities, the biggest impact has been a slower turnaround time due to lower workforce numbers allowed on-site. Other factors affecting test capabilities include travel restrictions, required direct personnel contact, and concerns of health risks associated with large chamber operations. Efforts are underway to continue to analyze and determine the COVID-19 risks associated with these operations.

This niche sector is also highly dependent on single and sole source manufacturers, which is common in the smaller, highly technical industrial base sectors. In many scenarios, this constraint can be directly attributed to deleterious U.S. government procurement practices, inconsistent funding and demand signals, and eroding manufacturing capabilities and the associated workforce. However, the primary constraint rests in DoD barriers that restrict entry into the industry and present qualification challenges, limiting competition within the base. When items are needed quickly, smaller companies (or those unfamiliar with the government procurement process) will struggle to compete. Procurement lead times, which can span to 18 months, discourage many small and non-traditional DoD businesses from entering into competition for CBRND products. This is a challenge because CBRND is a niche sector that depends on small businesses as important suppliers.

FY2020 Developments

During FY2020, there have been two policy and partnership developments within the CBRND Sector. First, the coronavirus pandemic necessitated a redesign of the federal and commercial CBRN testing laboratories certification process and policy. Second, PBA, in alignment with the CBRND CITE core competency requirements, established a PPP with a contractor for onsite production of CBRN large filters.

Laboratory Certification Process Redesign

The Quality Assurance (QA) branch of DEVCOM CBC is responsible for providing laboratory certification for both government and commercial CBRN testing laboratories. The onset of the coronavirus pandemic, and associated travel and health condition restrictions, constrained the ability of the QA branch to perform onsite laboratory certification. The affected customer base encompassed the DoD Shelf Life Program, Joint Program Executive Office Enterprise, and the Tank and Automotive Command (TACOM) Chemical Biological Directorate. The pandemic restrictions required the QA branch to redesign the process and policy. The QA branch, in collaboration with the customer base, developed a virtual laboratory certification process and policy. The virtual process has enabled effective risk management to ensure Warfighters and First Responders are issued conforming products. The versatility of the process has empowered the QA branch to continue supporting the DoD's CBRN program and the security of the nation.

Pine Bluff Arsenal CBRND CITE – Public Private Partnership

The organic industrial base CBRND CITE, PBA, has increased its efforts to provide a rapid capability response to any volatile supply chain challenges. The newly established PPP between PBA and a CBRN filter contractor leverages the technical capabilities of PBA's existing large filter production line and skilled workforce. The PPP filter production will occur during the night shift using contractor supplied metal frames and parts, with normal PBA filter production workload continuing during the day shift to ensure filter availability for national defense.

Sector Outlook

The coronavirus pandemic has impacted all sectors of the defense industrial base. For the CBRND Sector, this has manifested in an increased global demand and strain on supply chains for protective equipment. CBRND manufacturers have risen to the challenge and continued production in the midst of these challenges, yet the sector continues to find itself in a precarious position with a reliance on single and sole source providers for many products. It is imperative that the DoD proactively continues to manage the critical asset of PBA in order to provide improved capabilities to counter current and emerging CBRN threats.

Cybersecurity for Manufacturing

Sector Overview

The cybersecurity for manufacturing sector includes information and operational technology within contractor factories and across defense manufacturing supply chains.

Defense manufacturing supply chain operations rely on an immeasurablenumber of touch points where information flows through a network – both within and across the many manufacturers' systems that constitute the supply chain. Every one of these supply chain touch points represents a potential vulnerability to the security of our nation's defense production.

According to data released in late 2019 by the U.S. Census Bureau, approximately 291,000 manufacturing establishments operate in the United States.[13] Nearly 99 percent of those establishments are small and medium-sized manufacturers (SMMs) with fewer than 500 employees. Multiple data sources indicate that most SMMs are unprepared to deal with a cyber-attack. This problem is acute within defense manufacturing supply chains, where SMMs— often lacking basic cyber controls— constitute the bulk of the critical lower supply chain tiers.[14]

Most information that is generated, stored, and exchanged in the DIB is not classified. The protection of such unclassified, covered defense information, or CDI (including controlled unclassified information (CUI)), presents an enormous and complex challenge. Thirty-five percent of all cyberespionage attacks in the U.S. are targeted at the manufacturing sector.[15] Most of the manufacturing data of interest to adversaries is CUI, including design information; performance specifications; shop floor execution data; factory support information (e.g., financials, system status, and personnel); and supply chain operational information (e.g., invoicing, pricing, and contract volume). As such, cybersecurity for manufacturing presents a persistent, widespread, and complex challenge to the entire DIB.

Major Risks & Issues

Risk Archetypes

- Foreign dependency
- Product security

Awareness and Wherewithal of Small Defense Contractors to Implement Cybersecurity Protections

Both the public and private sectors recognize the importance of safeguarding informational and operational assets from cyber risks. However, cybersecurity has not become an ingrained norm in manufacturing, especially in small and medium-sized manufacturers. The Defense Federal Acquisition Regulations Supplement (DFARS) clause 252.204-7012 required defense contractors and subcontractors to implement the information security protections described in the National Institute of Standards and Technology (NIST) Special Publication 800-171 Revision 1, "Protecting Unclassified Information in Nonfederal Information Systems and Organizations" by December 31, 2017. Interactions with several thousand small manufacturers by the Department of Commerce (DoC) Manufacturing Extension Partnership National Network since 2017 reveals a lack of awareness and understanding of the DFARS cybersecurity requirement, and a deficiency of financial and technical resources necessary to manage cyber security risks. Compliance with the requirements by sub-tier suppliers, while increasing, remains relatively low and is not pervasive throughout defense supply chains.

Inadequate Focus on Manufacturing-Specific Cybersecurity Needs

Manufacturing is the second most heavily attacked sector in the economy (finance is the first), and the DIB is subject to continuous, coordinated cyber-attack campaigns by nation states. Unfortunately, most cybersecurity R&D is focused on information systems, without specific emphasis on the unique needs and operational technology aspects of the manufacturing sector.

If unaddressed, the industrial base faces a high likelihood of serious and exploitable vulnerabilities, while experiencing a reduction in the number of suppliers compliant with requirements and eligible to provide products and services to the DoD. This combination of risks will impact both the resilience of existing suppliers and the integrity of the supply chain.

FY2020 Developments

DoD issued an interim rule to amend the DFARS to implement a DoD Assessment Methodology and Cybersecurity Maturity Model Certification (CMMC) framework. This framework is intended to assess contractor implementation of cybersecurity requirements and enhance the protection of unclassified information within the DoD supply chain. This interim rule is effective November 30, 2020.

Building upon the NIST SP 800-171 DoD Assessment Methodology, the CMMC framework adds a comprehensive and scalable certification element to verify the implementation of processes and practices associated with the achievement of a cybersecurity maturity level. The CMMC is designed to provide increased assurance to the Department that a DIB contractor can adequately protect sensitive unclassified information, such as CUI and Federal Contract Information, at a level commensurate with risk, accounting for information flow down to subcontractors in a multi-tier supply chain. A DIB contractor can achieve a specific CMMC level for its entire enterprise network or for particular segments, depending on where the protected information is processed, stored, or transmitted.

The CMMC model consists of maturity processes and cybersecurity best practices from multiple cybersecurity standards, frameworks, and other references, as well as inputs from the broader cybersecurity community. The CMMC levels and associated sets of processes and practices are cumulative. Furthermore, the CMMC model includes an additional five processes and 61 practices across Levels 2-5 that demonstrate a progression of cybersecurity maturity.

Level	Description
1	Consists of the 15 basic safeguarding requirements from Federal Acquisition Regulation (FAR) clause 52.204-21.
2	Consists of 65 security requirements from NIST SP 800-171 implemented via DFARS clause 252.204-7012, seven CMMC practices, and two CMMC processes. Intended as an optional intermediary step for contractors as part of their progression to Level 3.
3	Consists of all 110 security requirements from NIST SP 800-171, 20 CMMC practices, and three CMMC processes.
4	Consists of all 110 security requirements from NIST SP 800-171, 46 CMMC practices, and four CMMC processes.
5	Consists of all 110 security requirements from NIST SP 800-171, 61 CMMC practices, and five CMMC processes.

Figure 7.8

DoD is implementing a phased rollout of CMMC. Until September 30, 2025, DFARS clause 252.204-7021, Cybersecurity Maturity Model Certification Requirements, is prescribed for use in solicitations and contracts. To implement the phased rollout of CMMC, inclusion of a CMMC requirement in a solicitation during this time period must be approved by USD(A&S).

CMMC will apply to all DoD solicitations and contracts, including those for the acquisition of commercial items (except exclusively commercial off-the-shelf items) above the micro-purchase threshold, starting on or after October 1, 2025. Contracting officers will not make an award, or exercise an option on a contract, if the contractor does not have current (i.e. not older than three years) certification for the required CMMC level. Furthermore, CMMC certification requirements must be applied to subcontractors at all tiers, based on the sensitivity of the unclassified information at the subcontractor level.

Sector Outlook

Gaps in cybersecurity protections among defense manufacturers can lead to widespread and persistent vulnerabilities in the DIB, contributing to the erosion of manufacturing, economic competitiveness, and national security.

Multiple approaches exist to manage cybersecurity risks within the industrial base, but not all are appropriate or even adequate to protect all levels of controlled information, including CDI and CUI. Three key issues – lack of uniform security implementation; inconsistent implementation of adequate security by defense suppliers; and reliance on self-attestation as indicated by current DFARS requirements – expose the manufacturing sector to cybersecurity risks. Further, the implementation of emerging technological systems in the DIB will exacerbate challenges to cybersecurity, and increase the stakes of malign technology transfer in the future.

Electronics

Sector Overview

The electronics sector manufactures products for a wide variety of end user markets, including consumer electronics, computers, automotive, industrial equipment, medical equipment, telecommunications, aerospace, and defense. Electronic systems and components are ubiquitous throughout all DoD weapons systems, but global military production represents only one percent of a market dominated by commercial devices.

Major Risks & Issues

Risk Archetypes

- Foreign dependency
- DMSMS

Decline of Domestic Semiconductor Manufacturing

Currently, the United States only holds a 12 percent market share in the global semiconductor manufacturing market. The dependence on foreign sources for semiconductor products continues to represent a serious threat to the economic prosperity and national security of the U.S., as much of the critical infrastructure is dependent on microelectronic devices. This threat will become more pronounced as emergent technology sectors, such as Internet of Things (IoT) and AI, require commodity quantities of advanced semiconductor components.

In addition, the diminished focus on domestic semiconductor manufacturing has contributed to the erosion of U.S. technological supremacy in advanced semiconductor manufacturing. The current industry leaders introducing new semiconductor technology nodes are Taiwan Semiconductor Manufacturing Company (TSMC), Ltd. (Taiwan) and Samsung Group (South Korea). These companies are several technology generations ahead of Intel Inc., the United States leader in semiconductor technology.

Counterfeited Electronic Components

The U.S. Navy studied counterfeit trends based on information provided by ERAI, an electronic part reporting and dispute resolution organization; their study consisted of 9,009 part reports and 2,593 company complaints. The study confirmed that integrated circuits (ICs) continue to be the most commonly counterfeited electronic components, identified in over 60 percent of all ERAI reports from 2018 through mid-2020. Multi-layer ceramic capacitors, a relatively simple part, are the second most-counterfeited part, making up approximately 15 percent of the reported suspect parts since 2018.[16]

DoD organizations continue to develop requirements to mitigate the counterfeit microelectronics risk. For example, U.S. Naval Sea Systems Command (NAVSEA) released NAVSEAINST 4855.40, *Counterfeit Materiel Prevention* in April 2019, with compliance becoming a part of NAVSEA Inspector General audits starting in October 2020. In November 2019, the Federal Acquisition Regulatory Council also issued a new regulation, FAR 52.246-26, which requires federal contractors to report any counterfeit or suspect counterfeit parts to the Contracting Officer and the Government Industry Data Exchange Program within 60 days of the finding.[17]

Decline of U.S. Printed Circuit Board (PrCB) Manufacturing

U.S. PrCB and PrCB assembly (PrCBA) manufacturers have sufficient technical capability to meet DoD's current advanced manufacturing technology needs, excluding organic IC substrates. However, this could change with a few acquisitions or closures.

The number of small and medium PrCB manufacturers supplying the DoD continued to diminish in 2020, falling by 16.3 percent and 25.6 percent in the last five years, respectively.[18] The DoD is at risk of losing capability due to the mergers and acquisitions of small domestic PrCB manufacturing companies that are purchased by larger companies. The small companies' niche products and services necessary for national defense systems may not provide sufficient revenue or opportunity for growth for their new, larger owners. This growth will further edge out the small PrCB manufacturers who provide essential products and services for national defense systems.

Fortunately, the DoD Executive Agent for Printed Circuit Board and Interconnect Technology (PrCB EA) is developing and promoting DoD policies and regulations that encourage trusted domestic PrCB manufacturing and reshoring, which could help alleviate this concern. In addition, DoD is investing in trusted domestic PrCB manufacturing by leveraging economic stimulus funding and the DPA Title III program.

Limited Domestic Capacity for Organic IC Substrate Manufacturing

Taiwan, South Korea, Japan, and China collectively produced over 90 percent of the $8 billion organic IC substrate production in 2018; the United States produced less than 0.1 percent that year.[19] Organic IC substrates are the most advanced PrCB interconnect technology in the market today and will enable next-generation technology. Substrate-like PrCBs (SLPs), essentially equivalent to organic IC substrate constructions, are becoming more common as the feature sizes in cell phone PrCBs continue to shrink.

The U.S. PrCB industry has not developed a significant capability to deliver production capacities of organic IC substrates due to high labor costs and the hyper-competitive environment created by Asia. However, a number of U.S. companies are starting to invest in this capability.[20, 21] Domestic and future DoD investments are crucial as Japan, a previously vital source for U.S. organic IC substrate supply, has recently announced it will not support production requirements for defense-unique microelectronics.

Obsolete Technology

DoD's acquisition and sustainment systems use microelectronic technology that is generations behind commercial technology. Due to the high cost of redesign, test, and requalification, most systems do not undergo technology refreshes, which would allow the insertion of new technology parts. This leads to obsolescence issues because the microelectronics industry does not have sufficient demand to continue producing these parts. DoD alone cannot sustain production. Therefore, many parts become obsolete, and programs are forced to do costly lifetime buys, or expensive redesign/requalification efforts to utilize a different part. These are usually not budgeted for by the programs, which makes it very difficult to address these issues.

A production line utilized by many DoD programs, including anti-tamper, missiles, platforms, space systems, and potential future strategic systems recently went end-of-life, requiring just such costly efforts. Better tracking of microelectronic parts by the Department, and better planning and budgeting by programs to insert new technologies, would allow DoD to respond to these issues in a more proactive way versus the costlier reactive efforts it usually undertakes.

Congressional Action

Congress has included a number of pieces of legislation in the draft FY2021 NDAA to address some of the issues noted in this report, including on-shoring microelectronics manufacturing capability, increasing funding for research and development of new microelectronics technologies, and requiring use of domestic PCBs in DoD systems. If the final legislation is targeted to the right risk areas, and appropriations are also provided, this could start to resolve some of the major issues outlined here.

FY2020 Developments

Mergers & Acquisitions

In the aerospace and defense sector, electronic equipment contributed 23 percent of total deal value in the first half of 2020 ($15.4 billion). The most noteworthy of these mergers and acquisitions were the BAE Systems Inc. acquisition of Collins Aerospace-Military – Military Global Positioning System business, and the Teledyne Technologies Inc. acquisition of Photonics Technologies SAS.[22]

In the microelectronics sector, two substantial mergers were announced that will have significant impact in their respective market segments:

- February 2020: Dialog Semiconductor (United Kingdom) announced the acquisition of Adesto (United States), a provider of analog and mixed signal application-specific semi-conductors and embedded systems for the Industrial IoT, for $500 million. According to Dialog, the acquisition will enhance Dialog's position in the Industrial IoT. Adesto is based in Santa Clara, California, employs 270 people, made approximately $118 million in 2019, and has a portfolio of solutions for smart building automation in the industrial, con-sumer, medical and communications markets.

- September 2020: NVIDIA, Inc. announced plans to acquire ARM Holdings from Softbank (Japan) for $40 billion. ARM technology is used in approximately 90 percent of all mobile applications and in many gaming platforms. NVIDIA has announced their plan to use ARM technology to accelerate next-generation data center technology, placing them in direct competition with Intel.

- October 2020: Advanced Micro Devices (AMD) announced plans to acquire Xilinx, Inc. for $35 billion. AMD is a direct competitor of Intel, engaged in the development of Central Processor Units, the core component in modern computers. Xilinx Inc. produces a class of semiconductor devices known as Field Programmable Gate Arrays that have extensive commercial and DoD applications. This merger would give AMD a significant competitive advantage over Intel, particularly in emerging markets such as IoT and large data applications.

The most substantial bare PrCB manufacturer acquisition in 2020 was the Summit Interconnect Inc. acquisition of Integrated Technology Ltd. in Canada.[23] Summit Interconnect now has four facilities, three in the United States and one in Canada. With annual total estimated sales of over $120 million, Summit Interconnect moved into the top four U.S. bare PrCB facilities.[24]

COVID-19 Impacts

The coronavirus pandemic has significantly impacted the U.S. electronics sector's ability to provide timely support and supply for national defense systems. The U.S. electronics sector has experienced:

- Heightened awareness of the sector's foreign dependency overall, but especially China.

- Product launch delays and cancellations (53 percent) and component cost increases (37 percent); [25]

- Onboarding new suppliers without approved vendor qualification processes in order to quicken access to critical inventory (31 percent). [26]

- Extending certifications and licenses for as long as six months, and delaying new certifi-cations (e.g., International Traffic in Arms Regulations, NADCAP, AS9100); and

- Decreasing 2020 capital expenditures in facility upgrades and new technology (26 per-cent), according to an IPC survey. [27]

The microelectronics industry, however, reported a more minimal impact. During an Industrial Base Council meeting on October 2, 2020, four commercial microelectronics companies (representing small, medium, and large microelectronics producers) provided their perspectives, discussing COVID-19 impacts to the commercial industry and their companies, and initiatives the U.S. government could take to help the microelectronics industry. The overall COVID-19 impacts described by the microelectronics companies were minimal.

New Programs/Initiatives

The PrCB EA facilitates access to reliable, trusted, and affordable PrCB fabrication, assembly products and technologies that meet the DoD quality, performance, and security requirements. The PrCB EA supports collaboration within and across DoD to conduct research, development, and sustainment efforts targeting Component-unique requirements.

The PrCB EA continued research and development activities in FY2020, focusing specifically on technologies that could enhance national defense systems. This research and development includes: performance and reliability assessments of additive manufacturing based electronics; manufacturing processes, patterning techniques, material sets, and equipment requirements that support PrCBs with less than ten micrometers line and space features; solder replacement technologies; reliability assessments on enabling technologies for 2.5D and 3D packaging; direct write substrates, and printed devices, including batteries, sensors, transistors, and energetics.

DoD is also investing in heterogeneous packaging through the State-of-the-Art Heterogeneous Integration Prototype (SHIP) Program, which is driving advanced microelectronic packaging technology. [28]

There have been several new budgetary developments within DoD in the electronics sector:

- The JIBWG collected, evaluated, and vetted critical electronics sector needs resulting from the coronavirus pandemic, and made recommendations to the IBC on CARES Act funding allocations. Roughly $80 million has been allocated to the electronics sector through the CARES Act.

- In June 2020, the bipartisan Creating Helpful Incentives to Produce Semiconductors (CHIPS) for America Act was introduced in the Senate and the House. This bill will provide significant federal investments to U.S. semiconductor companies to give them a technological edge in semiconductor materials, process technology, architectures, design, and advanced packaging to help restore U.S. leadership in semiconductor technology essential to national security.

- In October 2020, DoD awarded over $197 million to advance microelectronics technology and strengthen the U.S. microelectronics industrial base, which will underpin the development of other DoD technology priorities such as AI, 5G communications, quantum computing, and autonomous vehicles. Nearly $200 million will be issued through two DoD programs: The Rapid Assured Microelectronics Prototypes (RAMP) using the Advanced Commercial Capabilities Project Phase 1 Other Transaction Award, and the SHIP Program Phase 2 Other Transaction Award.

- The Presidential Determination authorizing the use of DPA Title III authorities to strengthen the domestic industrial base and supply chain for rare earth elements and to correct the industrial base shortfall for radiation-hardened electronics.

Sector Outlook

Trusted Certifications

To establish more comprehensive trust assurance within the U.S. PrCB industrial base, DoD in partnership with Institute for Printed Circuits (IPC) created IPC-1791 *Trusted Electronic Designer, Fabricator and Assembler Requirements*. The initiative aimed to develop a competitive network of trusted PrCB and interconnect technology providers. Efforts to keep IPC-1791 current continue: Revision A includes provisions for the certification of non-U.S. PrCB designers, fabricators, and assemblers that are sponsored by U.S. prime contractors; Revision B is currently under review and will expand requirements to include cable and wire harness assemblers, SLPs, and complementary Cybersecurity Maturity Model Certification requirements.

Additionally, section 224 of the FY2020 NDAA requires defense microelectronics products and services to meet trusted supply chain and operational security. A strategy is currently under development and will require implementation by January 2023.

Strategic Competition

"While we still design components and printed circuit cards in the U.S., the majority of fabrication, packaging, testing, etc., is done offshore," USD(A&S) Ellen M. Lord said at the Electronics Resurgence Initiative Summit. She offered some hope, adding that through public and private partnerships, the government can provide capital and a demand signal to encourage manufacturers to bring microelectronic production back to the U.S.[29]

While the global PrCB market continues to grow – from $30 billion in 2000[30] to over $65 billion in 2018,[31] the number of PrCB companies in North America has continued to decline, from over 1500 in 2000 to around 199.[32] While consolidations in the U.S. have strengthened some of the larger manufacturers, they have created a more challenging market for small PrCB manufacturers.

PrCBA manufacturing is often outsourced to electronic manufacturing service (EMS) providers. Of the top 20 EMS providers in 2019, four are based in the United States and eight in Taiwan.[33] Taiwan dominates the EMS market, leading in both revenue and number of facilities.[34] The current United States -China trade war has also prompted EMS providers to build plants outside of China, benefitting manufacturers in Vietnam and Malaysia.[35] An increase in EMS providers outside of China has provided the United States with considerable access to PrCBA manufacturing capability.[36]

The U.S. maintains a 45-50 percent combined market share in electronic design sectors such as electronic design automation and intellectual property core development. However, the U.S. market share of semiconductor manufacturing has declined from 37 percent in 1990, to 12 percent in 2020. Despite this trend, the U.S. currently maintains a combined 30 percent market share in the optoelectronic, analog, and discrete electronic component sectors. The U.S. manufacturing decline in semiconductor fabrication has benefitted large fabrication facilities in Taiwan, and more recently, China.[37] Global IC semiconductor sales in 2019 were $412.3 billion.[38]

The domestic semiconductor industry relies heavily on outsourced semiconductor assembly and test (OSAT) corporations to package and test semiconductor products. Currently, over 75 percent of electronic component packages and 98 percent of the testing performed by the OSAT sector occurs in Asian facilities.[39] This trend is expected to continue as leading edge semiconductor manufacturers, such as TSMC, are now engaged in the OSAT market.

Emerging Trends/Technologies

Finally, these emerging and foundational technologies will require the electronics sector to advance standard manufacturing processes, often necessitating investments, new processes, and new materials (Table 7.9).

Technology	Copper Interconnect/ Solder Joint Advances, Ruggedization	Thermal Management Advances	Improved Size, Weight, Power/ Finer Circuit Traces/ Smaller Vias	New Materials	Business Impacts	Advances in PrCB and PrCB Manufacturing
Hypersonics	X			X		X
Directed Energy		X		X		X
Advanced Communications			X			X
Space Offense and Defense				X		X
Unmanned Aerial Systems/ Autonomy	X		X	X		X
Advanced Robotics/AI	X		X	X	X	X

Table 7.9: Advances Required for Emerging and Foundational Technologies

Ground Systems

Sector Overview

Ground systems provide defense-unique products, integrating the functions of mobility, firepower, survivability, and communications into vehicle systems primarily for the U.S. Army and Marine Corps. These encompass tracked and wheeled vehicles for combat, combat support, and combat service support. The ground vehicle sector of the DIB has seen a drastic contraction of players in recent decades into what is now a small set of prime suppliers that design and manufacture Combat Vehicles (CV) and Tactical Wheeled Vehicles (TWV).

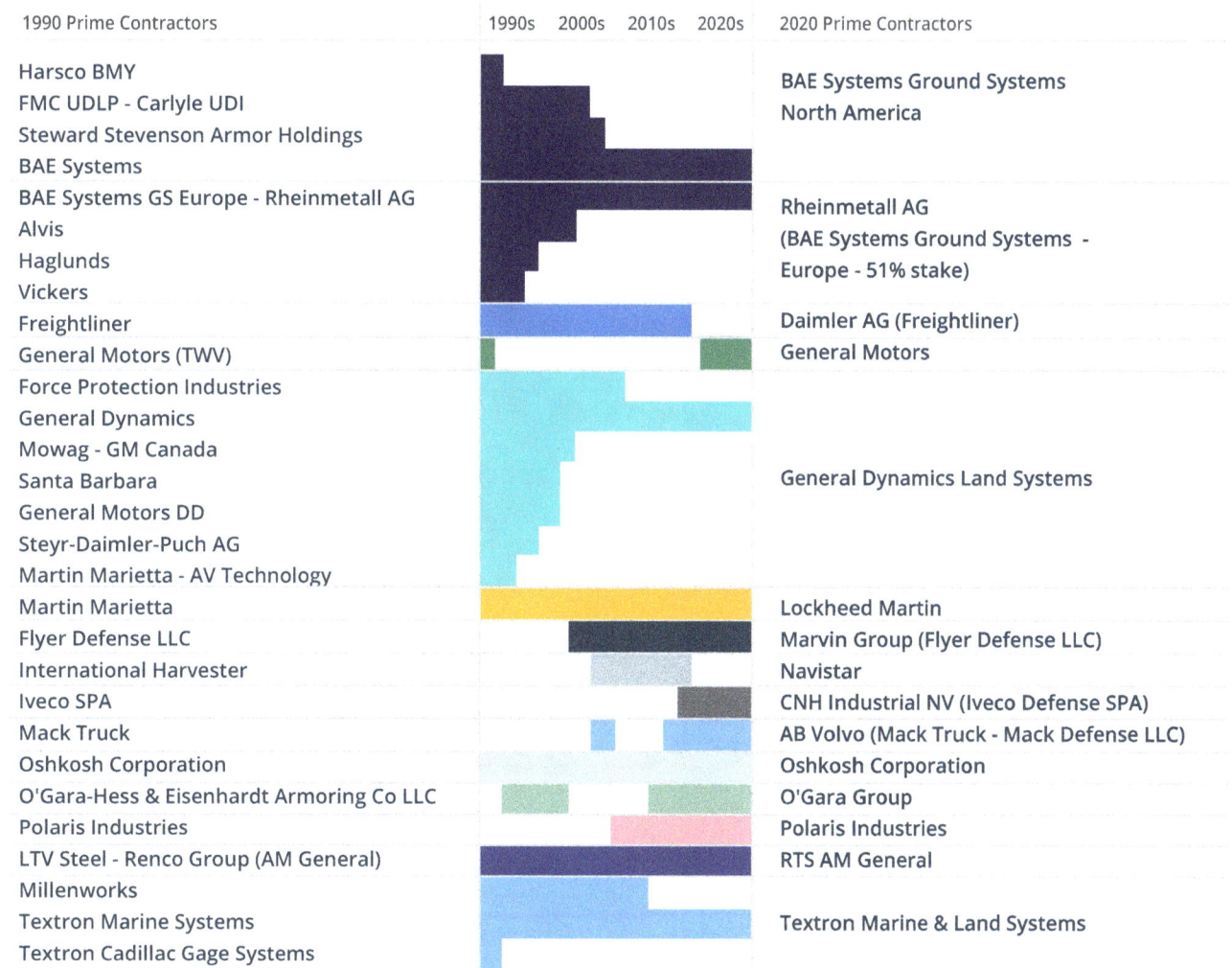

1990 Prime Contractors	1990s	2000s	2010s	2020s	2020 Prime Contractors
Harsco BMY					BAE Systems Ground Systems
FMC UDLP - Carlyle UDI					North America
Steward Stevenson Armor Holdings					
BAE Systems					
BAE Systems GS Europe - Rheinmetall AG					Rheinmetall AG
Alvis					(BAE Systems Ground Systems -
Haglunds					Europe - 51% stake)
Vickers					
Freightliner					Daimler AG (Freightliner)
General Motors (TWV)					General Motors
Force Protection Industries					
General Dynamics					
Mowag - GM Canada					
Santa Barbara					General Dynamics Land Systems
General Motors DD					
Steyr-Daimler-Puch AG					
Martin Marietta - AV Technology					
Martin Marietta					Lockheed Martin
Flyer Defense LLC					Marvin Group (Flyer Defense LLC)
International Harvester					Navistar
Iveco SPA					CNH Industrial NV (Iveco Defense SPA)
Mack Truck					AB Volvo (Mack Truck - Mack Defense LLC)
Oshkosh Corporation					Oshkosh Corporation
O'Gara-Hess & Eisenhardt Armoring Co LLC					O'Gara Group
Polaris Industries					Polaris Industries
LTV Steel - Renco Group (AM General)					RTS AM General
Millenworks					
Textron Marine Systems					Textron Marine & Land Systems
Textron Cadillac Gage Systems					

Figure 7.10 Contraction in Ground Vehicles Sector Primes
Source: DCMA IAG

Note: companies in the matrix have had production, development, or major vehicle modification contracts in the past decade

Combat Vehicles (CVs)

CVs are typically heavily armored and integrated with complex weapon systems, fire control, and sensors. This class of military ground vehicles tends to require defense-unique components with little commercial commonality. Although an assortment of other defense firms such as Lockheed Martin, SAIC, and Textron occasionally compete for selected CV programs as a prime or major partner, BAE Systems and GDLS largely dominate the combat vehicle subsector.

Tactical Wheeled Vehicles (TWVs)

While also designed to accommodate use in demanding military environments and missions, TWVs are usually platforms modified from commercial variants. As such, this class benefits from a shared industrial base supporting this subsector and the U.S. automotive market through complex supply chains, research and development operations, and shared assembly and production systems for component manufacturing. As a result, there is the equivalent of "warm basing" in the TWV market, where firms can maintain the expertise and product line capability to ramp up production of TWVs with minimal U.S. government or DoD involvement. Although current production of TWVs is dominated by two domestic suppliers, AM General and Oshkosh, there are multiple qualified vendors for the repair, refurbishment, and modifications business.

Major Risks and Issues

The primary risks in this sector fall into many of the risk archetypes developed in the EO 13806 report. The overall risk to this segment is moderate.

Risk Archetypes:

- Single source
- Fragile market
- Capacity-constrained supply market
- Gap in U.S.-based human capital
- Erosion of U.S.-based infrastructure

Single Source

The ground vehicles sector has evolved into a number of single source suppliers. The cyclical nature of shifting demand, declining budgets, and ever-changing requirements has driven market consolidation. As a result, DoD has only one qualified supplier for many of the platforms. Due to commonality of products across both defense and commercial product lines, the firms in the TWV market are not as segmented as those in the CV market.

Fragile Market

The ground vehicles sector is a fragile market due to the economic challenges created by the cyclic nature of demand, budgets, and requirements. Over the last few decades, budget reductions and uncertainty have resulted in delays and cancellations in new ground vehicle programs. This hinders both R&D and manufacturing technology supplier investment as well as the ability to incentivize new entrants.

Capacity Constrained Market

The segments of the ground vehicles sector remain capacity-constrained. Lack of continuous demand drives private industry to reduce excess manufacturing capacity and investments in DoD production lines. This issue is particularly acute in CV production where one U.S. manufacturer is responsible for producing approximately 80 percent of the U.S. Army's Armored Brigade Combat Team Vehicles as well as the Marine Corps' Amphibious Combat Vehicle. Rapid increases in demand for multiple new products continues to stress production capabilities at this manufacturing site, leading to program delays and quality control issues in multiple programs.

U.S.-Based Human Capital

The ground vehicles sector requires a steady flow of critical engineering and manufacturing skill sets to meet present and projected needs. Both CV and TWV markets require a new generation of skilled technicians, particularly in welding and machining, to meet future demands. These two critical skills are in short supply across all sectors of the DIB. The pipeline of trade schools and reputable technical education programs that once educated the older generations of the workforce is fragmented. If the eroding technical skill base is not addressed, the ground vehicle sector will not be able to maintain the workforce needed to keep up with demand. The CV market also requires unique engineering skills such as weapons systems engineers that are not needed in the commercial ground systems arena. These skills need to be nurtured by a suitable RDT&E base to support training the specialty engineers.

Erosion of U.S.-Based Infrastructure

Erosion of U.S. based infrastructure continues to impair the ability to maintain current capacity and prepare for future needs in the organic industrial base. By law, the DoD is required to manufacture large-caliber gun barrels at one organic arsenal. Much like the private sector, fluctuating DoD demand has resulted in higher operational costs, aging infrastructure, inability to retain human capital, and inconsistent production

management. The U.S. Army recently invested in new modern equipment for the arsenal. The DoD must continue to modernize the organic industrial base to ensure its fitness to sustain current programs and meet future surge requirements.

FY2020 Developments

The coronavirus pandemic had a major impact on all DIB sectors to varying degrees. A summary of the impact on the ground sector is below:

A number of program delays resulted in production backlogs and program cost increases. Prime contractors have refined their production operations to continue to work, making up the backlogs. The two key arsenals that support this sector are in the early stages of a five-year performance improvement plan, including process improvements and equipment upgrades to better support the needs of this sector.

Ground Vehicle Sector COVID-19 Impacts	Count
Number of Affected Ground Vehicle Programs	40
Number of Reported Facility Closures for Affected Programs	31
Additional Program and Facility Impacts: • Travel restrictions delayed program reviews • Supplier disruptions impacting production schedules • Employee absenteeism limiting production • Test range non-availability • As of October 13, 2020 there have been 118 ground vehicle sector industrial facility impacts and 301 temporary DIB closures due to the coronavirus pandemic with 1 current facility closure	

Figure 7.11, Source: DCMA IAG

Sector Outlook

The U.S. Army and Marine Corps have published long-term vehicle modernization strategies to align ground vehicle priorities with ground vehicle procurement profiles. In support of these strategies, new technology development is ongoing in support of increased lethality, supportability, and mobility.

Lethality	Survivability	Mobility
• 3rd Generation Improved Forward-Looking Infrared (U.S. Industry) • 30mm cannon upgrades for the Stryker • 40mm Cased Telescoping Armament System (UK/France) • Directed energy systems	• Advanced materials/structural fiber (U.S. Industry) • Active protection systems/ countermeasures (e.g., Trophy) (Raphael-Israel) • New electronic warfare (EW) systems to jam incoming missiles	• Hybrid electric and full electric propulsion (U.S. Industry) • Artificial intelligence for self-driving and situational awareness • Biofuels (DARPA) • Fuel optimization (Army Research Lab) • Ground X-Vehicle Technology (DARPA)

Figure 7.12, Source: DCMA IAG

During the upcoming FYDP period there is expected to be a decline in sector RDT&E that will require a greater focus on selective investment. Increased prototyping efforts can increase opportunities to practice critical design skills and capabilities for CVs and TWVs. The Army's Optionally Manned Fighting Vehicle program and the Marine Corps' Light Armored Vehicle replacement program will provide development opportunities for industry.

Across the FYDP, the CV production market is expected to grow as the modernization programs of the U.S. Army and U.S. Marine Corps mature and new platforms move into production.

The TWV market remains relatively stable and healthy due to its foundation in the commercial truck manufacturing sector. However, there is room for improvement to ensure the TWV industry is better able to leverage and rapidly employ innovative products and processes and critical skills between defense and commercial markets.

Machine Tools

Sector Overview

A machine tool is a power-driven machine that shapes or forms parts made of metal or other materials (e.g., plastics, composites) through processes including: turning, grinding, milling, stamping, drilling, forming, extrusion, injection molding, composite deposition, and additive manufacturing techniques. Modern machine tools leverage sophisticated industrial control systems, process parameter monitoring systems, and networked sensors. They incorporate advanced materials and precision components, as well as advanced lubricants, bearings, sensors, and coatings.

Machine tools provide the factory floor the foundation for leveraging advances in robotics, high precision automation, specialty materials, precision components, and additive, subtractive, and hybrid machining. Because machine tools support both prototyping and production operations for virtually all manufactured products, every commercial and defense manufacturer is a stakeholder in this sector.

The global machine tool sector is mature, but involves continuous innovation of new capabilities and features that drive competition. As Figures 7.13 and 7.14 show, in FY2019, China was the largest producer and consumer of machine tools. China designs, builds, and sells large volumes of relatively low-cost machine tools for consumption in the global market, and imports high-end machines from more advanced regions (notably Japan, Europe, and the United States).

FY2019 Top 20 Machine Tool Consumers

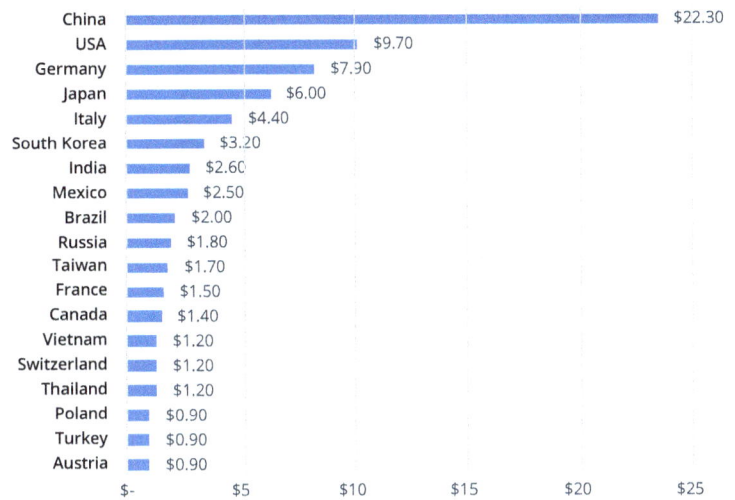

Figure 7.13: Global Machine Tool Producing Nations by Value[40]

FY2019 Top 20 Machine Tool Producers

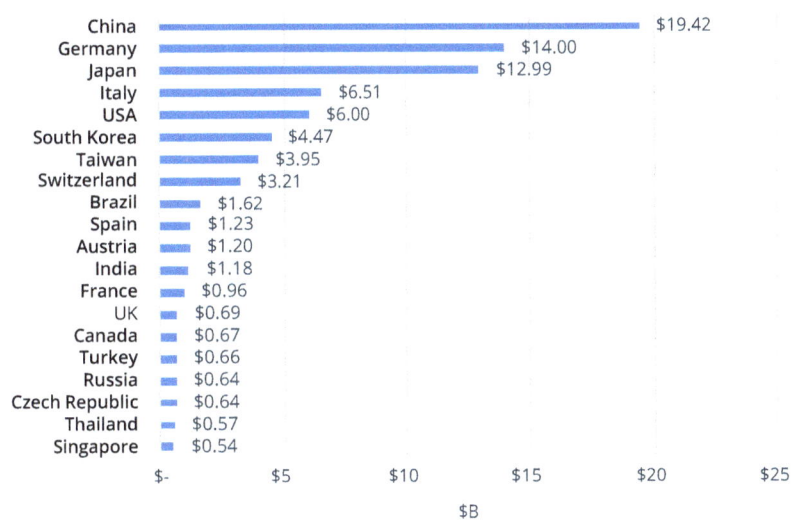

Figure 7.14: Global Machine Tool Consuming Nations by Value[41]

"Thus at the heart of the industrial health of any nation is its machine tool industry. It is no coincidence that the erosion of the machine tool industry parallels the decline of domestic manufacturing"[42]

Major Risks & Issues

Risk Archetypes:

– Foreign dependency
– DMSMS
– Gap in U.S.-based human capital

The risks detailed in the FY2019 version of this report still apply to the machine tools sector.

The playing field is still not level. In addition to widely documented and adversarial economic tradecraft, China's application of economic pressure on machine tool producing countries, especially in Asia, have steered products toward China. As Figure 7.15 shows, the U.S. has by far the worst machine tool trade balance in the list. Note that many countries with positive trade balances – such as Japan, Germany, Italy, Switzerland, South Korea, Spain, and Austria – are hardly low wage markets. However, all benefit from substantial national government support for machine tool sector R&D.

FY2019 Largest Trade Balances

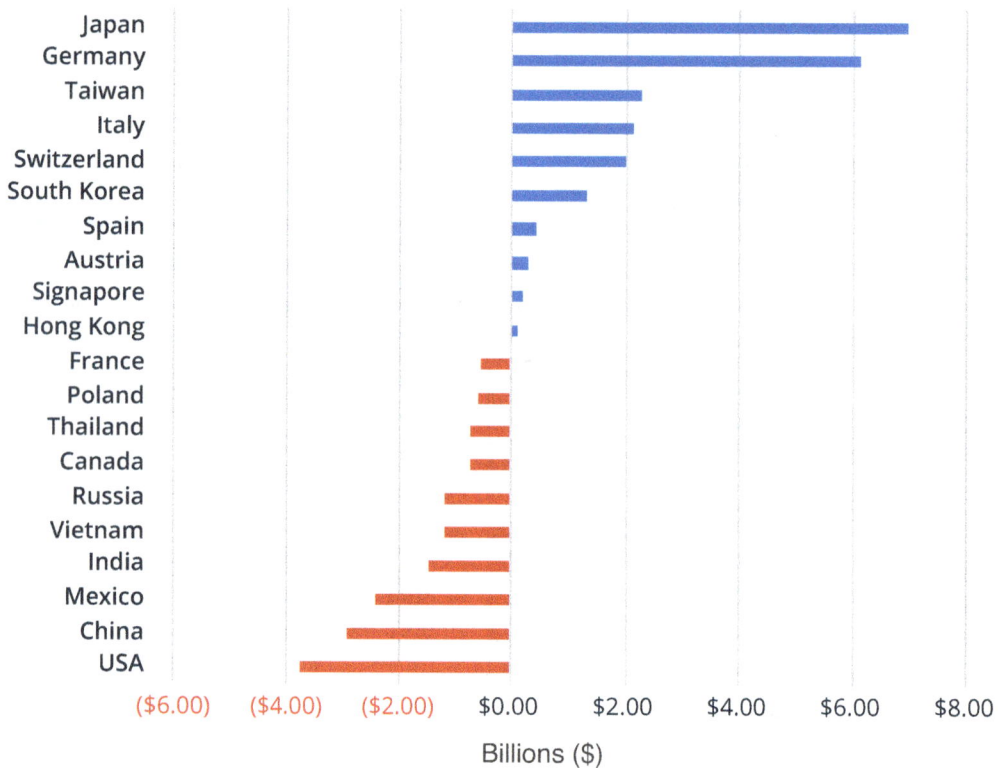

Figure 7.15: Trade Balances for Machine Tool Sector Nations[43]

The U.S. machine tool sector continues to lose diversity and capacity to international competition, industry consolidation, and business failure. The economic impacts of the coronavirus pandemic have made the situation much worse for the thousands of small "job shops" upon which the U.S. machine tool industry and the defense primes rely. Often, consolidations and failures have been the result of increased offshoring to low-cost providers to control costs and gain other tactical advantages. Offshoring can provide short-term benefits, but,

> "in such cases, corporate strategies often diverge from national interest, where better information on the effect of such decisions on the supply chain may lead to more mutually beneficial proactive decisions. It is also prudent to develop an ability to rapidly standup manufacturing capability in sectors that have been downsized in the U.S. or to develop new flexible manufacturing capabilities so that rapid reconfigurations can be realized."[44]

The U.S. still lacks a nationwide machine tool workforce development ecosystem operating at scale and velocity. This ecosystem is needed to replenish a shrinking, aging manufacturing workforce. Scale up of the current innovation ecosystem is required to revitalize our manufacturing base and attract talent through education programs that highlight the possibilities of machining careers. DoD and national efforts to overcome this weakness must address:

1. The cost of machine tool research in terms of equipment, space, and risk;

2. The fact that machine tool research is time-consuming but produces fewer publications—in journals with low impact factors;

3. Many university leaders view the machine tool sector as "old technology" and prefer to focus resources in "new" areas.

Supply chain impact, economic competitiveness, national security, and support and expansion of the innovation ecosystem are rarely considerations in university-sponsored research decisions.

FY2020 Developments

In March 2020, the IBAS Program and the Manufacturing Demonstration Facility at the Department of Energy's (DOE) Oak Ridge National Laboratory jointly launched "America's Cutting Edge" (ACE). ACE is the first in a nationwide network of regionally focused machine tool hubs. ACE has already made notable progress on three initial strategic research thrusts: develop technologies to increase productivity and efficiency of current machine tools; develop novel processes and control algorithms to enable hybrid manufacturing; and establish new machine tool metrology, designs, and controls for large components. In response to the coronavirus pandemic, ACE has also provided rapid tooling development for high-volume Personal Protective Equipment production, which provided key insights into control requirements for hybrid (additive plus subtractive) manufacturing.

In August 2020, the IBAS program awarded a National Imperative for Industrial Skills workforce development agreement to IACMI - The Composites Institute. This effort, which has the potential to impact all DoD manufacturing supply chains, operates in close partnership with ACE. It will implement a novel training experience that surpasses current computer-aided design/computer-aided manufacturing capabilities at the root of manufacturing.

Sector Outlook

The coronavirus pandemic is leading to decreases in machine tools sales and production. Factory shutdowns worldwide amidst the novel coronavirus pandemic led to months of abnormality in the manufacturing technology sector. As a result, the U.S. is seeing some of the lowest machine tool order numbers in the past decade. According to the Association for Manufacturing Technology (AMT), April and May 2020 produced the lowest monthly manufacturing technology order totals since May 2010. Table 7.16 below shows the described decline in FY2020 due to the coronavirus pandemic.

U.S. Manufacturing Technology Orders

Net New Orders for U.S. Consumption: Total National Orders ($ Thousands)

Date	Total Orders		Metal Cutting Machines		Metal Forming and Fabricating Machines	
	Units	Value	Units	Value	Units	Value
Aug-19	2,129	$380,406	2,077	$ 375,507	52	$ 4,898
Sep-19	2,269	$385,863	2,209	$ 376,460	60	$ 9,403
Oct-19	2,073	$391,208	2,009	$ 378,423	64	$ 12,785
Nov-19	1,970	$325,363	1,913	$ 311,072	57	$ 14,291
Dec-19	2,322	$387,583	2,255	$ 381,552	67	$ 6,031
Jan-20	1,729	$289,030	1,680	$ 282,453	49	$ 6,578
Feb-20	1,617	$283,167	1,593	$ 274,865	24	$ 8,302
Mar-20	1,754	$312,367	1,725	$ 309,088	29	$ 3,280
Apr-20	1,494	$235,062	1,467	$ 228,358	27	$ 6,704
May-20	1,602	$224,671	1,570	$ 217,941	32	$ 6,730
Jun-20	2,122	$343,158	2,088	$ 338,607	34	$ 4,550
Jul-20	1,840	$336,400	1,811	$ 331,806	29	$ 4,594
Aug-20	1,698	$297,769	1,679	$ 289,417	19	$ 8,351
Average	1,894	$322,465	1,852	$ 315,042	42	$ 7,423

Table 7.16: Net Orders for U.S. Consumption of Manufacturing Technology45

Indicators show that the industry is now improving as factories reopen. In May 2020, Oxford Economics analysts had predicted that the industry would be down 50 percent for FY2020 due to the uncertainty in the return to work across the country and worldwide. Instead, the expected loss is now half of that prediction. It is reasonable to expect that China's centrally planned and controlled economy and robust government support will afford it a significant short-term advantage in this area.

Last year's report emphasized the importance of the linkage between the ability to conceive, design, develop and manufacture advanced machine tools and national self-determination. FY2020's

coronavirus pandemic supported that lesson in stark terms. The inability to rapidly obtain tooling to produce the PPE and medicines required to keep American workers on the job crippled not only health care but all segments of the economy. The lack of a robust innovation ecosystem exacerbates the problem. The costs are measured not only in lost sales and production delays on major weapon systems, but also in the loss of the workers and firms that produce the products we need to prevail and thrive.

Technology Trends and Developments

For the next ten years, metal cutting tools (as opposed to metal forming or fabricating machine products), which accounted for over 97 percent of U.S. manufacturing technology orders in FY2020, are also expected to be a major product line due to the expected demand from industries such as automobiles and construction. Computerized Numerical Control tools will drive the machine tools market due to increased automation and digitalization across industries. They improve reliability and precision, and shorten production times. New COVID-19 inspired guidelines and regulations affecting worker spacing have made these capabilities even more attractive to customers and, hence, developers.

Materials

Sector Overview

The materials sector is among the most diverse sectors that the DoD assesses. It includes all elements of the periodic table in their natural and synthetic forms, as well as products throughout the materials supply chain through value-added processing, trading, and manufacturing into semi-finished products. The breadth of product coverage, global trade flows, and associated technical disciplines within the sector compels DoD to collaborate with non-defense agencies and private industry, both domestic and foreign, to ensure that the Materials Sector can support the requirements of the NDS.

The DoD largely relies on commercial markets and logistics networks to meet material demand. Since the end of the Cold War, U.S. reliance on foreign sources and globalized processing operations has accelerated. In general, this trend has decreased the cost of materials and opened new sources to U.S. manufacturers, with concomitant growth in U.S. import reliance and offshoring across the sector.

Major Risks and Issues

> ### Risk Archetypes:
>
> - Foreign dependency

In last year's report, the Department observed that the fundamental risk within the Materials Sector flows from the *U.S. private sector capability gap* between current, globalized supply chains and (A) current threats below the level of armed conflict and (B) serious threats in the event of armed conflict. The Department also highlighted three risk categories:

1. consolidation of supply chains in ownership, geography, and market access;

2. under-execution or lack of due diligence; and

3. lack of resilience.

These three risk factors remain in force, and the following new factors, accentuated by mobilization for COVID-19 response, have hampered the Department's ability to address them.

Acute Personnel Shortages

Upon the declaration of a National Emergency with respect to COVID-19, the Department mobilized substantial portions of its workforce to support HHS and FEMA. Within the OUSD (IP), this reorientation reflects the many additional duties performed by its personnel, particularly for DPA Title I and Title III. Similarly, the National Defense Stockpile (NDS) program repurposed its supply chain monitoring tools so the inter-agency could anticipate vulnerabilities in the Materials Sector as COVID-19 outbreaks progressed globally. Unfortunately, the NDS program was unable to make new hires or onboard newly-hired personnel in the COVID-19 telework environment, distributing current work and COVID-response tasks across a dwindling staff. As a result of these combined workforce constraints, DoD cancelled, deferred, or reduced its activities in the Materials Sector during FY2020, summarized in Figure 7.17.

Note: In House Report 116-442, the House Committee on Armed Services directed the Secretary of Defense to include a supply chain and vulnerability assessment for rare earth elements, tungsten, neodymium-iron-boron magnets, niobium, indium, gallium, germanium, and tin in this report, along with recommendations for stockpiling action for those materials and any other relevant materials. The Department has satisfied this reporting requirement with the submission of the Strategic and Critical Materials 2021 Report on Stockpile Requirements, in accordance with 50 U.S.C. 98h–5. However, the Department cautions that this report will be the last report of its type to Congress, pursuant to section 1061 of Public Law 114-328 (see Sector Outlook).

Cancelled Activities	Deferred Activities	Reduced Activities
- Meeting of the Strategic Materials Protection Board (10 U.S.C. 187)	- Time-Study for release of materials from the NDS under simulated National Emergency conditions (50 U.S.C. 98f) - Mobilization exercise for release of NDS materials under simulated National Emergency conditions (50 U.S.C. 98f) - Joint research and development activities with foreign allies under critical minerals Action Plans	- Meetings and reports for National Science & Technology Council action on critical minerals under Executive Order 13817 - Meetings and reports for the Federal Consortium for Advanced Batteries - Meetings and collaboration with foreign allies under critical minerals Action Plans - Acquisition policy and legislative proposal development

Table 7.17: Reduction in DoD Materials Sector Activities

As the Department returns to a normal work environment, many of these activities will be re-started, but the lack of workforce resilience is a significant risk in a future supply chain disruption event.

Significant Requirements Growth without Resourcing

In last year's report, the Department observed that Congress directed the NDS program to divert approximately 89.8 percent of the proceeds from its sales to other programs (see 7.18). Though Congress has halted these funding transfers, the NDS program remains undercapitalized, as described in reports under 50 U.S.C. 98h-5. The Department will deliver the final iteration of this report to Congress in early 2021 (see Sector Outlook).

Distribution Type	Total Amount (FY2003–FY2018) (Real $2018)	Average Annual Cash Flow (Real $2018)	Sample Activities / Accts.
To National Defense Stockpile Transaction Fund	$ 417.3M	$ 26.0M	– Material acquisitions – Qualification of new sources – Metallurgical R&D
To Non-Defense Accts.	($998.6M)	($62.4M)	– General Treasury Acct. – American Battle Monuments Commission (World War II Memorial) – Hospital Insurance Trust Fund – Federal Supplementary Medical Trust Fund
To Other Defense Accts.	($2,701.5M)	($168.8M)	– Foreign Military Sales Treasury Acct. – Reclamation purchases of electromagnetic spectrum – Defense Health Program – Military Service Operations & Maintenance accts.
Net Cash Flow to National Defense Stockpile Transaction Fund	**($3,282.8M)**	**($205.1M)**	

Figure 7.18: National Defense Stockpile Transaction Fund Distributions

Note: Total does not add due to rounding

Furthermore, as DoD and inter-agency supply chain assessments identify Materials Sector risk, the U.S. government routinely turns to the NDS for acquisition options. In addition to the previously-noted inadequacy of funding, the Department also observes that the NDS formerly held many of these at-risk materials.

For example, the Department of Commerce is investigating titanium sponge and vanadium under section 232 of *The Trade Expansion Act of 1962*. The NDS liquidated stocks of both materials during the post-Cold War sell-off, and to the extent possible within existing resources, the NDS program is increasing its stocks of these materials by reclaiming them from end-of-life weapon systems. Similarly, the NDS formerly contained approximately 14,000 tonnes of rare earth materials, equivalent to seven percent of today's global market. The Department submitted a legislative request to acquire rare earth materials for the NDS, but Congress has not adopted this provision for the FY2021 NDAA.

FY2020 Developments

The DPA Title III program issued multiple awards under Presidential Determinations related to neodymium-iron-boron (NdFeB) permanent magnet manufacture and strategic inventory demonstration. The DPA Title III program also issued one award using CARES Act funds to a domestic NdFeB manufacturer, whose critical manufacturing skills were at risk due to the onset of COVID-19:

- Urban Mining Company ($28.8 million), related to NdFeB magnet manufacture and maintaining critical workforce skills impacted by COVID-19
- TDA Magnetics LLC ($3.4 million) and Urban Mining Company ($1.7 million), related to the demonstration of a domestic NdFeB magnet supply chain and strategic inventory

The IBAS program also issued awards to the following vendors through its Cornerstone Other Transaction Agreement (OTA): Lynas Corporation ($0.65 million) and MP Materials ($0.66 million), for heavy rare earth separation technical development.

Sector Outlook

Funding and personnel constraints shape the Department's actions in the Materials Sector. Consequently, DoD's approach remains an exercise in economy of force, deploying against only the highest-risk materials with minimum levels of funding and time. Key activities in the Materials Sector are described below.

Defense Production Act (Title III) and the National Defense Stockpile

In the FY2021 President's Budget Request, the President recommended a significant increase to the base budget of the DPA Title III program. This funding increase aligns closely with pre-sequestration projections for the program ($185.8M forecast, versus $178.6 million requested, adjusted for inflation) (see Figure 7.19).

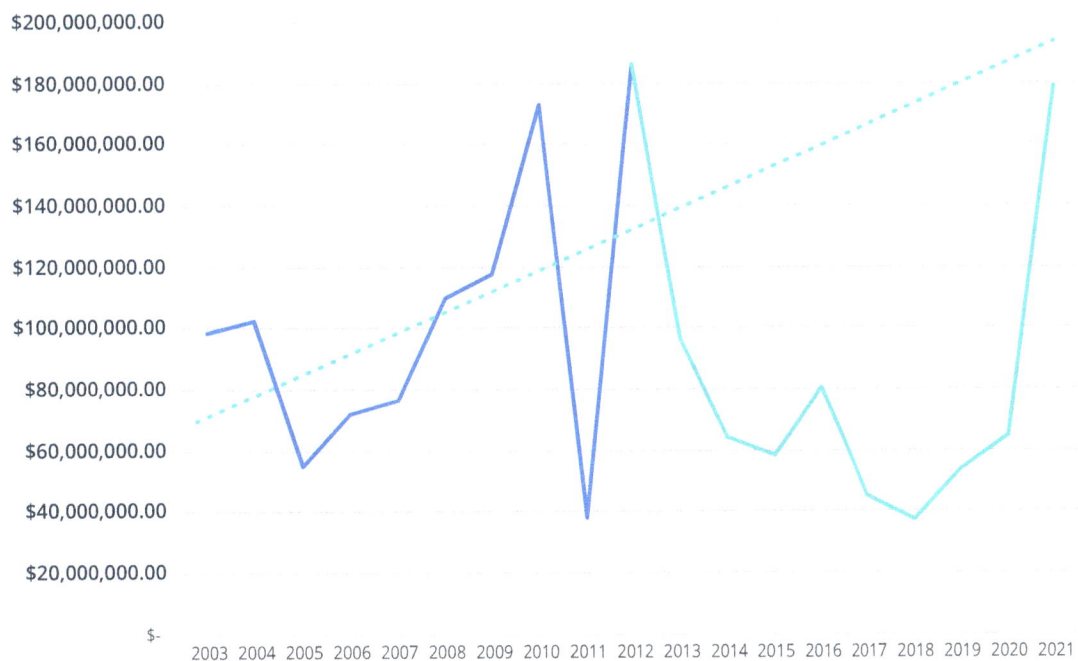

Figure 7.19: Defense Production Act Purchases Funding (Real $2019)

This resource influx will enable the DPA Title III program to execute against current Presidential Determinations far more effectively. However, the Department cautions that the FYDP for the Defense Production Act Purchases account in the FY2021 President's Budget Request returns to recent program lows, $45.9 million in FY2022 to $49.0 million in FY2025.

As noted in a prior section, the NDS program would like to re-acquire certain rare earth materials. The Department submitted a legislative proposal for the FY2021 National Defense Authorization Act to purchase (1) dysprosium, (2) neodymium-praseodymium (i.e., didymium) oxide, (3) NdFeB magnet block, (4) yttrium, and (5) samarium-cobalt alloy. Congress has not included this provision in legislation, and so, the Department is preparing follow-on legislative proposals to address this and other unmitigated Materials Sector shortfalls. Similarly, the Department notes the *Strategic and Critical Materials 2021 Report on Stockpile Requirements* (ref: 50 U.S.C. 98h-5) will be the last report of its type to Congress, pursuant to section 1061 of Public Law 114-328. This sunset provision notwithstanding, the Department will continue estimating Materials Sector shortfalls every two years, consistent with available funding and human capital.

U.S. Interagency and Allied Collaboration

The Department continues to leverage the partnerships forged in the execution of EO 13806 and E.O. 13817 to implement joint solutions, including:

- Sharing modeling best-practices, data, and data analytics approaches
- Pooling research and development funding to address common risks
- Enabling of defense and non-defense agencies in domestic and international fora

The Department maintains valuable partnerships with the Departments of State, Commerce, Interior, and Energy, as well as the U.S. Trade Representative, the DFC, and the Executive Office of the President, as well as our longstanding partnerships with NTIB members and other allies.

Modernization of Statutory Authorities for Materials Sector Mitigation

Major industrial base mitigation authorities for the DoD generally date to the Korean War-era or earlier. Some of these authorities are regularly re-authorized, but others have not undergone a meaningful reassessment since the 1970s. DoD is preparing legislative proposals for the modernization of many of these statutes, including the *Defense Production Act* and the *Strategic and Critical Materials Stock Piling Act,* and will seek appropriate stakeholder input to advance them for Congress' consideration.

Missiles and Munitions

Sector Overview

The missiles and munitions industrial base is comprised of both government-owned facilities (referred to as the 'organic' industrial base) and private sector companies engaged in the production of "smart" and "dumb" bombs.

- "Smart" bombs include tactical (cruise, air-to-air, air-to-ground, surface-to-air, torpedoes, mines, etc.) missiles, missile defense, strategic missiles, and has expanded to include hypersonic weapons.
- "Dumb" bombs include ammunition, mortars, artillery, tank rounds, naval gun/cannon rounds, etc.

However, the missiles and munitions sector definition could broaden through the 2020s due to changing technologies. Directed energy and cyber could enhance this sector by substituting non-kinetic weapons and effects for traditional missiles and munitions.

The sector is primarily defense unique and largely subject to wartime needs—meaning that procurement ramps up during wartime and declines when conflict ends. The market is defined and hampered by this conflict-reliant pattern, creating significant management and viability challenges for suppliers and their sub-tier suppliers.

Major Risks & Issues

Risk Archetypes:

- DMSMS
- Gap in U.S.-based human capital

Obsolescence & Lack of Redundant Capability

Specialty Chemicals from Foreign Sources: DoD relies on multiple non-domestic sources for many specialty chemicals, some from "non-friendly" sources. This presents a risk that supply could be disrupted during conflict, severely impacting our ability to produce munitions. OUSD (IP) is tracking development of advanced manufacturing technologies and scale-up efforts that could eliminate the need for foreign sources. Several DPA Title III efforts are scheduled for award during FY2021 to establish or evaluate domestic manufacturing capability for chemicals used in munitions. DoD investment in a series of flexible Pilot Scale Plants would also provide the capacity to address multiple critical obsolescent energetic materials within the organic industrial base, guaranteeing availability of these legacy materials as needed. These Pilot-Scale Plants would also provide a stable pipeline for rapid scale-up of next generational energetic materials for RDT&E. However, fully mitigating foreign dependency on specialty chemicals will require large investments (see Materials Sector Assessment).

Visibility into Sub-Tier Suppliers

Diminishing manufacturing sources and material suppliers (DMSMS), including obsolescence and single point failures: Due to the relatively low procurements of missiles, DoD relies on single source suppliers for many specialty materials, components, and end items, and obsolescence continues to be a major issue. These sole source components are critical pieces of the munition that are sometimes only available at government-owned facilities as manufacturers of last resort. Frequently, a component is too far down in the supply chain for DoD to have any visibility. Competitor nations are aggressively attempting to acquire critical sub-tier suppliers, either directly or through the higher-level ownership chain of the company, with limited visibility from DoD.

Loss of Design and Production; Aging Workforce

Hypersonics: Development and production of the many specialty materials and subsystems required for hypersonics is a niche area. The majority of the industrial base consists of small businesses that have focused their efforts on proving their technology and producing a handful of demonstration vehicles and glide bodies. Most of the workforce knowledge resides in these small companies. The traditional DoD industrial base is limited in production capability, resulting in large risks for cost, efficiency, and production. The industrial base is willing to self-invest in these capabilities, but a lack of definitive demand from DoD prevents them from justifying the business case necessary to do so.

Nuclear Modernization: Development and production of missiles as part of the Department's nuclear modernization efforts requires re-invigoration of certain industrial capabilities, which includes reconstituting a workforce that hasn't produced nuclear weapons in many decades.

Design and Manufacturing of Missiles and Munitions: Promising STEM and trade-skill oriented personnel are leaving the sector industry for other occupations. Individuals with these skills are becoming harder to recruit and retain due to barriers of pay, location, and cyclical sector demand. Increased engagement with the U.S, Manufacturing Institutes will support implementation of advanced manufacturing technologies, as needed, and strengthen and expand the capabilities of the US manufacturing workforce in key DoD technology areas.

Resilient Industrial Base: Surge and Gap Planning

Consistent Demand Signal: Conflict-driven procurements for missiles, munitions, and supporting energetic components make it difficult to maintain consistent and steady production demand. Steady demand enables industry to better plan for longer term stable production, negating the risk of the production line "going cold" (impacting readiness) and enabling greater surge capacity. However, U.S. government goals do not always align with industry goals.

Infrastructure: Manufacturing & Test Equipment, Test Ranges & Instrumentation

Hypersonics and Nuclear Modernization: Due to the decades-long lapse in hypersonic and nuclear weapon development and production, facilities and infrastructure (including unique production equipment) require reconstitution, major modernization, and increases in capacity. Test ranges and instrumentation also require significant capacity increases and/or modernization. Investment in both industry and organic DoD facilities is needed to achieve required capability and capacity.

FY2020 Developments

COVID-19 Impacts

COVID-19 has impacted the missiles and munitions sector less than other DIB sectors because it is nearly 100 percent DoD unique, unlike other areas which have been suffering due to the loss of commercial demand (e.g. Aircraft). There has been no decrease in the demand for missiles and munitions; this steady demand has kept the sector industrial base relatively healthy. In the spring and summer of 2020, some missile sector industrial facilities temporarily closed; however, all facilities reopened by September and remain open. Some impacts continue to be felt in program schedules and production deliveries, but the sector is better positioned should outbreaks increase again.

Ammonium Perchlorate (AP) Production

Ammonium Perchlorate is a critical energetic oxidizer with a decades-long history of use in rocket propellants, including space launch. Former suppliers have left the industry due to limited and inconsistent demand, which significantly reduced when the Space Shuttle program ended.

To address the AP supply issue, OUSD (IP) issued a Request for Information in 2017 seeking information about domestic AP sourcing. A business analysis was conducted for AP production on a GOCO plant and found not cost effective. One industry partner is developing a capability (online in late 2020) to produce AP from domestic materials, which will provide competition, supply stability, and reduce cost.

Energetic Materials

In addition to AP, the Department must address other critical energetic materials, such as Butarez, Potassium Nitrate, Zirconium, and Aluminum. A third of DoD's energetic material is produced overseas, and many materials have direct dependencies on China. Industry often chooses not to use domestic or allied sources of these chemicals even when available due to pricing.

The Critical Energetic Materials Working Group (CEMWG) executes a coordinated Department-wide approach to identify energetic materials and their ingredients that are at risk of becoming unavailable to the DoD. In 2019, CEMWG released a survey to government and industry to identify at-risk chemicals. The CEMWG found that the industrial base for chemicals was fragile, vulnerable to supply chain disruptions, dependent on foreign nations for a significant number of sole-source chemicals used in the majority of the DoD's munitions, reliant on obsolete specifications, and impacted by increasing environmental regulatory pressure within the U.S. and abroad. In January 2019, the President signed four Presidential Determinations to allow the use of DPA Title III funding to mitigate risk for critical chemicals for munitions.

Large Solid-Rocket Motors (LSRM)

To address the LSRM risk, Aerojet Rocketdyne (AR) is reconstituting LSRM manufacturing capability at its Camden, Arkansas facility. Northrop Grumman has announced its intent to include AR as part of its national team for ground-based strategic deterrent (GBSD), which should continue to provide DoD with two suppliers.

Production Capacity

DoD has conducted munitions war rooms to identify opportunities to accelerate munitions deliveries by either increasing production capacity or shortening lead times. These deep dives into each munition's industrial suppliers have been critical to identify and address capacity constraints and/or production bottlenecks. These efforts are labor and data intensive, which limits the Department's ability to execute war rooms to the highest risk items.

Sector Outlook

Missile budgets are expected to decline over the next few years, and then remain relatively stable through the next decade. The market for missiles and munitions has recovered from a decline in the early 2010s (in the wake of the 2008 recession) and the precision guided munitions market expanded by over 50 percent from 2014-2020.

Planned efforts in hypersonics and nuclear modernization will tap into new areas of the industrial base, but will also tax some of the existing base, particularly elements that support conventional missile production within the sub-tier supplier base. U.S. industry is willing to invest in production capacity and capability for hypersonics, but many suppliers are waiting on clear U.S. government plans and forecasts to justify the business case for these investments. A more detailed overview of the hypersonics industrial base is addressed in the Emerging and Critical Technologies section of this report.

The E.O. 13806 report, the CEMWG, and the war room process have improved visibility into the health of the missiles and munitions sector, and directed mitigation actions in several high-risk areas. The Department will continue to assess and mitigate higher-risk areas to improve the health of the industrial base, and continue to advocate for the strategic assessment, modernization, and expansion of U.S. and allied production capacity.

Nuclear Matter Warheads

Sector Overview

The Nuclear Matter Warheads Sector consists of U.S. government-owned, contractor-operated (GOCO) sites, and U.S. government furnished equipment used in the design, building, and testing of our nation's nuclear warheads. The U.S. nuclear deterrent is a lynchpin in defense planning and that of U.S. allies and adversaries. Nuclear weapons are designed and produced to meet an "Always/Never" standard:

1. They must always work when authorized by proper authority, and

2. They must never work in any situation or environment (normal, abnormal, or adversarial) without authorization by proper authority.

Supply chain availability and integrity are crucial to achieving the "Always/Never" standard, but an increasing set of risks threaten the integrity of the enterprise. Some of the associated research, development, production equipment, and software are designed and produced in-house by the DoD's organic industrial base. However, the majority is procured from outside vendors.

Major Risks & Issues

> ### Risk Archetypes:
> - DMSMS
> - Product security

Macro forces driving risk to the Nuclear Matter Warheads Sector are a reflection of the same forces driving risks to other sectors upon which the nuclear matter warheads sector is dependent (e.g. machine tools, electronics, and materials). Chief among those macro forces is the globalization of supply chains for software, materials, and equipment.

Clearable Workforce

The U.S. faces a diminishing supply of clearable labor with the advanced education and training necessary for designing, producing, and stewarding nuclear weapons. The primary source of that labor, U.S. colleges and universities, generate insufficient U.S. citizen graduates in STEM areas relevant to the nuclear enterprise. The U.S. also lacks labor with important trade skills, including welders. Additional challenges due to clearance requirements greatly reduce the available pool of labor.

Microelectronics/Electronic Components

Nuclear warheads depend on trusted sources of microelectronics and electronics. However, due to diminishing U.S.-based microelectronic and electronic manufacturing capability, it is challenging to ensure that finished assemblies, systems, and subsystems exclusively leverage trusted, discrete components.

Critical Materials

Various sole source materials, addressed through the Nuclear Posture Review, are unavailable through trusted sources in sufficient quantities to ensure a robust and independent nuclear capability throughout a weapon's lifecycle. The problem is exacerbated by policies and requirements that limit or place restrictions on procurement options (e.g. life of program buys).

Software Systems/Applications

Lack of trusted sources of software design tools, data management systems, manufacturing execution, and facility controls introduces risk to the nuclear weapons engineering environment. This problem is exacerbated by poor cybersecurity practices of many key software vendors.

Analytical and Test Equipment

Given current nuclear weapons test restrictions, specialized analytical and test equipment is essential to ensure the "Always/Never" standard. Components, subsystems, and systems must be tested to unique qualification standards, but the test equipment supplier base is increasingly globalized and not trusted, leading to uncertainty in testing.

FY2020 Developments

The Department of Energy (DoE)/National Nuclear Security Administration (NNSA) has several warhead modernization efforts underway and managing the supply availability and integrity is key for the successful completion of these efforts.

The B61-12 Life Extension Program (LEP) will integrate DOE efforts to extend the service life of the warhead with DoD efforts to develop a guided Tail Kit Assembly (TKA) required to maintain current B61 mission characteristics. Programmatic integration of the Air Force-led, joint DoD-DOE program is accomplished through the B61 LEP Project Officers Group and its subgroups. The U.S. Air Force is responsible for development, acquisition, and delivery of a guided TKA and for All Up Round technical integration, system qualification and fielding of the B61-12 variant on multiple platforms. The production effort for the B61 TKA includes the production and delivery of TKAs, accessories, spares, ancillary equipment, trainers, lot acceptance test assets, and support. The program received the signed Acquisition Decision Memorandum authorizing the B61 Mod 12 LEP TKA program to enter into the Production and Deployment phase on October 26, 2018.

The NNSA, in coordination with the DoD, is also extending the life of the W80-1 warhead as part of the W80-4 Life Extension Program. The W80-4 will be used on the Long-Range Standoff weapon which is expected to replace the legacy Air Launched Cruise Missile in mid-2020.

COVID-19

In 2020, the COVID-19 crisis presented a series of truly unprecedented challenges for the nuclear security enterprise and its workforce. The health and safety of our employees is and will continue to be the Department's main focus. Due to our critical national security missions, the NNSA could not and cannot temporarily cease operations until the crisis is over.

NNSA adopted a policy of maximum telework and social distancing to safeguard the health and welfare of the workforce, while also identifying a number of mission-critical activities that could not be performed remotely and needed to continue on-site. NNSA worked with its sites to set priorities and relied on them to make decisions based on the local situation and regulations to protect the workforce.

At the outset of the pandemic, NNSA directed the management and operating teams to continue production of the essential components and assemblies required to maintain critical missions. NNSA leadership is currently evaluating options to manage future impacts based on additional periods of COVID-19 limitations.

Sector Outlook

The Nuclear Matter Warheads Sector is increasingly challenged by reliance on foreign vendors for the supply and maintenance of advanced machine tools, and dependent on globalized complex supply chains for materials and components. Recent and ongoing life extension programs provide opportunities to address some of these vulnerabilities as new contracts and supply chains are developed.

Organic Defense Industrial Base

Sector Overview

The Organic Industrial Base (OIB) includes government-owned government-operated (GOGO) and government-owned contractor operated (GOCO) facilities that provide specific goods and services for the Department of Defense.

The OIB is comprised of resource providers, acquisition and sustainment planners, and manufacturing and maintenance performers in depots, shipyards, manufacturing arsenals, and ammunition plants. Collectively, the OIB provides maintenance and manufacturing services to sustain approximately 339,290 vehicles, 280 combatant ships and submarines, and over 15,340 aircraft and supporting critical safety items. Roughly $92 billion of DoD's total FY2019 $687.8 billion expenditure was applied to maintenance

Organic Manufacturing Arsenals, Major Depot Maintenance Facilities, and Ammunition Plants	
Army - Anniston Army Depot, Anniston, AL - Corpus Christi Army Depot, Corpus Christi, TX - Letterkenny Army Depot, Chambersburg, PA - Red River Army Depot, Texarkana, TX - Tobyhanna Army Depot, Tobyhanna, PA - Rock Island Arsenal, Joint Manufacturing and - Technology Center, Rock Island, IL - Watervliet Arsenal, Watervliet, NY - Pine Bluff Arsenal, Pine Bluff, AR - Crane Army Ammunition Activity, Crane, IN - Holston Army Ammunition Plant, Kingsport, TN - Iowa Army Ammunition Plant, Middletown, IA - Lake City Army Ammunition Plant, Independence, MO - McAlester Army Ammunition Plant, McAlester, OK - Milan Army Ammunition Plant, Milan, TN - Radford Army Ammunition Plant, Radford, VA - Scranton Army Ammunition Plant, Scranton, PN - Quad Cities Cartridge Case Facility, Rock Island, IL	**Navy** - Fleet Readiness Center East, MCAS Cherry Point, NC - Fleet Readiness Center Southeast, NAS Jacksonville, FL - Fleet Readiness Center Southwest, NAS North Island, CA - Portsmouth Naval Shipyard, Portsmouth, ME - Norfolk Naval Shipyard, Portsmouth, VA - Puget Sound Naval Shipyard and Intermediate Maintenance Facility, Bremerton, WA - Naval Surface Warfare Center Indian Head Division, Indian Head, MD - Pearl Harbor Naval Shipyard and Intermediate Maintenance Facility, Pearl Harbor, HI
Air Force - Ogden Air Logistics Complex, Hill AFB, UT - Oklahoma City Air Logistics Complex, Tinker AFB, OK - Warner Robins Air Logistics Complex, Robbins AFB, GA	**Marine Corps** - Marine Depot Maintenance Command, Albany Production Plant, MCLB Albany, GA - Marine Depot Maintenance Command, Barstow Production Plant, MCLB Barstow, CA

Figure 7.20

activities and services. DoD currently operates 17 major organic depot maintenance facilities and three manufacturing arsenals. Services provided within the OIB range in intricacy from daily system inspection and maintenance to Pilot Plant Scale-up, comprehensive depot-level overhaul, or rebuilding of engines and major weapon systems.

From a broader national security perspective, the OIB acts as an insurance policy to ensure a ready and controlled source of technical competence and resources. In doing so, the OIB executes sizeable legislatively and administratively directed production and maintenance workloads. Congress has developed an extensive framework of statutes that govern the establishment and workloading of core organic industrial capabilities, maximum yearly private sector industrial workload allocation, initial depot source of repair assignments, and subsequent movement of critical weapon system, engine, and component workloads. The OIB is positioned to provide the capacity and capability to support the readiness and materiel availability goals of current and future DoD weapon systems. However, FY2020 presented the OIB with both unforeseen and overarching, endemic risks and issues.

Major Risks and Issues

Risk Archetypes

- – Erosion of U.S.-based infrastructure
- – Sole source
- – Gaps in U.S.-based human capital.

Three primary macro forces and three key "risk archetypes," as categorized by the EO 13806 report, face the OIB. The macro forces include sequestration and uncertainty of U.S. government spending, the decline of U.S. manufacturing base capabilities and capacity, and diminishing U.S. STEM and trade skills. Three corresponding major risk types confront the OIB: 1) erosion of U.S.-based infrastructure; 2) reliance on sole source providers; and 3) gaps in U.S.-based human capital.

Erosion of U.S.-Based Infrastructure: The condition of the OIB continues to be encumbered by dated infrastructure, driven by longstanding investment trade-offs resulting in resourcing shortfalls. DoD is working to address both near and long-term OIB capability gaps through initiatives expected to improve strategy, policy, performance, resource advocacy, and outcomes. However, given the resources committed to infrastructure investment in DoD's OIB, operational drivers have strained the OIB more than the budget allows. The erosion of organic infrastructure continues to impact turnaround time and repair costs of both legacy and new weapon systems, decreasing operational readiness and impacting future deployment schedules. To address this risk, DoD is developing a congressionally mandated comprehensive OIB infrastructure improvement strategy that will drive increases in Joint Force readiness and materiel availability.[46] By introducing innovative process improvement and organizational solutions to be overseen by DoD-level governance, OIB infrastructure needs will receive greater visibility, increasing the likelihood of attaining required resourcing. Additionally, the introduction of a series of new state-of-the-Art Pilot-Scale Plants with flexible products & capacities would be an infrastructure solution to provide right-sized production capability for multiple legacy & emerging energetic materials with minimum facility investment by DoD.

Reliance on Sole Source Providers: The OIB supports the nation's defense industrial base manufacturing capability to provide operationally available scenario-tasked weapon systems. It is therefore imperative to ensure continuity of operational readiness of these facilities in order to meet both peacetime and surge requirements. OIB installations have been challenged in FY2020 and have experienced significant cost and schedule disruptions, resulting in both near and long term materiel readiness impacts for weapon systems across the Military Services. Due primarily to operational impacts of COVID-19, the viability of significant portions of sole source OIB capability has been threatened. To address this risk, the OIB must recover financial losses and pre-COVID military readiness rates.

Gaps in U.S. - Based Human Capital: The OIB confronts workforce skill gap risk throughout the sector. The emergence of new weapons system technologies, coupled with legacy system retirements, has driven a substantial disparity between skill requirements and workforce capabilities. Recruitment and retention of critical skill sets is also a primary OIB concern, mainly because of strong competition for skilled labor from the private sector and a lack of defense-specific skills. To mitigate this risk, several ongoing and interrelated mitigation strategies and initiatives are underway. For example, each of the Military Departments has implemented the direct hire authority provided by Congress to hire required OIB personnel. Innovative training approaches have been introduced to improve the OIB's recruitment of trained artisans that can provide significant and immediate impacts on productivity and readiness.

FY2020 Developments

Sector Outlook

The OIB, like most sectors of DoD's industrial base, faces considerable challenges. The OIB outlook, however, is that sound progress is possible and underway, driven by an unyielding focus upon National Defense Strategy imperatives. This section highlights three elements central to the way forward for the OIB.

First, new technologies and processes continually impact the strength and resilience of the OIB. Therefore, the OIB must continually refresh and modernize tools and processes used to retain materiel readiness. Within OSD, the Office of the Deputy Assistant Secretary of Defense for Materiel Readiness leads a broad set of maintenance technology and innovation initiatives in partnership with OUSD(R&E), the Military Departments, and industry partners. These initiatives focus on cross-cutting industrial base capabilities that enable the OIB to generate materiel availability at lowest cost, enable reduced repair cycle times, and provide higher reliability more safely. Examples of OIB innovations and technology development and insertion that will impact the future viability and effectiveness of the OIB include additive manufacturing, predictive maintenance, big data analytics, robotics and automation, non-destructive inspection, and advanced electronics diagnostics. A specific example of innovative OIB technology insertion is Intermittent Fault Detection Technology. Additionally, to address OIB obsolescence issues, the Department has developed a series of Pilot-Scaled energetic material facilities that could offer flexibility in the production of multiple products at varied scales.

COVID-19 Impacts

COVID-19 had major operational and budgetary impact on the OIB in FY2020. Reduced operational exercises, force training cancellations, and mission adjustments resulted in reduced production output throughout the OIB. COVID-19 workforce non-availability also decreased operations, both internal to the OIB and throughout its supply chains. Reduced demands/sales impacted the OIB's financing mechanism, the Working Capital Fund, by diminishing the fund's corpus and thereby increasing the cost of goods sold, while concurrently hampering annual throughput. Most installations have returned to pre-COVID production levels, and each Military Service war fighting domain, except for Navy (Air), expects to "carryover" some portion of their workload into FY2021. With delays in depot repair schedules, waivers may be required due to the carryover limits in the Financial Management Regulation. U.S. Navy ship maintenance is especially affected and may be unable to fully recover its schedule due primarily to physical shipyard constraints. To ensure the OIB returns to pre-COVID production rates, it is estimated that a fiscal solution that addresses approximately ten percent of the FY2019 total spend on DoD depot maintenance is required.

The second key emerging trend related to the OIB's outlook is that near-peer focused warfighting activities, particularly those related to posture, is becoming gradually more interlinked with OIB capability and capacity. In this contested logistics environment, weapon systems sustainment, and maintaining and building contingency bases and connected infrastructure is increasingly important. While progress is being made to improve OIB resilience in a near-peer contested logistics environment, the OIB must be postured with a new and constantly evolving set of decision support systems, supply chains, resourcing, and capability provision tools.

Finally, the OIB will be significantly shaped by investment choices, particularly in key elements of OIB infrastructure. This issue has been called into sharp focus with concern about possible shorting amounts of funding required for capital equipment purchases and the requirement of "heel-toe-funding," with many projects precisely timed. These require projects and regular maintenance to be executed and funded on schedule throughout the OIB.

Radar and Electronic Warfare

Sector Overview

Military radars and electronic warfare systems play a significant role in meeting our national security objectives. Radar is essential to detecting the presence, direction, distance, and speed of targets such as aircraft, ships, and weapons, and for controlling flight and weaponry. Radar achieves detection by transmitting electromagnetic waves that reflect off objects and return to the receiver to enable detection. Required to operate in the harshest environments to support combat operations, military radar system requirements are often more stringent than those imposed on commercial systems. Radar systems have many applications and can be used to detect slight changes to surfaces over time—allowing, for example, the detection of footprints of shallow depth.

Electronic warfare (EW) systems continue to become a more integral element of military weapon systems. EW refers to military action involving the use of electromagnetic energy and directed energy to control the electromagnetic spectrum or to attack the enemy. The purpose is to deny the opponent the advantage of, and ensure friendly unimpeded access to, the electromagnetic spectrum. This includes capabilities for electronic attack, electronic support, and electronic protection. EW systems are dependent upon technologies similar to those found in radar systems, including receivers and transmitters. They include countermeasure technologies such as chaff and flares, which can target humans, communications, radar, or other assets.

DoD has roughly 100 radar systems in development, production, or sustainment with a similar portfolio of electronic warfare systems. These systems provide critical mission capabilities and perform functions in four operational domains; land, air, space, and sea. There are a total of 23 firms that produce or have produced radars for the DoD. Three domestic suppliers dominate the domestic radar market and four domestic suppliers dominate electronic warfare systems. An emerging area of investment and interest is directed energy capability. Both laser and high power microwave systems are in the research and development phase, and these technologies and industrial base areas often align with the radar and electronic warfare industrial base risks.

Major Risks & Issues

Risk Archetypes

- Single source
- DMSMS
- Foreign dependency

The Radar and Electronic Warfare Working Group, which contributed to the September 2018 Interagency Task Force response to Presidential Executive Order E.O. 13806, identified several forces driving risk to DoD.[47] The working group identified five prioritized risks that drove mitigation efforts moving forward. In FY2020, three risks were paramount.

Availability of Electronic Components

This risk is driven by aging DoD systems which lead to obsolescence of available components, the fluidity of commercial technology, and decreasing U.S. industrial and manufacturing infrastructure.

Availability of Vacuum Electronic Device Materials, Components, and Manufacturing Sources

This risk is driven by requirements to leverage multiple sole and single source material suppliers both internal and external to the U.S., market fragility with the growth of the Gallium Nitride (GaN) Solid State based systems, and decreasing industrial and manufacturing infrastructure. Two high visibility material issues include: rare earth magnets that rely on raw material and metal oxides provided from China; and the lack of U.S. sources for high quality tungsten rhenium and thoriated tungsten wire.

Reduced Competition and Innovation for Tactical Radar and EW Systems

One example of this risk is the F/A-18 Actively Electronically Scanned Array (AESA). Similar AESA radars are being produced for other applications, but once the F/A-18 production ends, only a single qualified source remains.

FY2020 Developments

The onset of the coronavirus pandemic has negatively impacted the radar and EW sector, as well as the entire commercial and military industrial base; however, considerable work has been accomplished this fiscal year. Multiple programs across DoD have supported risk mitigation activities in the Radar and EW sector in FY2020.

Two programs of note that are focusing heavily on Gallium Nitride (GaN) technology (a significant enabler for AESA-based radar and EW systems) are the ManTech and Microelectronics Innovation for National Security and Economic Competitiveness (MINSEC) programs. Both of these programs are funding efforts related to GaN manufacturing. In one ManTech project, BAE Systems is partnering with the Air Force Research Laboratory (AFRL) to develop and mature an open-foundry 140 nm GaN Monolithic Microwave Integrated Circuits (MMIC) technology, with a focus on efficient power amplification at frequencies ranging from DC to 50 GHz, and a 90 nm technology targeted towards higher frequency applications.

The radio frequency and optoelectronic (RF/OE) technical execution area (TEA) of the MINSEC program develops and demonstrates secure access to SOTA foundries, designs, and intellectual property (IP). RF/OE investments enable next generation DoD programs with advanced sensors and communications, and bolster the underlying DIB. The RF/OE Community of Interest guiding these investments comprises over 60 subject matter experts, who gather at semi-annual TEA workshops to ensure alignment across services and industry.

To mitigate risk areas impacting the vacuum electron tube industry, multiple efforts were undertaken in FY2020. Perhaps the widest reaching effort was President Trump's July 2019 use of DPA projects to mitigate the reliance on foreign sources for rare earth elements. Presidential Determination letters were signed to enable risk mitigation in five focus areas:

1. Light Rare Earth Element Separation and Processing,
2. Heavy Rare Earth Element Separation and Processing,
3. Rare Earth Metals and Alloys,
4. Samarium Cobalt Magnets, and
5. Neodymium Iron Boron Magnets.

A DoD-wide technical working group led by the DPA Title III office is currently developing the required technical data packages to allow solicitation of these projects. In FY2020, two of the five topic areas were released for bids and have closed. Efforts are currently underway to finalize and announce the awards. Rare earth magnets and materials are required not only to support the vacuum electronics industrial base and the radar and EW community, but are required to support precision guided munitions, laser systems, sensors and actuators on airborne platforms, and future electronic propulsion systems.

Additional projects are currently being worked in FY20 to develop new sources and materials to mitigate the use of foreign-sourced thoriated tungsten and tungsten rhenium wire that is required for use in the vacuum electronics industry. The DLA and the DPA Title III program are supporting those respective efforts, which are scheduled to continue into FY2021.

Sector Outlook

The NSS and NDS emphasize the need for a strong, resilient defense industrial base and the E.O. 13806 report identified macro forces that have disrupted and deteriorated the U.S. radar and EW industrial base. In FY2020, the IBAS Program developed a Radar Supplier Resiliency Plan (RSRP), which was signed by USD(A&S) Ellen Lord, and delivered to the House and Senate Armed Services Committees.

The IBAS program formed a Joint Radar Industrial Base Working Group (JRIBWG) to support the development of the RSRP by researching core issues and identifying key leveraging opportunities. The RSRP identifies five radar sector challenges and five strategies to offset those challenges. It also identifies proposed projects to bolster the radar and EW industrial base and address risk areas identified in the Interagency Task Force response to EO 13806. As discussed in the RSRP, successful execution of the plan is dependent upon long-term fiscal comments required for the JRIBWG to strengthen and sustain the U.S. radar DIB.

Shipbuilding

Sector Overview

The shipbuilding industrial base is responsible for every aspect of shipbuilding, from design to decommissioning of aircraft carriers, submarines, surface ships, and their weapons and command and control (C2) systems. Over the past five decades, the industrial base has experienced significant consolidation. Fourteen defense-related new-construction shipyards have closed, three have left the defense industry, and one new shipyard has opened.

The sector includes shipyards – fixed facilities with dry docks and fabrication equipment – as well as manufacturing and other facilities that provide parts and services for shipbuilding activities. Today, the U.S. Navy contracts primarily with seven private new-construction shipyards, owned by four prime contractors, to build its future Battle Force, representing significantly less capacity than the leading shipbuilding nations.

There are also a number of smaller private-sector shipyards and facilities building non-battle force and unmanned vessels. Repair and maintenance is conducted at large and small private yards in addition to four public naval shipyards.

The shipbuilding industrial base can be further segmented by ship type: aircraft carriers, submarines, surface combatants, amphibious warfare, combat logistics force, and command and support vessels.

Major Risks & Issues

Risk Archetypes:

- Capacity constrained supply market
- Sole source
- Fragile market
- Gap in U.S.-based human capital

The major risks in the shipbuilding industrial base remained constant in FY2020. The diminishing domestic commercial shipbuilding sector continues to magnify these risks.

Capacity Constrained Supply Market

The increase in ship construction to reach a U.S. Navy fleet of 355 ships by 2035, and even greater growth beyond that, will strain the current U.S. shipbuilding sector. The resulting additional workload is a significant increase from current production levels and will challenge shipyards and their suppliers as they expand and adjust to meet larger production volumes. A new mix of vessels in the fleet will likely force incumbent shipyards to modify their business plans and facilities to meet these new demands. Shipyards and suppliers that don't currently participate in U.S. Navy shipbuilding will see new opportunities, particularly in small and unmanned vessels.

Sole Source Suppliers

The number of domestic suppliers at the lower tiers of the supply chain continues to decline. Due to macroeconomic forces, the Navy expects this trend to continue. The limited availability of suppliers requires the U.S. Navy to consider the workload and financial health of the supply chain when making procurement decisions. Low demand volumes in certain market spaces result in the selection of single or sole sources of supply for critical products, either out of necessity, or sometimes to promote resiliency during low production periods.

Fragile Markets

There are currently four prime contractors producing nearly all of the U.S. Navy's ships, and two that comprise the vast majority of shipbuilding sales. A limited number of yards, and the size and complexity of operations, makes it difficult for new businesses to enter the market. Only one shipbuilder is currently producing aircraft carriers, and only two are producing submarines, after a decision by the Navy to divide new work between Electric Boat and Newport News.

Unstable Demand

Fluctuation in planned modernization and procurement is also a long-term challenge, as changes in ship procurement plans impact the shipyards and lower-tier suppliers' workload. Battle Force 2045, discussed below, is an example of the Navy's changing requirements. This instability is necessary for the Navy to respond to emerging threats, but it results in financial risk to the industrial base as companies struggle to align their business decisions. The timing of ship procurements is also critical to achieve the stable workload required to support the viability of the shipbuilding industrial base and to sustaining a skilled workforce. Advanced procurement for long lead time material and economic order quantities, as well as multi-program material purchases, continue to be used to ensure stability in the industrial base.

Gaps in U.S.-based Human Capital

In addition to the challenges found in other manufacturing sectors throughout the U.S., shipbuilding has unique challenges, such as too few replacements for retiring workers, insufficient labor mobility, the perception of unattractive physical working conditions, and the cyclical nature of shipbuilding.

Shipbuilders and suppliers are stepping up recruiting efforts in response to these market realities. They are supported in many different ways by a multitude of entities including the OSD, the U.S. Navy, other federal agencies, state and local governments, and local and regional economic development initiatives. U.S. government support efforts typically include funding for capital investments to improve working conditions, training grants, and tax relief in exchange for meeting employment targets.

FY2020 Developments

New Programs or Initiatives

The Navy awarded the detail design and construction of the first Constellation Class guided missile frigate with options for up to nine more ships to the Marinette Marine Corporation. Another contract contains options for the design and construction of the first two Columbia Class ballistic missile submarines. Lead ship construction awards will occur in FY2021.

In October 2020, the Secretary of Defense unveiled Battle Force 2045. Derived from the Future Naval Force Study, which is still in process, it calls for a more balanced Navy of over 500 manned and unmanned ships. It retains the goal of reaching 355 traditional Battle Force ships by 2035. Highlights regarding shipbuilding include:

- A larger and more capable attack submarine force
- A potential reduction of nuclear powered aircraft carriers with an increased role for light carriers
- The addition of 140 to 240 unmanned and optionally manned vessels to perform a wide range of missions
- An increased number of small surface combatants
- Enhanced sealift capacity

In his remarks, the Secretary of Defense committed to increasing funding to shipbuilding accounts by harvesting reform efforts throughout the rest of the DoD. The end result will be a larger, more lethal, survivable, adaptable, sustainable, and modern force than we have seen in many years.

Industry Changes

The U.S. Navy continually monitors its industrial base, focusing on critical suppliers to ensure the supply of material and components for shipbuilding programs. There are constant changes in an industrial base with thousands of suppliers, but the health of the industrial base remained steady in 2020. The Navy is closely monitoring the purchase of AK Steel Corporation and ArcelorMittal USA by Cleveland-Cliffs Inc., which has traditionally been a mining company; and the purchase of Fairbanks Morse Engines, a critical supplier of medium speed diesel engines for the Navy, by Arcline Investments, a private equity firm.

Ship Awards and Deliveries

Despite the COVID-19 disruptions, the shipbuilding sector continued to deliver ships. Ten ships were delivered in 2020: two Virginia Class submarines (SSN 791 and 792), one America Class amphibious assault ship (LHA 7), one Arleigh Burke Class destroyer (DDG 119), three littoral combat ships (LCS 19, 22, and 24), one Lewis B Puller Class expeditionary sea base (T-ESB 5) and two Spearhead Class expeditionary fast transports (T-EPF 11 and 12).

In FY2020, the Navy awarded a multi-year contract for nine Virginia Class submarines (SSN 802-810) through FY2023 with an option for an additional ship. All but one of these ships will have the Virginia Payload Module. The Navy awarded the first of its new Constellation Class guided missile frigates (FFG 62) with options for nine additional ships. One San Antonio Class amphibious transport dock (LPD 31) along with two Navajo Class towing, salvage, and rescue ships (T-ATS 9 and 10) were also awarded in FY2020. Contract options were exercised for one John Lewis Class fleet replenishment oiler (T-AO 210) and one Arleigh Burke Class destroyer (DDG 135).

Sector Outlook

Strategic Competition

China has the largest navy in the world with a battle force of approximately 350 vessels, including major surface combatants, submarines, ocean-going amphibious ships, mine warfare ships, aircraft carriers, and fleet auxiliaries. China's 2019 defense white paper described the People's Liberation Army Navy (PLAN) as speeding up the transition of its tasks from "defense on the near seas" to "protection missions on the far seas." The PLAN is an increasingly modern and flexible force that has focused on replacing its previous generations of platforms in favor of larger, modern multi-role combatants. This modernization aligns with China's growing emphasis on the maritime domain and increasing demands for the PLAN to operate at greater distances from mainland China.[48]

The shipbuilding sector of the DIB is perhaps unique in that the U.S. is not a major contributor to the global commercial market. The U.S. accounts for less than one percent of commercial shipbuilding by tonnage. China is the world's leader with South Korea and Japan rounding out the top three shipbuilding countries. Major changes to the current relative production levels of today's major shipbuilding countries is unlikely.

The largest contributing factor of declining U.S. competitiveness in global shipbuilding has been state intervention from competitor countries. China's shipbuilding industry benefits from a robust domestic industrial economy that provides raw material and components to shipbuilders. It is China's long-term goal to have an entirely self-reliant defense industrial sector, and they have established market leading positions in many heavy industries that support shipbuilding. As an example, China is the world's largest steel producer and user by a large margin.

Given current macroeconomic conditions, China is expected to continue to out-build the United States in terms of ship quantities. The U.S. Navy will continue to use its technological advantages to maintain superiority in the maritime domain.

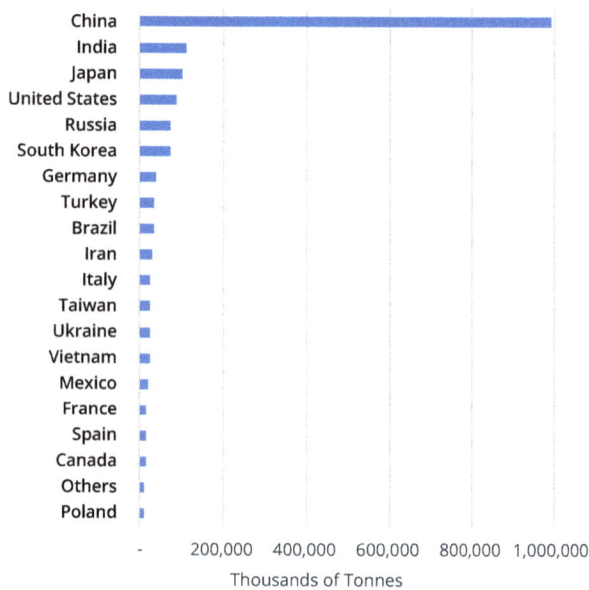

Figure 7.21: FY2019 Top Crude Steel Producers[49]

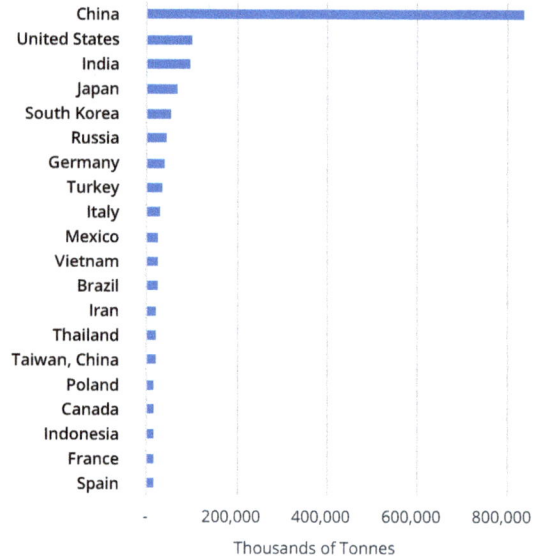

Figure 7.22: FY2018 Top Steel Users (Finished Products)[50]

Software Engineering

Sector Overview

Software engineering is the application of a systematic, disciplined, quantifiable approach to the development, operation, and maintenance of software. Software engineering capability includes the processes, resources, infrastructure, and workforce competencies to enable systems to meet operational mission requirements and evolving threats. Challenges within this sector have evolved significantly over the last several decades as the demand for engineering professionals and the DoD policy and processes for software failed to keep pace with the current and future digital transformation of the modern battlefield.

Software is in virtually every piece of electronics in the form of firmware, operating systems, and applications. This includes DoD weapon systems, mission support systems, maintenance systems, and business systems. Today's modern weapon systems rely heavily on software to provide functionality. For example, the F-35 is estimated to rely on software for 90 percent of its avionics specification requirements. This has grown significantly over the last four decades when the F-15A had just 35 percent software reliance in 1975.

Unlike physical hardware, software can be delivered and modified remotely, facilitating rapid adaptation to changes in threats, technology, mission priorities, and other aspects of the operating environment.

Software for many weapon systems is being sustained with processes developed decades ago for hardware-centric systems.

Unfortunately, software for many weapon systems is being sustained with processes developed decades ago. In addition, much of DoD policy remains hardware-centric, despite software providing an increasingly larger percentage of system functionality. In today's fast-paced,

changing environments with mounting cyber threats, software engineering for software-intensive systems should utilize agile software development methodologies and development, security and operations (DevSecOps) processes, and apply contracting practices capable of rapidly delivering incremental and iterative changes to the end-user. Efficiencies gained with the widespread adoption of these processes will help to alleviate the shortfall of qualified software professionals within the DIB as addressed in the following section.

Major Risks & Issues

Risk Archetypes:

- Gap in U.S.-based human capital
- Foreign Dependency

Since software is pervasive throughout military systems and technologies, the impacts within the software engineering industrial base manifest themselves across the traditional sectors. The Software Engineering Working Group, which contributed to the September 2018 Interagency Task Force response to EO 13806, assessed impacts across sectors; as such, software risks are included in each of the sectors' inputs.[51,52]

Diminishing U.S. STEM skills, and U.S. government business practices and policies are both driving risk within the software engineering industrial base.

Government Practices & Policies

Policy, roles, and responsibilities for software engineering at the DoD level are not clearly established to effectively represent software equities at the acquisition policy and program levels. The DoD lacks a unified software engineering policy, which has produced inconsistency in practices and policy implementation across the services. Despite its prevalence, engineering sustainability of software-intensive systems during the requirements, design, and development processes has also received limited focus and priority. Collectively, these factors have negatively impacted the successful development and sustainment of software across the Department.

The DoD has also struggled to track and manage its inventory of software, which is immense and continually growing. There is limited visibility and understanding at the enterprise level of the total size, complexity, and characteristics of the inventory, which may exceed one billion lines of custom developed software code. A unified source of clear software engineering policy would aid in a unilateral implementation of appropriate practices across the industrial base.

STEM Workforce

Exacerbating the need to strengthen organic software expertise is the national STEM shortage. Today's education pipeline is not providing the necessary software engineering resources to fully meet the demand from commercial and defense sectors, and resources required to meet future demands continue to grow.

STEM covers a diverse array of professions, from electrical engineers to researchers within the medical field, and includes a range of degree levels from bachelor's to PhD. Seven out of ten STEM occupations were related to computers and information systems, with nearly 750,000 of them being software developers. Demand across all STEM sectors is not consistent; there is a surplus of PhDs seeking positions as professors in academia, while there is a shortage of individuals with electrical engineering PhDs who are U.S. citizens.[53]

The development and sustainment of increasingly complex software-intensive weapon systems requires skills from both the engineering and computer science fields. The STEM shortage cannot be addressed solely by hiring more computer programmers. Modern software-intensive systems rely a great deal on skilled software system engineers with in-depth knowledge of the systems and environments in which the software operates (e.g., avionics

systems, electronic warfare, weapons, and space systems). The intersection of these disciplines creates a specialization that results in a limited resource pool when compared to the requirements of commercial software application developers. Between 2014 and 2024, job openings are projected to exceed one million for computer occupations and half-a-million for engineers.[54]

The STEM shortage is even more challenging for the DIB, which requires most employees to obtain security clearances, necessitating U.S. citizenship. Students on temporary visas in the U.S. have consistently earned 4-5 percent of bachelor's level STEM degrees awarded in U.S. colleges and universities. In 2015, these students earned a substantially larger share (11-13 percent) of bachelor's degrees in industrial, electrical, and chemical engineering. The number of STEM bachelor's degrees awarded to students on temporary visas increased from about 15,000 in 2000 to almost 33,000 by 2015.[55]

The U.S. is also graduating fewer students with STEM degrees as a percentage of population compared to China, and the trend continues to worsen. The population of China is four times that of the U.S., but is producing eight times the number of STEM graduates. The U.S. no longer has the most STEM graduates worldwide and is being rapidly outpaced by China. In 2016, the U.S. had the third most STEM graduates worldwide with 67.4 million graduates compared to China with 78.0 million.

The software engineering crisis in the DIB will not be corrected until significant effort is placed on updating software policy and processes, and more importantly, placing significant investment in software engineering education and retention initiatives. Greater attention must be paid to workforce concerns in the Software Engineering sector to maintain and develop the intellectual capital necessary to create and sustain war-winning weapon systems for the modern battlefield.

FY2020 Developments

In May 2019, the Defense Innovation Board released a report, "Software is Never Done: Refactoring the Acquisition Code for Competitive Advantage," resulting from the Software Acquisition and Practices (SWAP) study.[56] The congressionally mandated study (Section 872 of the FY2018 NDAA) outlines the importance and pervasiveness of software in modern DoD systems and emphasizes the need to decrease cycle time and develop digital talent and the enduring qualities of software that differentiate it from the hardware paradigm. Implementation of the lines of effort recommended by this study is currently underway.

In a memorandum released in October 2019, USD(A&S) Ellen Lord, released interim policy and guidance on establishing direction, responsibilities, and procedures for the management of the Software Acquisition Pathway (Recommendation A1 from the SWAP study).[57] As actions are undertaken to implement the recommendations from this study, such as the issuance of DoD Instruction (DoDI) 5000.87, "Operation of the Software Acquisition Pathway," in October 2020, the implications cast a wide net over the policy status quo. The impacts on software engineering in the DoD promulgated by these actions reflect a growing acknowledgment of the significance and prominence of software throughout the Department.

The coronavirus pandemic exposed the importance of a robust infrastructure to enable remote work. At the onset of the crisis, tremendous efforts were made to shore up the gap in capability to effectively support the mission. The software sector quickly adapted to the sudden shift in culture and applied significant resources toward improving the resilience of the new normal. While challenges remain, the urgent requirements driven by the pandemic acted as a forcing function to address a necessary shortfall in capability.

The DoD Enterprise DevSecOps Initiative, a joint program with the OUSD (A&S), DoD's Chief Information Officer (CIO), Defense Information Systems Agency (DISA), and the Military Services established teams (i.e., CloudOne, PlatformOne by LevelUp) focused on deploying hardened software factories for both existing and new environments within days instead of years (see Figure 7.23). These initiatives pulled together top talent from across the DoD, tasked with enabling the infrastructure and associated tools needed by modern software engineers to rapidly deliver software capability for the warfighter.

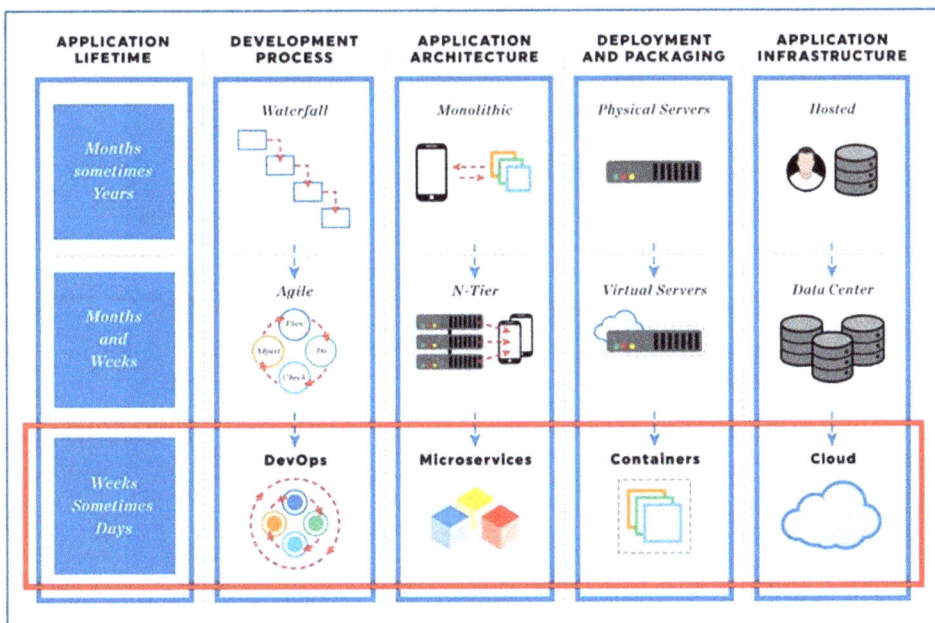

Figure 7.23, Source: DoD Enterprise DevSecOps Initiative (DSOP)[58]

Software Engineering organizations across the services continue to focus on growing the workforce. Notably, the Software Engineering Groups of the Air Force Sustainment Center grew the organic workforce by eight percent in 2019, to a total workforce of 4500+ software engineers and computer scientists supporting over 250 distinct software projects.

Sector Outlook

From the perspective of the warfighter, adaptation at the speed of relevance is a matter of necessity to stay ahead of the ever-increasing pace of deployment practiced by our near-peer adversaries while maintaining compliance with applicable statutes. As the software engineering profession embraces cloud-based development environments with increasingly automated pipelines (enabling vastly shorter delivery cycles), policies must be updated to reflect this paradigm shift.

Along with the change in technologies and methods that the software engineering community is adapting by, comes a requirement for a workforce with the necessary talents to effectively employ these enablers. The production of engineers and scientists with U.S. citizenship, and the skills necessary to successfully develop and sustain the software required by the DoD

in modern environments, is not keeping up with demand. As of 2017, American students make up barely 21 percent of the computer science student body and 19 percent of electrical engineering majors among our nation's universities (see Figures 7.24 and 7.25).[59] Emphasis must be directed toward inspiring the next generation to pursue STEM careers, especially in software engineering.

This issue directly threatens U.S. national self-determination in commerce and geopolitics. The STEM shortage in the DIB is quickly approaching crisis status. As stated by Arthur Herman, "We are fast approaching another Sputnik moment, we can't afford to ignore."[60] The U.S. must create a state-of-the-art STEM education strategy to cope with this reality.

Computer Science:
Full-Time Graduate Students 1995-2015

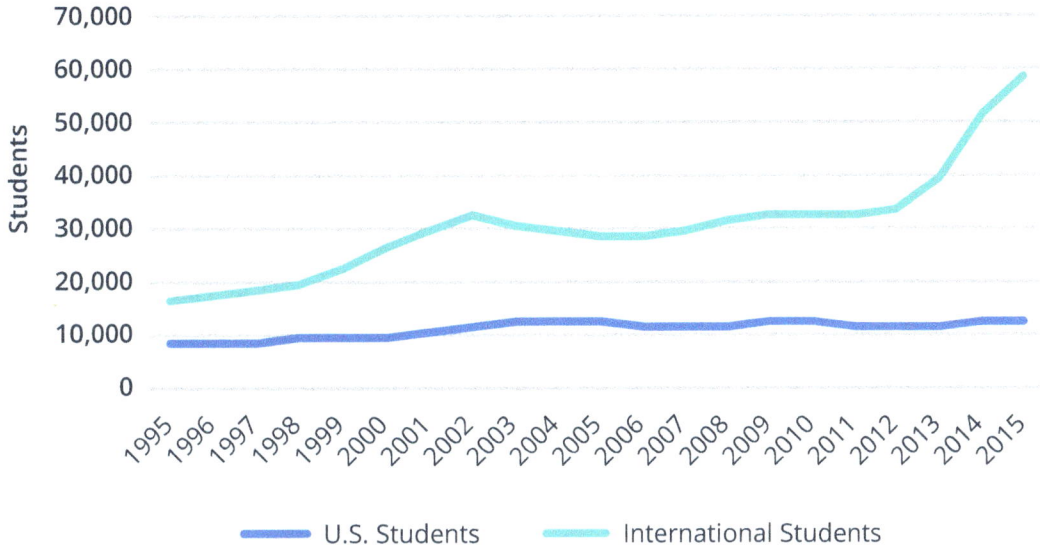

Source: National Science Foundation, Survey of Graduate Students and Postdoctorates, NFAP calculations. U.S. students include lawful permanent residents

Figure 7.24, Source: National Science Foundation, Survey of Graduate Students and Postdoctorates, NFAP calculation. U.S. students include lawful permanent residents.

Electrical Engineering:
Full-time Graduate Students: 1995 to 2015

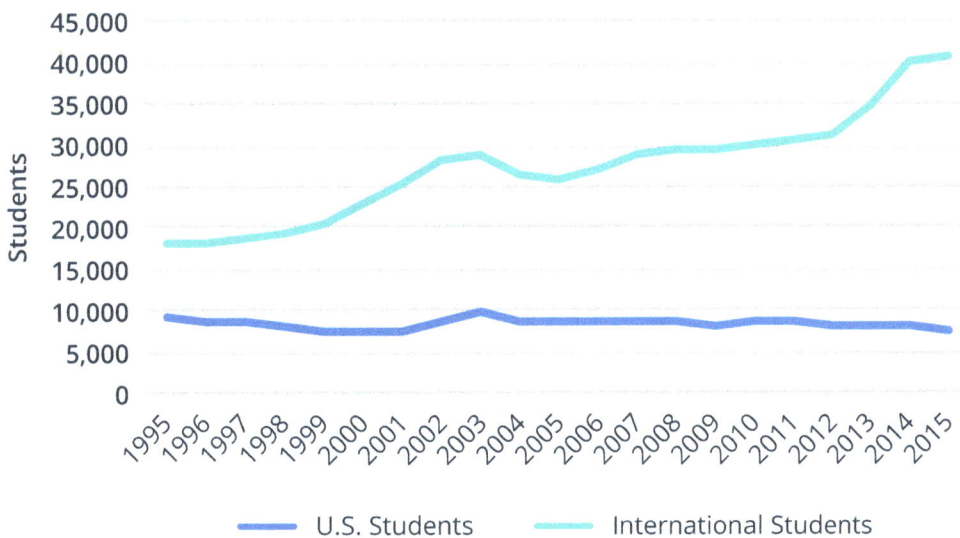

Source: National Science Foundation, Survey of Graduate Students and Postdoctorates, NFAP calculations. U.S. students include lawful permanent residents.

Figure 7.25, Source: National Science Foundation, Survey of Graduate Students and Postdoctorates, NFAP calculation.[61] U.S. students include lawful permanent residents.

Soldier Systems

Sector Overview

Soldier systems are the diverse products necessary to maximize the warfighter's survivability, lethality, sustainability, mobility, combat effectiveness, and field quality of life by considering the warfighter as a system. This sector includes the weapons, body armor, clothing, footwear, radios, sensors, power supply, shelters, food, and other items essential to executing U.S. military missions—from snipers to tankers to airmen to divers.

Most soldier systems have significant commercial overlap. The commercial market provides stabilizing revenue for existing defense contractors and opportunities for new players to modify commercial gear for the defense market. Companies in the sector navigate a variety of challenges, including:

- technical advancement at funding levels typically well below major defense programs;
- stringent quality control and affordability challenges in high volume production;
- legislation and regulation promoting domestic sourcing and restricting technology proliferation;
- unique defense requirements that can rapidly evolve with a wartime threat; and
- defense demand volatility that varies proportionally with operational tempo.

The advanced designs and novel industrial capabilities needed to preserve U.S. warfighter tactical advantage require a skilled workforce and modernized factories.

Major Risks & Issues

> ### Risk Archetypes:
>
> - DMSMS
> - Single source
> - Sole source
> - Foreign Dependency

Industrial capability gaps in the Soldier Systems sector reduce assurance that the warfighter is prepared to successfully execute defense missions in any operating environment. Risks include single sources of supply, capacity constraints, foreign dependency, market fragility, and diminishing manufacturing sources and material suppliers. The case studies below illustrate risks that may warrant government action.

Erosion of the U.S. Textile Industry

Textiles are an integral component of many defense systems. In addition to uniforms, tents, parachutes, and backpacks, textile applications also include composite and non-woven structures such as Kevlar body armor, fiberglass in drones, and carbon fiber in advanced aircraft. Between 1995 and 2009, the U.S. textile industry suffered a historic contraction, and Asian markets now dominate global textile supply.

DoD is reliant on single and foreign sources of supply, and competes with global commercial demand for adequate production capacity. However, U.S. manufacturers face a competitive disadvantage in workforce and raw material costs and availability. DoD has relied on a sole source for Service Dress Uniform fabrics for a number of years, as well as sources of fibers that protect against flame and ballistic threats, and many other essential components. As a result of DMSMS from domestic suppliers, DLA has considered seeking a Domestic Non-Availability Determination for Service Dress Uniforms.

Erosion of U.S. Rechargeable and Non-Rechargeable Battery Industry

Military-unique battery requirements can differ from commercial demands in size, quality, safety, power density, weight, and environmental ruggedness. Lack of stable production orders, inadequate research and development investment, and disjointed acquisition strategies have resulted in lost capability and capacity, increased surge lead times, workforce erosion, and inhibited private investment.

Surge capacity-limiting constraints occur at several points along the value chain, from raw material to final battery assembly. Most battery configurations are produced by single sources of supply. The rechargeable battery market is dominated by commercial demand and primarily foreign sourced. Domestic rechargeable battery producers cannot compete in production volume, labor availability, or cost.[62]

Most domestic lithium ion cell packagers rely on foreign suppliers. Rapid expansion of the electronic vehicle market is likely to exacerbate these risks, especially if designs deviate significantly from military requirements, foreign markets drive adoption, or foreign competitors lead the way in manufacturing infrastructure investment.

Erosion of U.S. Photonics and Optics Industries

Photonics and optics are technology drivers for warfighter sensing and laser systems. Sensing technologies and applications have expanded exponentially over the last few decades and are increasingly integrated into every facet of warfighting. Unfortunately, U.S. value-added manufacturing has eroded over the last 20 years, threatening assured access to new optics and photonics.

Competitor nations are investing in key manufacturing infrastructure and have lower-cost human capital, which provides a competitive advantage. Human capital gaps in skilled blue-collar workers, and clearable U.S. nationals with advanced degrees in optics and photonics, constrain the domestic defense industry. Additionally, rapid technology proliferation brings a risk of parity with competitor nations in the market. The result is U.S. reliance on foreign sources for key technologies for defense systems like night vision.

Future advancements in flexible displays, OLEDs, and quantum mechanics offer opportunities to regain international competitive leadership in both technical innovation and manufacturing. While display alternatives may exist, there is only one known domestic source of OLED microdisplays. The DoD has made investments to manage the risk, is actively engaged with suppliers, and is monitoring the niche industry closely.

Government Business Practices

Commercial items modified to meet military specifications may still require unique-enough industrial capabilities to oppose market dynamics and fuel industrial base risk. The military specifications qualification processes can cause barriers to entry and source of production technical risks. Where significant differences exist between commercial solutions and defense products, the government is left to sustain the capability and capacity needed for production. While this is necessary in some cases, it is costly and impractical across the broad soldier systems portfolio.

In a few cases of high-volume soldier systems (e.g. body armor, uniforms, batteries, etc.), a small industrial base is further divided by contract awards to produce Service-specific variants of comparable products. Disjointed acquisition strategies can unknowingly create single sources, decrease demand signal strength and visibility, increase logistics burden, and create industrial base risk. As part of the planned risk management actions in the sector, DoD will evaluate joint requirements and acquisition strategies with an objective to create a more cohesive demand signal to industry and to adjust requirements to better align with market-stable solutions as appropriate.

FY2020 Developments

Operational Transition

The soldier systems sector is emerging from a long-term sustainment effort focused on immediate warfighter needs. Many programs have met or are approaching their acquisition objectives, which triggers a natural peacetime cycle of decreased defense spending/demand. In the past, periods of decreased defense spending have led to industry consolidation, reduction in capacity, loss of capability, reduced capital investment, and a transition toward commercial investments in order for industry to remain viable.

Peacetime industrial readiness losses have historically been recovered or replaced by alternatives as the U.S. enters other large-scale military engagements. Future soldier systems objectives include lightening the soldiers' load, developing modular/flexible/agile materiel solutions, and taking advantage of advancements in sensor technology and materials engineering.

Sector Outlook

Strategic Competition

U.S. competitors continue to modernize their capabilities to challenge U.S. technological leadership and interests across a broad industrial spectrum. Russia has been modernizing its soldier systems ensemble in a coordinated, modular, and evolutionary program called "Ratnik" - or "Warrior" - reported over the last five years. The program integrates and upgrades all aspects of soldier systems. The latest generation integrates exoskeletons, advanced sensing, and unmanned systems, paralleling the U.S. Special Operations Command's Tactical Assault Light Operator Suit.[63,64] Since 2010, Russia has significantly modernized its ground forces and ground troop tactics.[65]

China's PLA Army (PLAA) is the world's largest standing ground force, with approximately 915,000 active-duty personnel in combat units. Recent structural changes to PLAA organization and tactics aim to develop more mobile and modular units. To assist in the transformation, the PLAA is also modernizing command, control, communications, computers, and intelligence systems to enhance its forces' interoperability. PLAA forces stress the importance of ISR and leveraging information to enable future combat.[66]

China's industrial policies and national priorities are focused on advancement in areas that will enhance its soldier systems capabilities; quantum communications and computing; innovative electronics and software; automation and robotics; specialty materials; nanotechnology; batteries, power, and alternative energy; and neuroscience, neural research, and artificial intelligence.[67]

Commercial Demand Dominance

DoD competition with commercial demand continues to impact textiles, batteries, and night vision technologies, and other industry subsectors. Although commercial demand can provide stabilizing revenue to industry during periods of reduced DoD demand, it also reduces the DoD's influence on the market and ability to drive investment in the development of next generation technology.

When military and commercial requirements differ substantially, or if shared resources are scarce, commercial market dominance can directly impact lead time, surge capacity, and the sustainment or development of defense-unique industrial capabilities. Often DoD is left to adapt to commercial market-driven changes, and only when unacceptable levels of industrial base risk arise may DoD intervene to sustain critical industrial capabilities.

Space

Sector Overview

The space industrial base includes the satellites, launch services, ground systems, satellite components and subsystems, networks, engineering services, payloads, propulsion, and electronics that support National Security Space (NSS) missions and operations. These systems provide an emergent capability and strategic advantage to U.S. forces.

Demand for space capabilities and services—and resulting capability development— is increasingly driven by foreign and domestic commercial markets.

> "Rapid increases in commercial and international space activities worldwide add to the complexity of the space environment. Commercial space activities provide national and homeland security benefits with new technologies and services and create new economic opportunities in established and emerging markets. The same activities, however, also create challenges in protecting critical technology, ensuring operational security, and maintaining strategic advantages."
>
> – 2020 Defense Space Strategy

Certain NSS performance requirements and capabilities are also particularly stringent or unique, and require support outside of the growing commercial/civilian space ecosystem. The DoD space industrial base remains a niche market with very specialized and capital-intensive requirements that are not efficiently managed through individual program investments. Many current and planned systems also rely on dated technology and practices, as well as fragile or foreign sources.

Reliance on foreign sources for critical technologies, competition from subsidized lower-cost imports, and erratic demand from the NSS enterprise will erode essential space capabilities and critical skills, and threaten future access to space qualified domestic industrial sources. However, due to capital intensive requirements, individual programs are reluctant to invest in, and qualify, new technology and sources. This creates a need to sustain fragile domestic sources and to qualify new technologies and sources for next-generation systems.

Major Risks & Issues

Risk Archetypes

- Foreign dependency
- Erosion of U.S.-based infrastructure
- Product security
- Fragile suppliers
- Gaps in U.S.-based human capital

The Space Industrial Base Working Group (SIBWG) assesses risks within the space industrial base, develops mitigation plans, and promotes management and procurement practices across the DoD and the intelligence community (IC) to ensure access to technologies critical to the NSS community. SIBWG members—government and industry stakeholders— identify and pursue risk mitigation efforts to protect the U.S. space industrial base through cost-sharing contracts between the government and private industry.

The SIBWG currently tracks 119 essential space capabilities with identified supply chain risks. The following technologies exhibit specific risks impacting the space industrial base:

Precision Gyroscopes

Precision Gyroscopes are a critical component of the attitude determination, stabilization, and inertial navigation system on spacecraft, launch vehicles, and missiles. Three types of gyroscopes (ring laser, hemispherical resonating, and fiber optic) are commonly employed in space systems.

- Hemispherical resonating gyroscopes are an older technology mainly used on non-agile satellites and only one domestic provider remains— with limited production capacity.
- Fiber optic gyroscopes are employed in high performance agile spacecraft and missile applications. Although there are three domestic suppliers of fiber optic gyroscopes, they rely on key components (integrated optics chips and laser diodes) experiencing supply issues that threaten the viability of domestic product lines.

Space Qualified Solar Cells

Space qualified solar cells are optimized for specific environments required for NSS and National Aeronautics and Space Administration (NASA) missions, which hinders the transfer of technology to terrestrial applications and often prevents providers from diversifying to reduce risk and burden. The space industrial base is developing advanced cells to provide weight savings, decrease stowage footprint, and enable higher-power missions. However, foreign suppliers are also developing high efficiency cells, while marketing internationally at lower costs.

U.S. providers are dependent on NSS procurement funding, whose batched orders are generally low volume, low margin, and with inconsistent demand. As a result, they have struggled to remain competitive. During the coronavirus pandemic, the DPA Title III team made critical investments in the domestic space qualified solar cell market to maintain production capacity.

Traveling Wave Tube Amplifiers

Traveling Wave Tube Amplifiers (TWTAs) improve radio frequency spectrum access and increase bandwidth in military satellites. Recent commercial market downturns have resulted in layoffs and skills gaps in the space TWTA workforce. A sole domestic supplier competes with a single foreign source for production of all space qualified TWTAs. Although some U.S. programs are required to use a domestic source, the foreign source offers more competitive products and pricing. Having a strong domestic source would reduce dependence on the foreign source and ensure availability of NSS specific TWTAs.

FY2020 Developments

COVID-19 Impacts

The long-term impacts of the coronavirus pandemic are still unclear, but the DoD will monitor the sector closely. Potential areas of concern include a slowdown in capital expenditures and more rapid industry consolidation than originally anticipated. For example, the Organization for Economic Co-operation and Development (OECD) has expressed concern that COVID-19 could disproportionally affect space start-ups. The uncertainty associated with COVID-19 could cause constraints in the ability of start-ups to raise the capital required to bring innovation to the market. This could open a window of opportunity for the rapidly growing Chinese commercial sector to weaken the U.S.'s position as a commercial space leader.

Sector Outlook

Defense Space Strategy

The June 2020 Defense Space Strategy identifies four lines of effort (LOE) for the development of a "secure, stable, and accessible space domain":

1. Build a comprehensive military advantage in space;
2. Integrate space into national, joint, and combined operations;
3. Shape the strategic environment; and
4. Cooperate with allies, partners, industry, and other U.S. Government departments and agencies.[68]

The December 2019 establishment of the U.S. Space Force as a separate Service branch may bring attention to the risks facing the space industrial base and establish a more strategic investment and development approach. The SIBWG will continue to play a critical role in the Space Strategy and the fourth LOE in particular. Whereas investment by individual programs tends to result in program specific architectures, cooperation across government and industry is necessary to:

- Identify and support cross-cutting technologies and priorities;

- Invest in areas and technologies where commercial demand is insufficient, or DoD-unique components exist;

- Maintain or improve hard-to-reconstitute manufacturing processes to avoid schedule and cost impacts associated with re-establishment; and

- Anticipate technology requirements to maximize investment across space programs.

A clear strategy will help inform investment and policy priorities across the NSS enterprise and guide the actions of the SIBWG in support of a stronger space industrial base.

Commercial Space

The commercial space sector will continue to play an increasing and critical role in NSS, including space launch. The United States is an overall world leader in commercial space, but near peer competitors such as China are rapidly expanding their commercial space industrial bases.[69] The DoD, in coordination with other Federal Agencies such as the DoC and NASA will continue to leverage, support, and promote the commercial space industry, where appropriate. There are potential areas of support where the DoD and partner agencies can positively help the U.S. commercial space industry. For example, recent economic analysis by the U.S. Air Force Office of Commercial and Economic Analysis and the MITRE Corporation highlight that government support of the launch industry, coupled with commercial efforts to reduce space launch costs and increase reliability, is effective in helping U.S. commercial launch service providers gain additional global market share. However, the U.S. government should simultaneously be aware of the likely oversaturation of launch service providers, especially small launch providers, when considering the foreseeable Total Addressable Market for space launch.[70]

Workforce

Sector Overview

The DIB relies on a force of skilled workers to provide and support the products and services required to meet the U.S. government's national security needs. This shrinking workforce comprises 1.1 million designers, engineers, manufacturing and production workers and maintainers, information technology developers, and members of DoD's organic industrial base. It is a key element of the nation's critical infrastructure.

In the last several years, changing economic and national security policies have sharpened executive and legislative branch focus on the state of the DIB workforce. The combination of Presidential Executive Orders seeking to re-shore manufacturing and of ambitious production goals such as the Navy's 530-ship fleet initiative have given industry reasons to consider sizable new investments in manufacturing operations, shorter and more reliable supply chains, and advanced production technologies.

Such efforts require marked increases in the DIB's capacity and resilience. In turn, those objectives require producing more workers trained in the skilled trades or in STEM. Unfortunately, many young Americans have developed unfavorable impressions of careers in manufacturing and the trades. These impressions have been reinforced by educational policies that steer students toward four-year college programs. Meanwhile, STEM-focused programs at American universities, "are confronting a dearth in American talent generation and retention, and much of that shortfall is filled with foreign students, a large share of them from China."[71]

Major Risks & Issues

> ### Risk Archetypes:
>
> - Gap in U.S.-based human capital
> - Foreign dependency
> - DMSMS

Domestic manufacturing output grew in 2019 and early 2020, but the DIB's overall capacity to prevail against strategic competitors was still uncertain even before the coronavirus pandemic. The pandemic highlighted long standing critical risks and issues related to the supply chain for workers and materials. Many of these issues are the result of economic realities that favored off-shoring over the use of domestic supply chains for materials and workers, and investments in services rather than manufacturing; despite some marginal changes, policy incentives largely failed to overcome these issues.

The DIB workforce still suffers from the persistent issues highlighted in the 2019 version of this report. Candidate pools of potential workers are shrinking due to adverse demographics and persistent biases against industrial trades careers among parents and educators. Meanwhile, the mismatch between 1) technological knowledge and skills required by evolving manufacturing sectors and 2) suitable training programs is growing. Decades of neglect have left the robust system of technical schools the nation once relied upon for industrial training badly weakened. Finally, the existing workforce is rapidly aging out, taking irreplaceable tacit knowledge with them. Programmatic responses to education and training needs still largely focus on four-year STEM-based programs rather than digital industrial skills on the factory floor.

FY2020 Developments

In the short run, DoD's COVID-driven reinforcement of the DIB's critical infrastructure status helped limit, but could not eliminate, production losses and schedule delays in major defense programs. The coronavirus pandemic caused "demand crash," affecting commercial manufacturers and their suppliers, had pronounced adverse effects on the small, medium, and large defense suppliers that rely on commercial work to maintain economic viability over time. The coronavirus pandemic also highlighted the adverse impacts of dependence upon foreign sources of low cost labor and materials, especially China. Defense executives recognized the long-term threat of adversary influence on critical supply lines.

The COVID-19 effects notwithstanding, the USD(A&S)'s Office of Economic Adjustment (OEA) and IBAS programs executed key efforts to mitigate DIB workforce risks.

Service-Level Efforts

In keeping with priorities articulated by executives, workforce-related efforts undertaken by the U.S. Services due to the coronavirus pandemic focused on *retaining* rather than growing or enhancing the industrial workforce. In a few cases, these efforts supported the movement of workers from crippled commercial-side efforts to explicit defense work. Most other Service-level investments tied to DIB workforce development requirements are in individual weapon system acquisition and sustainment programs versus broad, defense-wide strategic workforce development efforts.

A&S Initiatives

As previewed in the FY2019 Industrial Capabilities Report, the IBAS program formally launched its 'National Imperative for Industrial Skills' initiative in FY 2020, making ten awards for prototyping agreements across the nation (approximately $30 million in total federal funding), testing various segments of the Industrial Skills Workforce Development Ecosystem Model (see Figure 7.26). Several of these awards are the result of direct partnerships with the military departments. The initiative is the Department's effort to reawaken the nation's commitment to the manufacturing and industrial skills needed to build next-generation weapons and platforms. The effort aims to promote the prestige of manufacturing and associated careers, accelerate the delivery of workers into and through training and education pipelines, and elevate U.S. manufacturing to a world-leading status. Through it, the Department consciously recognizes the nation's workforce development pipelines as vital supply chains.

The National Imperative is a logical outgrowth of 'ProjectMFG,' a highly successful and continuing series of competitive events intended to generate interest in manufacturing and industrial skills and associated careers (described in last year's report). In FY2020, the IBAS program conducted ProjectMFG events in Alabama, New York, California, Tennessee, and Virginia. Additional planned events in Texas, Ohio, and the National Finals in Illinois were cancelled due to COVID-19. ProjectMFG has been refined to support competition using virtual arenas.

OSD's OEA is designed to support long-term community investments that strengthen national security innovation and expand the capabilities of the defense industrial ecosystem. The OEA awarded six Defense Manufacturing Communities Support Program grants (totaling $25 million in federal funding) to entities in Pennsylvania, West Virginia, Ohio, Utah, California, Alabama, and Connecticut, each of which helps to advance that community's local and regional defense industrial workforce development ecosystem in unique ways.[72] Each awardee was required to provide substantial cost share.

Sector Outlook

The Department will continue to assess the immediate and long-term DIB workforce impacts from the coronavirus pandemic, while also addressing more long-term and systemic shortfalls in the workforce development pipelines that supply and sustain these vital resources. Shortages of skilled labor and its impact to the production schedule and cost of major weapons and platforms will continue to be a source of concern to both the DIB and the Department. Dependent upon access to sufficient financial resources, in FY2021, the IBAS program office will expand the National Imperative for Industrial Skills initiative by making additional awards and funding optional tasks on already-awarded agreements. IBAS will continue to seek and leverage partnerships across the Services through the 'Cornerstone' OTA membership consortium.

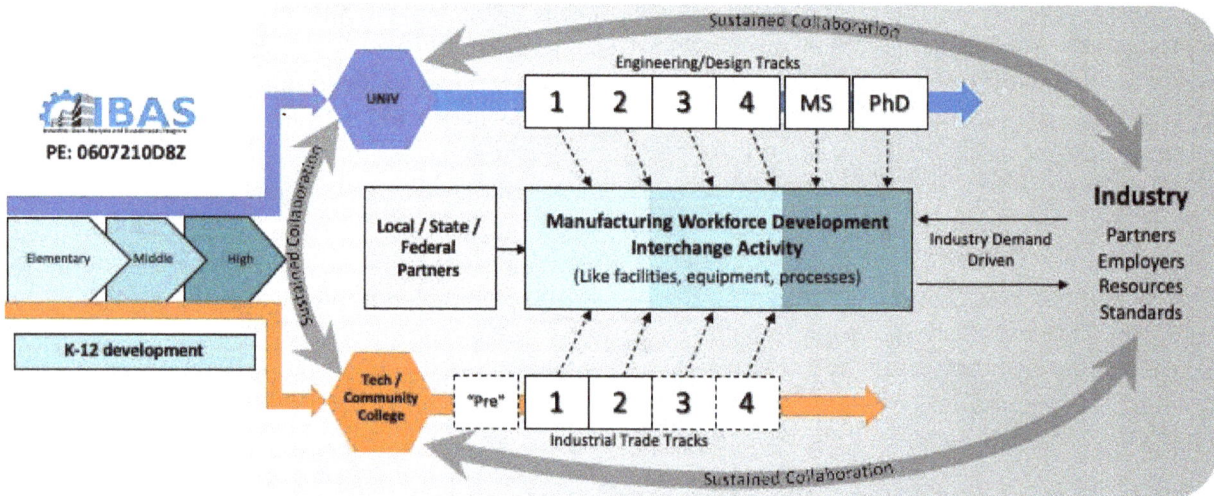

Figure 7.26: Graphic representation of the "Industrial Skills Workforce Development Ecosystem" as envisioned by the National Imperative for Industrial Skills.

CRITICAL AND EMERGING TECHNOLOGIES

CRITICAL AND EMERGING TECHNOLOGIES

Introduction

The Technology, Manufacturing, and Industrial Base (TMIB) Office within OUSD(R&E) is responsible for creating strategies within the industrial base to develop, manufacture, and sustain current and emerging technologies to retain U.S. advantage. TMIB uses emerging technology assessments to translate technology requirements into manufacturing and industrial base requirements. Figure 8.1 outlines the assessment methodology employed by TMIB to provide a full overview of the technology from a manufacturing and industrial base point of view and create technology and industrial base protection and promotion strategies.

Technology Characterization

- Determine military advantage, assess technical maturity, and understand challenges

- Understand near-peer & adversary perspectives, strategies, investments

Development & Testing

- Assess government and industry laboratories and engineering centers

    • Identify requirements for workforce skills, engineering tools, facilities, technical challenges

    • Identify test requirements-infrastructure, skills, tools

Production & Supply Chain

- Assess industry production capabilities & supply chain capacities

- Identify critical companies and expertise, existing relationships, mergers and acquisitions

Future State of Technology

- Assess future state of technologies, capabilities, and interdependencies

- Identify economic strategies/ investments, scalability of emerging technologies, and maintain technological advantage

Figure 8.1: Types of Technology and Manufacturing Studies

These strategies protect and promote the DIB by mitigating risks, exploiting opportunities identified in emergent technology assessments, and providing support for the development and execution of technology modernization activities and priorities.

The following section of the report includes an overview of the critical and emergent technologies currently in the research and development phase, including current and future initiatives to promote and protect the technology innovation base.

Biotechnology

Biotechnology, or biotech, refers to the engineering of biological systems and processes to produce a wide range of products, as well as utilizing biological data to enable technological advances. DoD investments in biotechnology will result in enhancements to warfighting materiel and systems, warfighter health and performance, military medicine, and chemical and biological defense. For example, biotechnology can enable the Department to: source mission-critical materials without relying on fragile supply chains; develop materials with novel properties to enhance performance in systems ranging from hypersonics to ships and submarines; and greatly reduce logistical timelines and burden for deployment and resupply

by providing point-of-need manufacturing. The mastery of this emerging technology will have an outsized impact on national security. It is critical that the United States and its allies prevail in the race for biotech, as China has publicly stated that it intends to "win" the bio-revolution and signaled willingness to use biotechnology against their adversaries without respect for protocols, conventions, or human rights.

The DoD Biotechnology modernization strategy identifies initial key areas to develop to create a pipeline to rapidly transition science and technology (S&T) toward fieldable products and capabilities, as shown in Figure 8.2.

A deliberate shift toward bioindustrial manufacturing could reduce DoD dependence on sole source and foreign suppliers through the use of engineered organisms as factories to produce a wide range of downstream products, including materials that cannot be manufactured using alternative approaches. However, DoD efforts have focused largely on developing capability at the laboratory level, and commercial applications of engineering biology are still in early stages of market expansion. A clear limitation in growth of this technology segment relates to facilities and know-how for scaling biomanufacturing from the

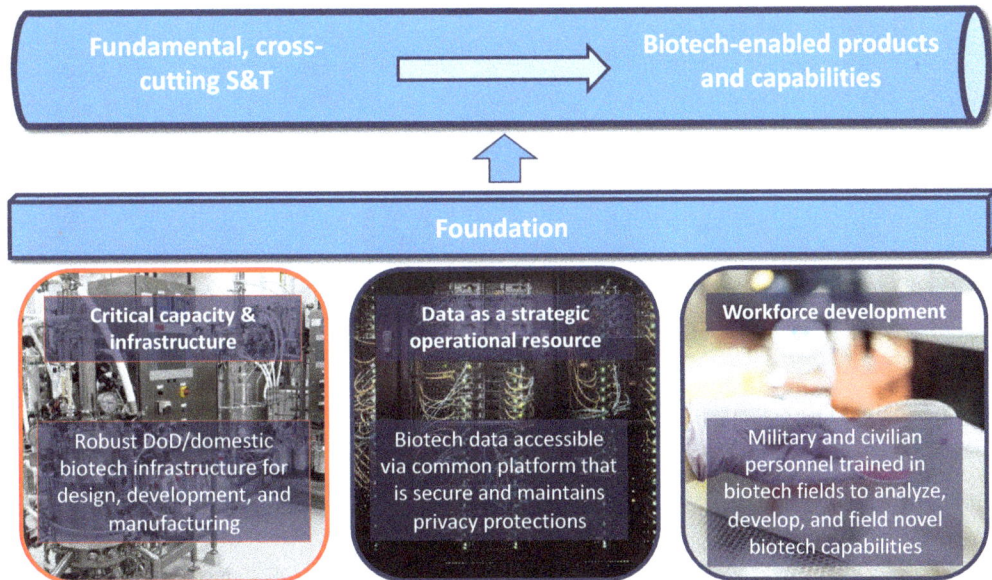

Figure 8.2

laboratory to commercial production; a valley-of-death exists for most companies between federally funded proof-of-concept work and demonstration, scale-up, and production.

To mitigate this challenge, the DoD Manufacturing Technology Office, along with the Principal Director for Biotechnology within OUSD (R&E), awarded a 7-year Cooperative Agreement worth $87 million to BioMADE to develop a Manufacturing Innovation Institute dedicated to biomanufacturing for non-biomedical applications. Focus areas for BioMADE will include: 1) the development of better tools for scale-up manufacturing, 2) improvements in down-stream processing techniques, and 3) the ability to rapidly assess and characterize biomanufactured products. Collectively, these efforts will reduce the cost and time to achieve robust biomanufacturing, with a focus on fostering and sustaining a globally competitive U.S. manufacturing base.

As biotechnology continues to develop, the DoD faces several key risks related to gaps in domestic workforce, national and international standards, and robust biosecurity to prevent misuse of the technology by adversaries. The coronavirus pandemic further underscores U.S. and global vulnerabilities to biological threats. The DoD can play a key role in contributing to national and international standards for responsible use of biotechnology, and ensuring that the technology is broadly available, safe, and secure by developing innovative approaches to address biosafety, biosecurity, and biocontainment.

To support Biotechnology development, OUSD(R&E) TMIB is leading two assessments to quantify: 1) domestic bioindustrial manufacturing capacity, and 2) the current and future biotechnology workforce. These assessments aim to develop an understanding of gaps and needs, and create recommendations for mitigation measures necessary to ensure a robust bioindustrial manufacturing base and advance the broader U.S. bioeconomy.

Fully Networked Command, Control, and Communications

Fully Networked Command, Control, and Communications (FNC3) technology encompasses the capability to acquire, process, and disseminate information across force elements.[73] The DoD requires reliable interconnection of diverse platforms and systems across all domains and operating environments as defined in the NDS. Existing capabilities require sufficient protection against threats that are increasing in pervasiveness and effectiveness. OUSD(R&E) will mature and transition the overall FNC3 architecture and associated technologies via a strategy that fosters distinct but inter-related R&D efforts across the physical, network, and application layers. The DoD FNC3 strategy will result in a resilient DoD-wide command, control, and communications (C3) system, while also enabling interoperability and connectivity between every system and platform.[74]

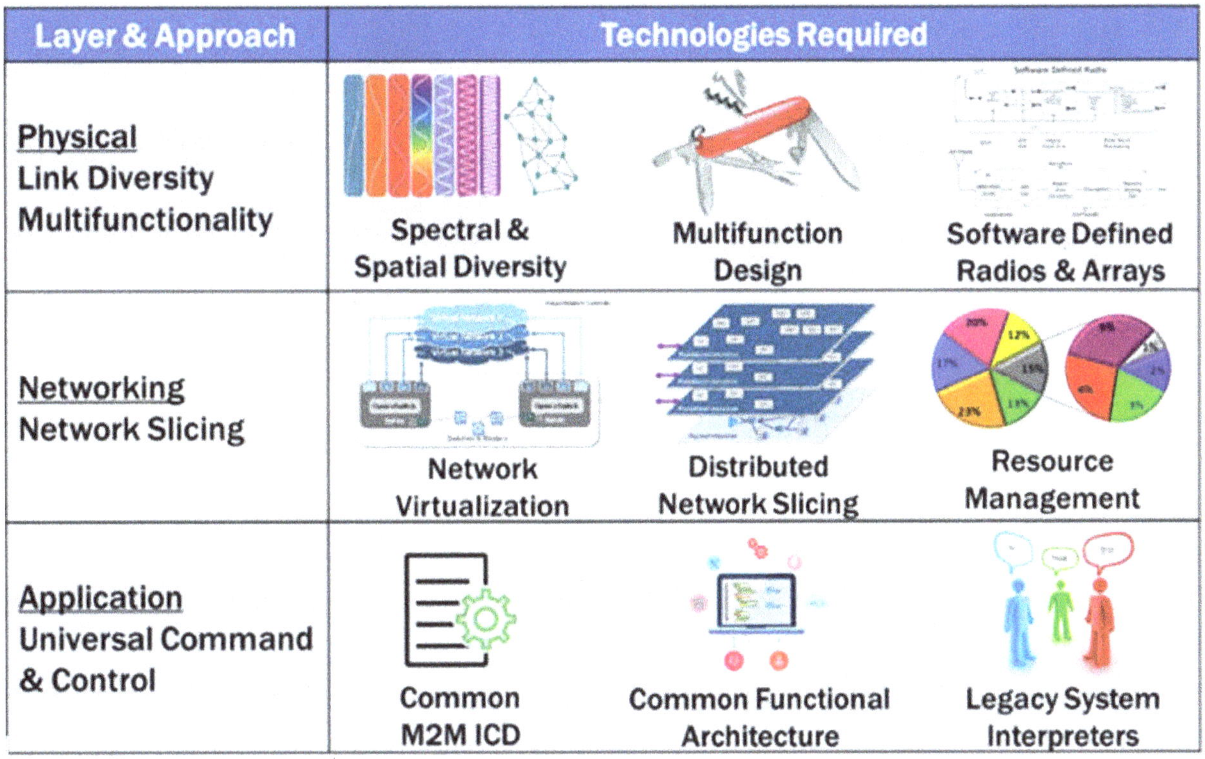

Layer & Approach	Technologies Required		
Physical Link Diversity Multifunctionality	Spectral & Spatial Diversity	Multifunction Design	Software Defined Radios & Arrays
Networking Network Slicing	Network Virtualization	Distributed Network Slicing	Resource Management
Application Universal Command & Control	Common M2M ICD	Common Functional Architecture	Legacy System Interpreters

Figure 8.3: FNC3 Strategy[75]

The existing C3 innovation and industrial bases are healthy. However, while commercial products benefit from the use of open architectures, common interfaces, and fixed infrastructure, DoD C3 systems require unique, military-specific applications to be effective. Today's military C3 systems were designed and developed with incompatible requirements and are unable to efficiently exchange information.[76] DoD will leverage existing commercial technologies and best practices to solve the two biggest challenges facing the DoD's existing C3 systems: interoperability and resilience in highly contested environments. The FNC3 strategy takes advantage of all available link diversity to provide resilience while also promoting interoperability and connectivity between every system and platform.[77]

To transition capabilities to the warfighter, FNC3 is coordinating with key DoD stakeholders, including the OUSD(A&S), DoD CIO, the Joint Staff, Space Development Agency, and the Services to guide the transition of FNC3 capabilities into appropriate acquisition programs, standards, and operational architectures. The Joint All-Domain Command and Control (JADC2) Cross-Functional Team chartered by the Deputy Secretary of Defense has adopted the FNC3 strategy as its long-term technological baseline. JADC2 will also provide the ability to connect distributed sensors, intelligence, information, data, and effects from all domains to tactical and strategic decision makers; JADC2 will provide this capability at the scale, tempo, and timing required to accomplish the commander's intent, agnostic to domains, platforms, or functional lanes.[78]

DoD will continue to collaborate with industry stakeholders to identify and implement C3 industrial base vulnerability mitigation efforts, leveraging investment programs such as Defense-Wide Manufacturing Science & Technology (DMS&T), ManTech, IBAS, and DPA Title III to protect the FNC3 industrial base from challenges, and to bridge the gap between S&T and production.

In FY2020, OUSD(R&E) TMIB initiated a multi-phased industrial base assessment focused on discovering commercial trends that support the FNC3 strategy; determining capabilities and vulnerabilities related to delivering the technologies required; identifying risks and opportunities; and making recommendations to enhance the existing C3 supplier base. Initial findings include actionable approaches to achieving interoperability across DoD-wide platforms (including legacy) using analytics, network management techniques, modular approaches to interoperable architectures, and data management strategies. The FY2021 assessment outcomes will identify DoD and commercial technology development investment trends, and will provide recommendations on how to improve the DoD FCN3 strategy by leveraging what industry has already invested in, and by focusing next on military-unique capabilities that must be incentivized.

Hypersonics

Hypersonic weapons achieve sustained flight within the atmosphere with speeds near, or above, five times the speed of sound. There is a focus on the tactical capability that these types of weapons bring to theater or regional conflicts. These weapons provide quick response and high speed, are highly maneuverable, and difficult to find, track, and kill. DoD is modernizing our offensive and defensive force structure to both utilize and deter this capability. Example programs for the U.S. investment in hypersonics strike systems are shown in Table 8.4.

The Department is identifying issues, risks, and opportunities to advance hypersonics capabilities with the objective of creating near- and long-term investments strategies. DoD's ability to develop and field hypersonic capabilities requires a robust industrial base positioned to design and test hypersonic systems. IB capability must also sustain the anticipated U.S. production demand in support of the DoD strategy for accelerated development and fielding of hypersonic strike weapons as shown in Figure 8.5.

Hypersonic Development Program	Service/Agency	Capability
Long Range Hypersonic Weapon	US Army	Intermediate Range Strike
Conventional Prompt Strike	US Navy	Intermediate Range Strike
Air Launched Rapid Response Weapon(ARRW)/Tactical Boost Glide (TBG)	US Air Force/DARPA	Medium Range Strike
Hypersonic Air-breathing Weapon Concept	US Air Force/DARPA	Medium Range Strike
STANDARD Missile-6 (SM-6 Blk1B)	US Navy	Medium Range Strike

Table 8.4: Hypersonics Programs

Accelerated Development and Fielding of Hypersonic Strike Weapons			
Phase 1: Concept and Technology R&D *Develop the enabling technologies and concepts necessary to underpin future hypersonic systems*	Phase 2: Weapon System Rapid Prototypes *Accelerate future hypersonic weapon system prototype development*	Phase 3: Accelerated Fielding Plan *Field hypersonic strike weapon prototype capabilities in meaningful numbers*	Phase 4: POR Fielding Plan *Establish programs of record to build warfighting inventory and implement capability phasing plans*
Foundational S&T, Industrial Base and T&E Investment Plans			

Table 8.5: Hypersonics Development and Transition Phases

In 2019, the Defense Contract Management Agency's Industrial Analysis Group (DCMA IAG) and the Air Force's Office of Commercial Economic Analysis performed studies focused on the capabilities, capacity, and financial health of the hypersonics IB. Major findings of the reports included the need for immediate and continued investments in infrastructure, development activities, manufacturing, and workforce development to ensure a healthy and resilient IB. Recent industrial base assessments have also identified capabilities essential to achieve a robust hypersonics industrial base, including:

- Stable sources of critical materials such as ceramic matrix composite material sources (fibers, pitch resin, etc.)

- Industry access to test facilities and broad access to test results

- An ability for multiple hypersonics programs to compete for the same supply chain of traditional weapons system prime and sub-tier contractors

- Access to proprietary processes in a small number of critical small businesses

- A robust technical workforce of weapon systems engineers and supporting skilled trades workers

- Robust and resilient verified design tools and techniques

The development of the Hypersonics Science and Technology roadmap has also identified a short list of immediate investment opportunities that are required to increase the capability and health of the hypersonics IB.

In July 2020, a Presidential Determination for use of DPA authorities for the industrial base production of ultra-high and high temperature composites for hypersonics, strategic missiles, and space launch systems was signed to address future capacity needs. Additionally, further investment opportunities are being explored and implemented to advance manufacturing technologies for additive manufacturing of high temperature metals, ceramic matrix composites, and modeling and simulation methods. The OSD ManTech office projects Manufacturing of Carbon-Carbon Composites for Hypersonic Applications will continue to advance methods and processes to more affordably and rapidly produce carbon-carbon components for hypersonic systems. These investments will greatly improve the ability of the industrial base to design and test systems, and provide quantities needed for near-term demonstration and early operational capability milestones. They will also contribute to the ability to produce larger production quantities in the future.

In support of the Principal Director for Hypersonics, the TMIB office within OUSD(R&E) and the OUSD(A&S) Industrial Policy office are working to develop an IB roadmap and conduct assessments in support of the acceleration of hypersonic strike capability described in the Figure 8.5. This effort will identify actions and investment strategies necessary to meet the hypersonics capability required to meet DoD's goals. To execute this, a Hypersonics War Room (HSWR) was established with members from OSD and the Services. The HSWR conducts deep dives into the industrial base, especially at the sub-tier level, to visualize the emerging results of the roadmap development and mitigation activities. This effort has and will continue to focus on the current supply chain to identify areas of opportunity. Additional planned and future IB assessments will facilitate data gathering and analytics, and support fact-based decisions on investments in key areas of the hypersonics IB. Future work to develop requirements and acquisition strategies for Programs of Record will be informed by the HSWR to help accelerate delivery of operational capabilities to the warfighter.

Microelectronics

Microelectronics is a subfield of electronics that relates to the study, manufacture, and microfabrication of electronic designs and components with very small feature sizes. Typically, this refers to micrometer-scale to nanometer-scale products. These devices are typically made from semiconductor materials and many components of normal electronic design are available in a scaled down microelectronic equivalent. These include transistors, capacitors, inductors, resistors, diodes, insulators, and conductors.

Microelectronics have evolved rapidly as the demand for inexpensive and lightweight equipment has increased; they have also been incorporated into countless DoD systems. However, the DoD modernization ability is jeopardized by foreign microelectronics (ME) production, actions, and investments. To mitigate this, DoD must develop and deliver next generation microelectronic technologies to enhance lethality, ensure critical infrastructure, and achieve economic competitiveness.[79]

In a recent DoD News article, "DoD Adopts 'Zero Trust' Approach to Buying Microelectronics," Dr. Lewis, the DoD's Director of Research and Engineering for Modernization, stated that microelectronics are in nearly everything, including the complex weapons systems DoD buys, such as the F-35 joint strike fighter. He further stated, "Our goal is to allow the Department of Defense to purchase on the commercial curves...that will put us on...par with our strategic competitors."[80]

Microelectronics are critical to advancement of emerging technologies like AI, 5G and quantum computing, as well as critical components in weapons systems. Commercial market forces continue to lead in the consumption of microelectronics and therefore are driving the industry.

FY2019 Total Global Semiconductor Demand Share by End Use [81]

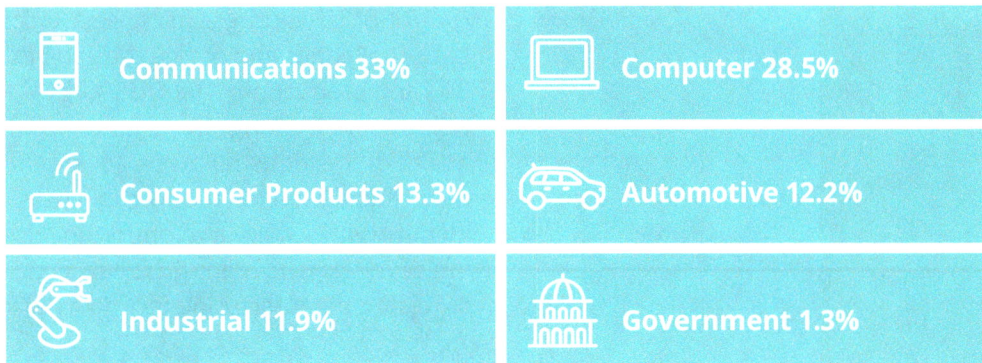

Communications 33%

Computer 28.5%

Consumer Products 13.3%

Automotive 12.2%

Industrial 11.9%

Government 1.3%

Figure 8.6

To respond to market forces, the microelectronics industry must always be state-of-the-art. Approximately every two years, the industry moves to the next technology node, bringing benefits which generally include improved size, weight, speed, and power consumption. The current SOTA for microprocessors is five nanometers, and is reserved for the highest volume commercial customers. Unfortunately, these improvements have resulted in increased costs, particularly in the area of design.

The United States still leads in the design of SOTA microelectronics, but Asia has nearly 80 percent of the outsourced aspects of semiconductor production. This includes foundries, and assembly and test functions. "The U.S. currently maintains a stable chip manufacturing footprint, but the trend lines are concerning. There are commercial fabs in 18 states, and semiconductors rank as our nation's fifth-largest export. However, significant semiconductor manufacturing incentives have been put in place by other countries, and U.S. semiconductor manufacturing growth lags behind these countries due largely to a lack of federal incentives."[82] During FY2020, the microelectronics sector experienced an increase in the numbers of both CFIUS and export control cases. The majority of the cases were related to components for 5G. The health of the U.S.-based microelectronics industry is being balanced against policy changes to protect the technology.

DoD relies on the Defense Microelectronics Activity Trusted Foundry Program to provide access to trusted microelectronics and services through their network of accredited suppliers. DoD plans to make use of chiplets and advanced packaging to fill the need in the short term, until there is either a domestic source of SOTA microelectronics, or Quantifiable Assurance reaches sufficient maturity to allow the use of any foundry. The Trusted and Assured Microelectronics program is pursuing an effort to both define Data-Driven Quantifiable Assurance and create the methodology for a zero-trust risk-based approach for supply chain protection and assured access to SOTA microelectronics technology and electronic components.

The Defense Advanced Research Projects Agency (DARPA) Electronics Resurgence Initiative is attempting to forge collaborations among commercial industry, the DIB, universities, and the DoD to innovate a fourth wave of electronics progress. The five year, up to $1.5 billion initiative, to enable far-reaching improvements in electronics performance, is halfway to completion with much of the focus area in microelectronics.[83]

DoD is continuing to collaborate to identify and implement mitigation efforts. OUSD(A&S) and OUSD(R&E) are leveraging several investment programs such as DMS&T, ManTech, IBAS, and DPA Title III, to address microelectronics industrial base challenges and bridge the gap between S&T and production. The OUSD(R&E) TMIB will assist in creating strategies to promote the health of the industrial base, advance technology maturation, monitor supply chain risks, and identify issues, risks, and opportunities related to the development, manufacturing, and sustainment of related manufacturing technologies.

Machine Learning/ Artificial Intelligence (AI)

Artificial intelligence refers to the theory and development of systems able to perform tasks that normally require human intelligence, including perception, learning and reasoning, human-robot interaction, and other major processing and reasoning tasks, with the aim to improve efficiency and effectiveness across DoD.[84,85] Machine learning (ML) refers to the field of computer science concerned with creating programs that "learn" from data using a large and evolving set of techniques grounded in statistics and mathematical optimization. AI uses machine learning technologies to enable a multitude of capabilities.[86] DoD is currently developing AI for various military applications, such as intelligence, surveillance, and reconnaissance, logistics, cyber operations, command and control, and semiautonomous and autonomous vehicles.

While military AI technology is still in a stage of infancy, DoD is pursuing AI algorithms developed for ISR and for autonomous vehicles as two key AI capabilities, among others. The Army, Air Force, DARPA, DISA, Navy, and OSD all have AI/ML development projects in progress to further mature AI technology. For example, the U.S. Air Force program Project Maven integrates AI into systems for insurgent target identification through the use of AI algorithms, computer vision, and machine learning,[87] with the goal of automating the processing, exploitation, and dissemination typically done by human analysts, thus increasing efficiency.[88] DARPA has AI/ML programs, such as the Air Combat Evolution (ACE) program, which is developing an AI fighter pilot with human-machine teaming to reduce the cognitive load on the pilot during dogfights.[89] The U.S. Army is researching reinforcement learning approaches to enable swarms of unmanned aerial and ground vehicles to accomplish various missions, minimizing performance uncertainty. The U.S. Army Research Laboratory is also investigating deep recurrent neural networks to improve the learning and prediction algorithm for optimal coordination of autonomous air and ground vehicles.[90]

The DoD AI strategy identifies initial key areas to develop to maintain a competitive advantage in AI, including AI capabilities, determining a common foundation, cultivating the AI workforce, engaging in partnerships, and leading in AI assurance. In particular, a common foundation across DoD with a joint AI development platform and DoD shared data, AI evaluations, and AI solutions will enable the rapid transition of AI research breakthroughs to edge developers.

As AI/ML technology continues to grow in terms of development and strategic importance, the DoD AI/ML industrial base faces several key risks: gaps in U.S.-based human capital, variable ease of adaptability of commercial AI technology, and potential product security issues. Product security is one of the main risks for AI/ML systems, as they are vulnerable to theft and exploitation due to being primarily software-based. The U.S.-based human capital gap is also a risk, with DoD and the defense industry facing challenges in recruiting and retaining personnel with AI expertise compared with the commercial sector. In addition, there has been a decline in the domestic AI workforce due to the rise of international graduates in U.S. research institutions and universities, who then frequently return to work overseas or at companies in competition with U.S. AI/ML companies.[91]

DoD also faces a challenge in leveraging commercial technology for military applications, as innovation in AI is currently dominated by private companies that work with open-source, general purpose AI software libraries. There is a wide variance in how easily commercial AI technology can be adapted for DoD, with certain algorithms requiring only minor data adjustments and others needing significant changes in order to be used in complex military environments. In addition, existing DoD processes may be at odds with commercial companies' safety and performance standards and their acquisition processes. These factors can inhibit the smooth transfer of commercial AI technology to DoD.[92,93]

DoD continues to identify and implement mitigation strategies to support AI/ML development and is leveraging ManTech investment programs to further develop technologies in the AI/ML investment area. TMIB is leading an AI/ML industrial base assessment to develop recommendations for the design of a DoD AI/ML open-market model, based on feedback from industry and other stakeholders. This assessment has the goal of increasing competition and reducing development cost to move more viable capabilities into DoD.

Quantum

Quantum Information Science is the study of how quantum physics can be exploited for the collection, manipulation, storage, retrieval, analysis, movement, dissemination, and protection of information. DoD research indicates that advancing capabilities of quantum technologies will benefit critical mission spaces.[94] DoD is interested in military applications of quantum information science that will provide technological advantage over alternative approaches.[95] Consequently, there is a push toward ultra-sensitive devices that increasingly rely on quantum phenomena to achieve advances in precise timing and navigation, sensing, computing, and networking.[96]

The Department is currently pursuing four key technical areas: atomic clocks, quantum sensors, quantum computers, and quantum networks.[97] Atomic clocks and quantum sensors will deliver new and assured precision, position, navigation, and timing capabilities, as well as improved intelligence, surveillance, and reconnaissance, allowing our forces to continue operations in GPS-denied theaters. Quantum computers are projected to provide high-performance computing, solving hard mathematical problems that are intractable for a traditional computer. Quantum

networks are expected to profoundly impact a number of DoD missions, including timing, sensing, computation, and communications in the long-term, potentially delivering resource multiplying effects for other quantum technologies to solve DoD's challenging analytical problems.[98]

Some of these areas have reached higher technology readiness levels (e.g., atomic clocks and vapor cell magnetometers), while others are in the earliest stages of proof-of-principle development (e.g., quantum computers and entangled quantum networks).[99] For example, in the case of quantum sensor technologies, commercial companies are starting to make quantum products, and the technology is progressing towards military utility. Although atomic clocks and magnetometers have been in use, other sensors (e.g., gyros, accelerometers, and gravimeters) are still in development and not yet fieldable. Other quantum technologies such as quantum computers and quantum networks are still in their infancy and exist primarily in labs.

Additionally, these quantum technologies differ in the anticipated impact to the military. As Figure 8.7 depicts, technologies vary from low military impact with low readiness level (e.g., entangled sensor networks) to high military impact with high readiness levels (e.g., GPS atomic clocks).[100]

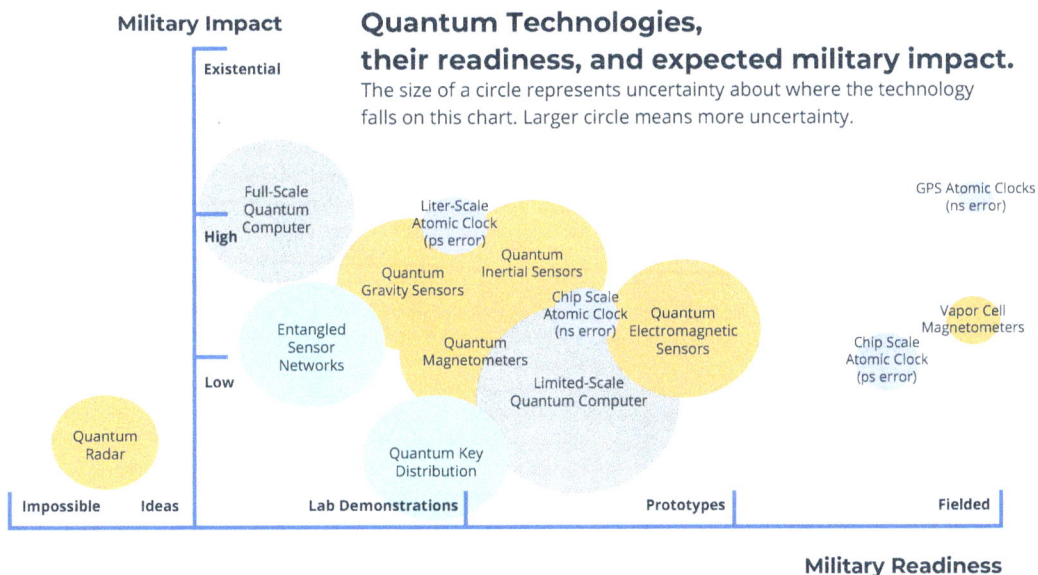

Figure 8.7 Quantum Technologies Military Readiness

To mature quantum technology, the OUSD(R&E) Roadmap for Quantum Science highlights key long-term military challenges with technical goals, including:

- Synchronized timing in denied environments;

- Precision targeting, positioning, and navigation in denied environments;

- Military advantage for intelligence, surveillance, and reconnaissance;

- Access to high performance computing for military applications; and

- Survey cryptographic solutions for military communications.

For example, the U.S. is reliant on precision time-keeping and communications synchronization. Atomic clocks provide a non-GPS alternative to position, navigation, and timing solutions in denied environments and offer size, weight, and power improvements over currently available timing solutions. Therefore, one key focus area is to mature atomic clocks with novel characteristics of military relevance and reduced cost. To this end, the DoD is making substantial investments in the development of novel atomic clock technologies, as well as low-cost, chip-scale atomic clocks.

Various actions the Department is taking to mitigate national security risks to quantum technology include: monitoring the development of a potential "quantum winter", actively promoting realistic expectations of the maturity of the science, staying abreast of the health of the quantum science industrial base and workforce, and continuing to partner with academia and industry to develop quantum science. The term "quantum winter" has been coined to describe a possible time period in which the public hype of the potential in quantum computing outpaces the maturity of the applications. Gartner's "hype cycle" describes the effect of inflated expectations and ensuing disillusionment, which has been seen before in emerging technology areas.[101] This may cause U.S. investors to reduce their investments, negatively affecting large companies and start-ups, making them vulnerable to acquisition by

strategic competitor nations, and resulting in the loss of intellectual property, equipment, and talent. DoD assesses that current elevated levels of commercial investment are unsustainable, given the limited commercial utility of quantum computing. Existing levels are only sustainable if there is a major breakthrough, and DoD continues to monitor the situation to keep abreast of and mitigate developments.

DoD is in a position to help the country weather a "quantum winter" by maturing and transitioning practical applications for quantum technology, thereby decreasing the perception gap. DoD will continue to issue realistic timelines for quantum technology development. For example, industry claims that quantum desktops will be available in five years; these claims are unreasonable and DoD is in a position to clarify this information. As an additional measure, DoD is also tracking the health of the quantum science industrial base and workforce.

It is important for DoD to understand the current health of the quantum science industrial base to mitigate risks. Quantum information science is a relatively new technical focus area for consumers, with an emerging supply chain. To gain this understanding, DoD is sponsoring a RAND Corporation assessment of the robustness of the U.S. industrial base in quantum technology. Potential focus areas for this assessment include: the robustness of supply chains; academic research activity; commercial deployment; strength of international collaborations; technological breadth of investments; dedicated public funding (total investment and sustained level of funding over time); academic, industry, and/or government integration; and prioritization by national leadership.[102]

DoD's legacy of more than twenty years of quantum information science research, including both internally at Service labs and by funding external talent, has created a wide breadth and scope of expert-quality quantum workforce nationally. Continuation of these efforts will allow the pool of talent to encompass the full quantum product life-cycle. Figure 8.8 illustrates the generalized job ratio and role requirements of the workforce necessary to support the product's full life cycle.

In the coming decades, as technology matures and moves through its life-cycle from concept to commercialization, the challenge will lie in shaping the workforce to address the specific needs that will arise.

Since much of quantum technology is early in its lifecycle, DoD has endeavored to balance technology promotion efforts and technology protection efforts. A correct balance would allow for the industrial base to have access to the best talent available globally, while mitigating the risks of technology transfer to strategic competitor nations. The DoD is in the process of assessing and understanding what the future quantum workforce will comprise. The study will identify projected gaps in industry-level capabilities, competencies, and occupations required to fulfill mission objectives. This assessment will also make recommendations for broad-based strategies to mitigate those gaps.[103]

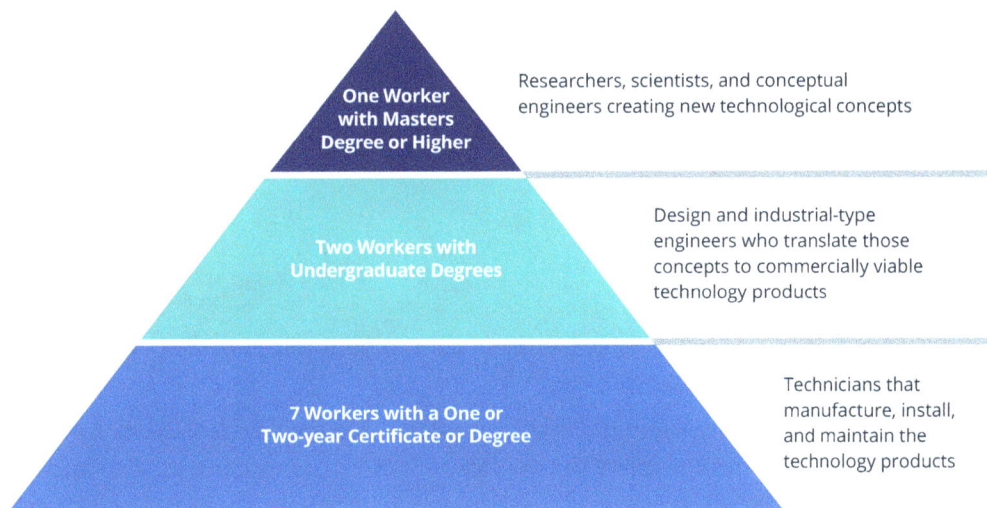

One Worker with Masters Degree or Higher — Researchers, scientists, and conceptual engineers creating new technological concepts

Two Workers with Undergraduate Degrees — Design and industrial-type engineers who translate those concepts to commercially viable technology products

7 Workers with a One or Two-year Certificate or Degree — Technicians that manufacture, install, and maintain the technology products

Gray, K. & Herr, E. (2006). Other Ways to Win: Creating Alternatives for High School Graduates. Third Edition. Thousand Oaks: Corwin Press

Figure 8.8: U.S. Job Ratio for the Product Life-Cycle Workforce

Directed Energy (DE)

Directed Energy is an umbrella term referring to technologies that produce concentrated electromagnetic (EM) energy and atomic or subatomic particles. A directed energy weapon (DEW) is a system using DE primarily as a means to incapacitate, damage, disable, or destroy enemy equipment, facilities, and/or personnel.[104]

DoD is currently pursuing two key types of DEWs: high energy lasers (HEL), which offer precise laser beams that can reversibly dazzle or permanently burn and damage targets; and high power microwaves (HPM), which produce radio- and microwave-frequency beams that can engage multiple targets at a time and disrupt their electronic systems. Both weapon systems offer the distinct advantages of deep magazine, low cost-exchange ratio, and speed-of-light engagement, and can be employed across all warfighting domains to counter threats of evolving quantity (e.g., swarms of unmanned aerial systems or fast inshore attack craft), speed (e.g., hypersonics), and lethality (e.g., highly maneuverable cruise missiles and intercontinental ballistic missiles).[105]

The U.S. Army, Navy, Air Force, Marines, Special Operations Force, and other DoD Agencies have development programs underway to mature both HEL and HPM weapon systems.[106] For instance, the Navy has installed Optical Dazzler Interdictor (ODIN) counter-sensor lasers aboard three Arleigh Burke-class guided missile destroyers, the first of which was USS Dewey. Five additional installations will follow in the next couple of years.[107] Multiple DEWs, including the High Energy Laser (HELWS), High Power Microwave (PHASER), and Tactical High Power Operational Responder (THOR), have also been recently deployed overseas for 12-month field assessments in which Warfighters will evaluate their performance and benefit.[108] Table 8.9 shows other operational experiments. Results of these assessments will provide insight on the DE capability to counter UAS and shape the way forward for their use.

HELWS	Raytheon HEL using invisible beams of light to neutralize hostile UAS; mounted on a Polaris MRZR all-terrain vehicle
PHASER	HPM developed by Raytheon that uses microwave energy to disrupt drone guidance systems, with the capability to address UAS swarms; mounted on a shipping container-like box
THOR	Counter-swarm HPM developed by AFRL, intended for airbase defense; stores in a 20-foot transport container

Table 8.9: DEWs deployed for operational experimentation[109]

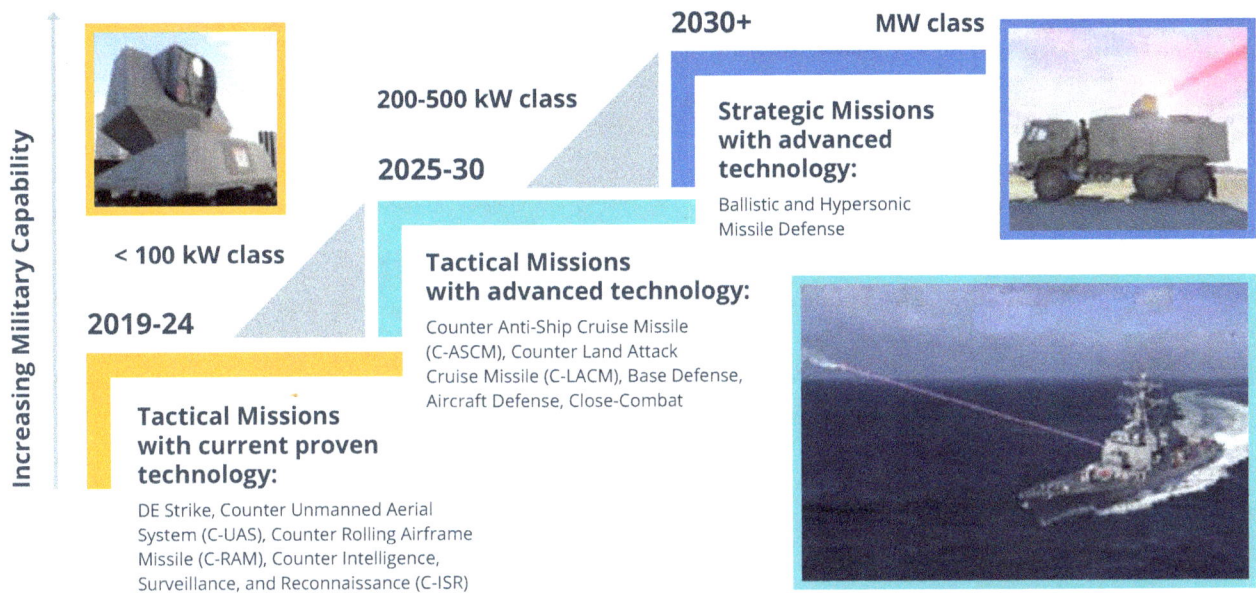

2030+   **MW class**

200-500 kW class

2025-30

Strategic Missions with advanced technology:

Ballistic and Hypersonic Missile Defense

< 100 kW class

2019-24

Tactical Missions with advanced technology:

Counter Anti-Ship Cruise Missile (C-ASCM), Counter Land Attack Cruise Missile (C-LACM), Base Defense, Aircraft Defense, Close-Combat

Tactical Missions with current proven technology:

DE Strike, Counter Unmanned Aerial System (C-UAS), Counter Rolling Airframe Missile (C-RAM), Counter Intelligence, Surveillance, and Reconnaissance (C-ISR)

Increasing Military Capability

Figure 8.10: DoD HEL Roadmap[112]

Overall, DoD is focusing its near-term efforts on fielding capabilities for tactical missions with proven technologies. However, as Figure 8.10 shows, the DE technology roadmap includes the development of advanced technologies extending into the next decade. Among the DoD roadmap efforts[110] is the HEL Scaling Initiative which intends to increase HEL power levels from around 150 kW, as is currently feasible, to around 300 kW, a level at which cruise missiles could potentially be intercepted, with the potential to scale to 500+ kW.[111]

To facilitate the implementation of these future technologies, the roadmap also establishes a DE reference architecture to identify components and subsystems around which DoD can standardize. Such standards[113] will enable a modular open systems approach and reduce costs by allowing components to be bought and used by multiple programs.[114]

As the DoD demand for DEWs increases, it faces key industrial base risks related to supplier financial health, specialized equipment and skills, production capacity, foreign dependence, and single source suppliers. The primary challenge is adapting commercially available production methods to meet DE-specific products, while accomplishing high-rate, low cost production.

Fabrication of many DE components necessitates a high degree of touch labor using highly specialized skills and equipment unsuitable for any level of quantity production due to the significant cost and lead times involved.[115] This is further exacerbated by the many single and sole source suppliers currently providing critical DE components. While these suppliers are adequate for a number of demonstrator systems, there is a risk that they will not be able to meet program needs as the Military Services ramp up DE system production rates.

Domestic manufacturing insufficiencies have increased the U.S. dependency on foreign goods, such as raw substrate materials for optics and laser components, and tooling and equipment required for manufacturing of DE components. Not only does this dependence expose the supply chain to foreign influence, but it also has the potential to impact component and other downstream activity lead times, and the ability to meet necessary yield rates.

Underlying a number of industrial base risks are shortfalls in the workforce. The U.S. faces a diminishing supply of clearable labor with the advanced education and training necessary for designing, producing, and stewarding DE systems. The DoD DE community faces workforce skill gaps across the board, as the emergence of new weapon technologies, coupled with retirements, has caused a significant mismatch between skill requirements and workforce capabilities. Recruitment and retention of critical skill sets are concerns, partially because of sharp competition for labor with the private sector. Training the new workforce is essential, and improving the organic industrial base's opportunity to recruit already-trained artisans would have significant and immediate impacts on productivity and readiness.

DoD is continuing to collaborate to identify and implement mitigation efforts, leveraging several investment programs such as DMS&T, ManTech, IBAS, and DPA Title III, to apply towards DE industrial base challenges and bridge the gap between S&T and production. The TMIB office is also leading a DE industrial base assessment to identify issues, risks, and opportunities related to the development, manufacturing, and sustainment of this technology. The assessment findings will be used to create strategies to promote the innovation base and advance technology maturation.

5ᵗʰ Generation (5G)

The 5th generation (5G) of cellular networking infrastructure will use a combination of frequencies from multiple bands to maximize throughput. In addition to traditional macro cell towers, 5G will also use a large number of much smaller micro cells for new millimeter wave spectrum bands to create a blanket of ultrahigh-speed network coverage, providing significant improvements in capacity and latency that will enable connections to and control of many types of devices, not just cellphones. 5G will bring about wireless, ubiquitous connectivity across humans, machines, and the Internet of Things. Representative emerging and future applications are listed in Tables 8.11 and 8.12. Some commercial carriers have already started rolling out 5G networks in the U.S.

DoD will adapt 5G and next generation technologies to "operate through" congested and contested spectrum, in spite of compromised networks, to ensure maximum readiness, lethality, and partnering among allies. 5G prototyping and experimentation will be conducted in collaboration with the defense industry and commercial suppliers to accelerate U.S. prominence in the 5G global ecosystem.[116]

Segment	Drivers	Enablers	5G Requirement
Education	Remote delivery Immersive experiences	Video streaming Augmented reality/ Virtual reality	Large bandwidth Low latency
Manufacturing	Industrial automation	Massive IoT networks	High connection density Ultra reliability Low power consumption
Healthcare	Remote diagnosis and Intervention Long term monitoring	Video streaming Augmented reality/ Virtual reality Embedded devices, Advanced robotics	Low power High throughput Low latency
Smart Grid	Intelligent demand/ supply control Powerline communication	IoT sensors and networks	High reliability Broad coverage of network Low latency
Entertainment	Immersive gaming and media Industry Multimedia experience at 4k, 8K res.	Video streaming Augmented reality/ Virtual Reality	Large bandwidth Low latency

Table 8.11: Emerging applications and services enabled by 5G[117]

Segment	Drivers	Enablers	5G Requirement
Automotive / Autonomous Cars	Collision avoidance Intelligent navigation and transportation systems	Vehicle-to-vehicle (V2V) Vehicle-to-infrastructure (V2I) and other intelligent transport systems (ITS)	Large bandwidth and low latencies (< 5 ms) and high connection reliability (99.999%)
Smart Cities	Connected utilities, Transportation, Healthcare, Education and all amenities	Massive IoT networks Automation Cloud infrastructure Artificial intelligence	Large bandwidth High throughput High connection density Low latencies

Table 8.12: Envisaged Future Applications[118]

To support the new 5G capabilities, more of the radio frequency spectrum must be made available. The Federal Communications Commission is working to make additional spectrum available for 5G services and have prioritized auctioning high-band and mid-band spectrum.

Commercial 5G

U.S. commercial carriers are rolling out 5G across the low-band, mid-band, and high-band ranges of frequencies. However, the coverage is not widespread, particularly in the high-band, and it may not be available in all markets for a few more years. In addition, few devices are commercially available to take advantage of the new technology, although that is changing rapidly.

There are several new technologies that are becoming mainstream and enable the next generation of applications. Though many of these enablers have been in industry for a while, there are new applications utilizing these technologies and generating business value. Key enablers and their impact on 5G are as follows:

Robotics and drones — Industrial automation and healthcare will be two main areas where advancements in robotics will play a major role. In addition, an important use case for 5G will be drones and autonomous aerial vehicles. For example, future UAVs will deliver products and perform surveillance, disaster relief, etc. Currently, the ecosystem is exploring the use of 4G networks

to enable complex flight operations that are safe (e.g., avoiding collisions with buildings, airplanes, and each other). 5G enhancements will further enable this effort and disrupt many current business practices.[119]

Virtual/augmented reality — A new set of end-user devices enabled with virtual-reality capabilities, augmented reality (with digital view on a physical view), and haptic feedback are becoming popular with education, gaming, and real-world simulations. These devices are wirelessly connected and need low latency and high reliability to enable real-time experiences.[120]

AI — Advances in deep learning have allowed for very complex algorithms being applied in everyday applications. The petabytes of data generated by networks and services on the internet and otherwise have made this possible. AI will drive applications like autonomous cars, robotics, automation, and several intelligent applications on mobile devices. AI will also be the key driver for self-optimizing networks that will allow 5G networks to respond to issues of congestion, failures, and traffic spikes.[121]

Department of Defense

Recently, DoD announced the award of over $600 million in contracts to 15 prime contractors to perform testing and evaluation of 5G technologies at five military installations across the United States. Work on the test sites will last approximately three years, with the sites expected to be set up within the first year and full-scale experimentation planned by year two. The photograph in Figure 8.13 is the AN/FPS-117 engineering facility at Hill Air Force Base, Utah – one of the 5G testing sites.[122]

Figure 8.13: The AN/FPS-117 engineering facility at Hill Air Force Base, Utah, one of the DoD 5G testing sites[123]

There are three key thrust areas that the military is pursuing in regards to 5G networking: *Accelerate, Operate Through, and Innovate. Accelerate* includes the hastening of DoD's use of 5G technologies; *Operate Through* ensures that DoD networks are secure and will have the ability to operate wherever and whenever the military goes; and *Innovate* focuses on next generation technologies (6G, 7G, etc.) to position the U.S. for the future. 5G technology is vital to maintaining the U.S. military and is a transformational technology critical to DoD modernization.[124] The economic advantages of 5G technology will be the advent of ubiquitous connectivity, and the connectivity of everything, everyone, everywhere through wireless communications.

Autonomy

"Autonomy" describes systems capable of performing assigned tasks without continuous human control. Autonomous systems include a level of perception and decision-making that allows them to adapt their performance to changing conditions, rather than completing procedural tasks. These systems have limited human guidance, though they are dependent on human guidance at some level.[125]

The strategic goals for DoD's autonomous system portfolio include building a more lethal force, strengthening the operational pull for autonomy, and accelerating DoD adoption of autonomous capabilities. To achieve these goals, DoD has identified two key areas: Manned-Unmanned Teaming (MUM-T); and Machine-Machine Teaming (M2M). MUM-T is a systems architecture that enables synchronized performance of the warfighter, manned and unmanned vehicles, robotics, and sensors to achieve enhanced situational understanding, greater lethality, and improved survivability.[126] Similarly, M2M involves synchronizing machines, such as manned and unmanned vehicles, robots, and sensors.

In the near-term, the DoD is focusing on the development of autonomous robotic platforms, swarm agents, and autonomous ISR applications. The Army, Air Force, DARPA, DISA, Defense Threat Reduction Agency, Navy, OSD, and USSOCOM all have autonomy development and research projects to further mature autonomy technology. For example, the U.S. Army began a research project on ground robot autonomous systems with the ability to receive demonstration commands from a human, enabling increased human-machine teaming.[127] The U.S. Army also has the Robotic Combat Vehicle program and with their Ground Vehicle Systems Center, they have developed autonomous software for their unmanned vehicles to enable them to autonomously explore, follow a human-designated route, and adapt to unplanned obstacles.[128]

As DoD increases its demand for autonomous systems, the Department faces several key industrial base risks, particularly related to foreign dependencies and the gap in U.S.-based human capital. Foreign dependencies exist on the technologies needed to enable autonomy, leading-edge graphics processing units (GPUs), field-programmable gate arrays (FPGAs), and application-specific integrated circuits (ASICs) – many of which have AI-specialized versions – as Taiwan and South Korea control a large percentage of chip fabrication factories. However, even for U.S.-based semiconductor manufacturing, there is a reliance on rare earth metal imports, which can cause long lead times and high expenses in the development and fabrication of autonomous systems.[129,130]

DoD also faces a gap in human capital, due to the displacement of U.S. students in autonomy at research institutions and universities by international graduates. This gap is also caused by the large proportion of international graduates who return overseas or work for foreign companies that compete with U.S. companies.

In addition, one of the main risks the Autonomy sector faces are threats of intellectual and corporate theft. Autonomy relies heavily on software, which is frequently threatened by theft and exploitation due to network vulnerabilities. Both hardware and software components of autonomous systems face persistent, advanced threats, network penetration, and forced technology transfer and theft.[131]

DoD continues to identify and implement mitigation strategies aimed at enabling autonomy development, and leverages the ManTech investment program to further develop technologies in the autonomy area, particularly in human machine teaming and collaborative robotics. The Advanced Robotics for Manufacturing Institute (ARM) is a public-private partnership leading collaboration in robotics and workforce innovation that is working to accelerate U.S.-based autonomy development and manufacturing. DoD is also continuing to oversee the health of the autonomy industrial base and monitor supply chain risks.

Cyber

DoD defines cyberspace as a global domain within the information environment, consisting of: the interdependent network of information technology (IT) infrastructures and resident data, including the Internet; telecommunications networks; computer systems; and embedded processors and controllers. All aspects of DoD joint operations rely in part on cyberspace, which is the domain within the information environment that consists of the interdependent network of IT infrastructures and resident data. It includes the Internet, telecommunications networks, computer systems, and embedded processors and controllers. Cyberspace operations (CO) refer to the employment of cyberspace capabilities to achieve objectives in or through cyberspace.[132]

Cyber is a unique military operational domain with significant security challenges and potential leap-ahead capabilities for military operations, requiring enhanced command and control, situational awareness, and autonomous operations.[133] The ability to gain and maintain the U.S. technological edge in cyberspace in the face of rapid evolution is essential to maintaining mission readiness. To ensure the country's safety in the cyber era, priority actions of the U.S. government include: identifying and prioritizing cyber risks; building defensible government networks; deterring and disrupting malicious cyber actors; improving information sharing and sensing; deploying layered defenses; improving attribution, accountability, response, integration, and agility; and strengthening cyber workforce.

- Preserving U.S. overmatch in and through cyberspace is an explicit objective of the 2018 National Cyber Strategy.[134] These actions are categorized as offensive, defensive, and cyber security:[135]

- Offensive DoD Cyber Strategy focuses on increasing force lethality through accelerated capability development, innovation, agility, automation, and analysis; deterrence; alliances and partnerships; organizational practices; and workforce issues, including force structure, training, and qualifications.

- Defensive options including design for security, resilience, and survivability; training, awareness; and cyber hygiene. Design for resilience applies at all levels, from the simplest components and their underlying technologies to the most complex integrated system of systems, as well as all enabling technologies that make them possible.

- Cybersecurity refers to the prevention of damage to, protection of, and restoration of computers, electronic communications systems/services, and wire communication, including information contained therein, to ensure its availability, integrity, authentication, confidentiality, and nonrepudiation (DoDI 8500.01).

The U.S. influence in cyberspace is linked to its technological leadership. Accordingly, the U.S. government is making a concerted effort to protect cutting-edge technologies, including from theft by our adversaries, and to support those technologies' maturation, and, where possible, reduce U.S. companies' barriers to market entry.[136] DoD is focused on preventing cyber vulnerabilities within the cyber operations infrastructure, the industrial base, enterprise IT and business systems, and infrastructures required for integration and testing. Other DoD objectives include defending U.S. critical infrastructure, both DoD and non-DoD assets, and securing DoD information and systems against malicious cyber activity. The March 2020 U.S. Cyberspace Solarium Commission report advocates a strategic, "layered cyber defense," approach aimed at promoting responsible behavior by U.S. personnel, enhancing cyber resilience and security to deny benefits of cyber-attacks, and imposing costs to adversary attacks short of armed conflict.[137] The report also suggests continual assessment of cyber vulnerabilities of all U.S. weapon systems, and an overall force structure assessment in light of continuously increasing mission requirements and expectations for cyber defense.[138]

The United States must protect sensitive emerging technology R&D from adversaries who seek to acquire intellectual property and gain an unfair advantage. To achieve this, DoD will invest in cyber defense, resilience, survivability, and the continued integration of cyber capabilities into the full spectrum of military operations. Investments will prioritize developing resilient, survivable, federated networks and information ecosystems from the tactical level up to strategic planning. Investments will also prioritize capabilities to gain and exploit information, deny competitors those same advantages, and enable the DoD to provide attribution while defending against and holding accountable state or non-state actors during cyberattacks.

The present and future cyber workforce will require, in addition to the basic cybersecurity and software engineering knowledge, a much broader and deeper understanding of analytics and key technologies, such as autonomy, human-machine interaction, and artificial intelligence. Key focus areas include acknowledging a need to address cyber defense with an "Always-On" 24/7/365 mentality. Continuing to add security controls on top of security controls (*e.g.,* multi-factor authentication) only provides limited symptomatic relief without addressing the need for people to change the way they think about being responsible for security. The DoD is collaborating with the NSA to develop curricula for learning and development, laboratory and training exercises, research opportunities, and competitions, to provide the future cyber workforce with relevant experiences in the practice and leadership of cyber security and resilience. These efforts will facilitate both the growth and readiness of the DoD cyber workforce.

SUPPORTING ACTIONS AND AUTHORITIES

Defense Priorities and Allocations System

Program Objective

The purpose of the Defense Priorities and Allocations System (DPAS) is to assure the timely availability of industrial resources to meet current national defense and emergency preparedness program requirements, and to provide an operating system to support rapid industrial response in day-to-day operations and national emergencies. The Defense Production Act of 1950 authorized the President to require preferential treatment of national defense programs. DPAS establishes procedures for placement of priority ratings on contracts, defines industry's responsibilities under rated orders, and sets forth compliance procedures.

Rating Determinations

All prime contracts, subcontracts, or purchase orders in support of an authorized program are given a priority rating.

A DX rating is assigned to those programs of the highest national priority. Per DoD 4400.1-M, USD(A&S) has authority to validate the request for a DX rating. If deemed necessary, the USD (A&S) will nominate the suggested program for a DX rating to the Secretary of Defense for approval. The DPAS team continues to educate the Services and DoD agencies on DPAS authorities including the differences and applicability of DO, DX, and SPA. The Department strives to minimize the use of DX ratings and SPAs because they can be disruptive to the commercial and Defense industrial base. Additionally, overuse of DX ratings will dilute the strength and effectiveness of the priority and therefore negatively impact the ability of the Department to surge in the event of a National Emergency; if everything is a priority, then nothing is a priority.

DO Rating	DX Rating	Special Priorities Assistance (SPA)
A DO priority rating gives the DoD preference over all unrated orders Because of DoD's mission, all procurement contracts should contain a "DO" priority rating DO rated orders have equal priority among other DO rated orders, but have priority over unrated orders	Assigned to programs with the highest national defense urgency Takes preference over DO rated orders and unrated orders with the same delivery dates DOES NOT move the order in front of orders with the same rating with earlier delivery dates ONLY the Secretary or Deputy Secretary of Defense can grant a DX priority rating designation to systems or programs with the highest national defense urgency	SPAs alleviate schedule delivery conflicts during high demand periods where there are competing requirements for the same resources SPA requests should be timely for the DoD or the Department of Commerce to effect a meaningful problem resolution, and must establish that: 1. There is an urgent need for the item; and 2. The applicant has made a reasonable effort to resolve the problem

Security of Supply Arrangements

DPAS Ratings are only enforceable for companies subject to U.S. law. Since the U.S. DIB sources from a global market, the DoD enters into Security of Supply Arrangements (SOSAs) with several nations to ensure the mutual supply of defense goods and services. These bilateral arrangements allow the DoD to request priority delivery for DoD contracts, subcontracts, or orders from companies in these countries. Similarly, the arrangements allow the signatory nations to request priority delivery for their contracts and orders with U.S. firms. The DoD currently holds nine SOSAs with U.S. allies and partners, and continues to evaluate opportunities to expand SOSAs to other allied countries.

FY2020 Accomplishments

In 2020, the DPAS program worked closely with the DoD Services and industry partners to resolve a number of Industrial Base issues, resulting with little to no impact to DoD programs. In 2020, a number of DoD programs experienced delivery date conflicts which were resolved amicably between the DoD and its suppliers through education, communication, and cooperation. This outreach lead to the resolution of a potential production shutdown impacting DoD, and Allied readiness, and industry partners.

Established in 2019, the DPAS Enterprise Board (EB) continues to work collaboratively to provide a more responsive process to address national security requirements, including an enterprise-level approach to evaluate DX ratings, and assigning resources to mitigate competing cross-service requirements. The EB has added two new Services members to increase visibility and collaboration among OSD and the Services.

COVID-19 Actions

In response to COVID-19, the Department of Defense, in conjunction with FEMA and HHS, worked to prioritize production and construction equipment using the DPAS authority. The DPAS team worked closely with the DPA Title III Office to award and fund industrial expansion projects, and ensure the awardees were able to receive the production and construction equipment needed to meet the demands of the nation. DPAS, or DPA Title I, continues to support the whole-of-government effort to combat the coronavirus pandemic.

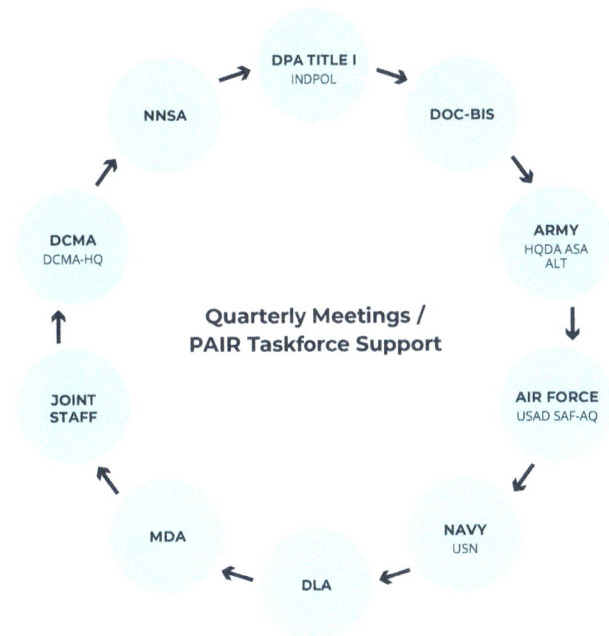

Quarterly Meetings / PAIR Taskforce Support

DPA TITLE I — INDPOL · DOC-BIS · ARMY HQDA ASA ALT · AIR FORCE USAD SAF-AQ · NAVY USN · DLA · MDA · JOINT STAFF · DCMA DCMA-HQ · NNSA

DPA Title III

Program Objective

The Office of Industrial Policy administers the DPA Title III program, consistent with the Secretary of Defense's duties as the Fund Manager under 50 U.S.C. 4501 *et seq.* Title III provides the President broad authority to ensure timely availability of domestic industrial resources essential for the execution of the U.S. National Security Strategy through the use of tailored economic incentives, including:

- Purchases/Purchase commitments,
- Developing production capabilities and commercializing emerging technology,
- Loans/Loan guarantees, and
- Installing Production Equipment in Government- or Privately-Owned Facilities.

The Title III program predominantly executes against defense industrial base shortfalls. However, the program has a broader statutory mandate, authorizing non-defense agencies to mitigate their industrial shortfalls pertaining to homeland security and critical infrastructure, in sectors defined by the Department of Homeland Security.

Throughout FY2020 in response to the national emergency from COVID-19, the DPA Title III program executed at unprecedented scale and speed to mitigate industrial shortfalls within the DIB and the healthcare sectors. Using supplemental appropriations from the CARES Act, the DPA Title III

Overview
Legislative Authority: Title III of the Defense Production Act of 1950
Established: 1950, reauthorized in 2018
Oversight: A&S Industrial Policy

program allocated $676 million to DIB mitigation, $213 million to the healthcare sector, and $100 million to a Federal Credit Loan program, to make loans supporting the national response and recovery to the COVID-19 outbreak or the resilience of any relevant domestic supply chain.

Presidential Actions

Under the program's peace-time functions, the President must issue a determination and notify Congress of an industrial base shortfall prior to initiating investment actions under Title III. In FY2020, the President issued one determination, related to high temperature materials for hypersonic weapons.

The President also issued a Proclamation declaring a national emergency with respect to the COVID-19 disease. This declaration, combined with the Public Law 116-136, authorized the use of extraordinary authority under Title III for rapid, large-scale investments to prevent, prepare for, and respond to COVID-19 (see 2020 Overview). The President also declared a national emergency under the International Emergency Economic Powers Act, concerning adversarial exports of critical minerals.

Sustain Critical Protection	Commercialize R&D Investments	Scale Emerging Technologies
"To create, maintain, protect, expand, or restore domestic industrial base capabilities essential for the national defense."	"From Government sponsored research and development to commercial applications;" and "from commercial research and development to national defense."	"For the increased use of emerging technologies in security program applications and the rapid transition of emerging technologies."

Investment Areas

DPA Title III projects address three broad priority areas, as defined in section 303(a) of the Defense Production Act:

FY20 Presidential Actions:

1. Presidential Proclamation 9994: Declaring a National Emergency concerning the Novel Coronavirus Disease (COVID-19) Outbreak

2. Executive Order 13911: Delegating Authority under the Defense Production Act with respect to Health and Medical Resources to respond to the spread of COVID-19

3. Executive Order 13922: Delegating Authority under the Defense Production Act to the Chief Executive Officer of the United States International Development Finance Corporation to respond to the COVID-19 Outbreak

4. Presidential Determination: Ultra ultra-high and high temperature composites

5. Executive Order 13953: Addressing the Threat to the Domestic Supply Chain from Reliance on Critical Minerals from Foreign Adversaries and Supporting the Domestic Mining and Processing Industries

2020 Overview

– At end of FY2020, DPA Title III portfolio included 87 projects, leveraging over $2.1 billion in government and industry funding to increase the lethality and readiness of the nation by strengthening the DIB and responding to the coronavirus pandemic

– In support of E.O. 13806, President issued one Presidential Determination supporting the hypersonic industrial base

– New projects in FY2020 strengthening the domestic industrial base in key sectors, including rare earths, microelectronics, strategic materials, space, aircrafts, and power storage.

Appropriations on the DPA Fund Since FY2010, in Millions [139]			
Fiscal Year	Law	Appropriation Amount	a. In FY2014, FY2015, and FY2016, Congress also authorized DOE to transfer up to $45 million to the DPA Fund from each FY appropriation from the Energy Efficiency and Renewable Energy account. These transfers were made by DOE, for a total of $135 million.
2010	P.L. 111-118, 123 Stat. 3422	$150.7	
2011	P.L. 112-10, 125 Stat. 51	$34.3	
2012	P.L. 112-74, 125 Stat. 800	$170.0	
2013	P.L. 113-6, 127 Stat. 291	$223.5	
2014	P.L. 113-76, 128 Stat. 98	$60.1a	
2015	P.L. 113-235, 128 Stat. 2246	$51.6a	
2016	P.L. 114-113, 129 Stat. 2345	$76.7a	
2017	P.L. 115-31, 131 Stat. 242	$64.1	
2018	P.L. 115-141, 132 Stat. 458	$67.4	
2019	P.L. 115-245, 132 Stat. 2995	$53.6	
2020	P.L. 116-93	$64.4	

Committee on Foreign Investment in the United States

Objective

The Committee on Foreign Investment in the United States (CFIUS) is an interagency committee authorized by statute to review certain transactions, mergers, and acquisitions that either could result in foreign control of a U.S. business or real estate property, or which are non-passive, non-controlling investments in certain critical or emergent technology companies. In 1988, Congress enacted the Exon-Florio amendment adding section 721 to the Defense Production Act of 1950, which authorized the U.S. President to investigate the effect of certain foreign acquisitions of U.S. companies on national security and to suspend or prohibit acquisitions that might threaten to impair national security. The President delegated this investigative authority to CFIUS.

CFIUS is comprised of nine voting member agencies (the Department of the Treasury (CFIUS Chair); the Departments of Commerce, Defense, Energy, Homeland Security, Justice, and State; the U.S. Trade Representative; and the White House Office of Science and Technology Policy), two ex-officio members, and five White House offices.

Legislative Authority: § 721 of the Defense Production Act of 1950

Established: 1988

Oversight: Foreign Investment Review, A&S INDPOL

Within the Office of Industrial Policy, the Foreign Investment Review (FIR) team serves as the DoD's CFIUS representative and acts as the principal advisor to USD(A&S) on foreign investment in the U.S. As the DoD CFIUS representative and central point of contact, FIR coordinates departmental participation across more than 30 DoD component organizations (DoD stakeholders) to identify, review, investigate, mitigate, and monitor inbound foreign direct investment in the U.S. FIR relies on DoD stakeholders for the technical expertise needed to analyze the threats, vulnerabilities, and consequences associated with foreign investment into the U.S.

Review Process

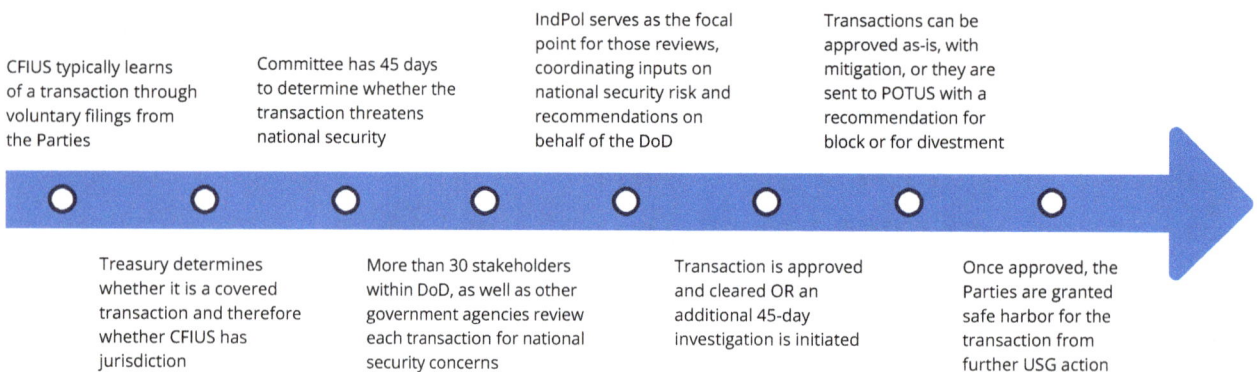

CFIUS typically learns of a transaction through voluntary filings from the Parties

Committee has 45 days to determine whether the transaction threatens national security

IndPol serves as the focal point for those reviews, coordinating inputs on national security risk and recommendations on behalf of the DoD

Transactions can be approved as-is, with mitigation, or they are sent to POTUS with a recommendation for block or for divestment

Treasury determines whether it is a covered transaction and therefore whether CFIUS has jurisdiction

More than 30 stakeholders within DoD, as well as other government agencies review each transaction for national security concerns

Transaction is approved and cleared OR an additional 45-day investigation is initiated

Once approved, the Parties are granted safe harbor for the transaction from further USG action

FIRRMA

On August 13, 2018, President Trump signed the Foreign Investment Risk Review Modernization Act (FIRRMA) into law. FIRRMA expands the scope of reviewable transactions to address a new set of national security concerns and strengthens the ability of CFIUS to protect national security.

Before FIRRMA, CFIUS jurisdiction had remained virtually unchanged in the 30 years since Congress first passed the Exon-Florio Amendment (the statutory cornerstone of CFIUS). Since that time, the nature of foreign investments in the U.S. and the national security landscape have shifted significantly.

FIRRMA expanded CFIUS jurisdiction to four new types of covered transactions: certain real estate interests; non- controlling "other investments" in certain U.S. businesses; changes in a foreign investor's rights; and any other transaction, transfer, agreement, or arrangement designed or intended to evade or circumvent the application of previous rules governing CFIUS.

1. Critical Technology: The definitions and standards for critical technology were not updated with the Rules. However, subsequent Notice of Proposed Rulemaking to update the standards for filing critical technology-related mandatory declarations was published on May 21, 2020. The Department of Commerce continues its rulemaking efforts to characterize emerging and foundational technologies and to align associated critical technologies with applicable export control laws.

2. Critical Infrastructure: FIRRMA expands CFIUS jurisdiction to review non-controlling investments in U.S. businesses that own, operate, manufacture, supply, or service certain components of the defense industrial base, energy infrastructure, communications networks, financial services, transportation services, and water and wastewater systems.

3. Sensitive Personal Data: The rules expand CFIUS jurisdiction to review non-controlling investments in U.S. businesses that collect sensitive personal data. Sensitive personal data includes financial information, health information, communications, geolocation data, biometric or genetic data, and security clearance information.

4. Real Estate: FIRRMA allows review of commercial real estate transactions within certain proximities to named military installations.

FIRRMA does not change the longstanding open investment policy of the U.S. The U.S. continues to welcome foreign investment as a vital part of a robust economy.

Office of Small Business Programs

Objective

The Office of Small Business Programs (OSBP) maximizes prime and subcontracting opportunities for small business to respond to current and future Warfighter requirements. The complexity of DoD requirements and contracting processes can preclude new entrants to the defense market. This is particularly true of small businesses that do not have the manpower and resources necessary to navigate and compete for defense contracts.

The October 2019 DoD Small Business Strategy focuses on three objectives:

1. Creating and implementing a unified management structure across DoD's small business workforce.

2. Ensuring that the Department's small business activities align with the 2018 National Defense Strategy and other guiding documents.

3. Strengthening DoD's ability to support the warfighter through supporting small businesses

The following programs help bring new business into the DIB by creating a pathway for non-traditional contractors to participate and succeed.

Mentor Protégé Program

DoD's Mentor Protégé Program (MPP) has successfully helped more than 190 small businesses fill unique niches and become part of the military's supply chain. The MPP supports eligible small businesses to expand their footprint in the defense industrial base and become reliable government contractors. Protégés work side by side with established defense contractors to

MPP

Legislative Authority: §831 of the FY1991 NDAA

Established: 1990

Oversight: Industrial Policy

IIP

Legislative Authority: 25 USC Section 1544

Established: 1997

Oversight: Industrial Policy

develop technical capabilities. Mentors, typically large defense contractors, can leverage the nimble and agile nature of small businesses and their technologies, services, and cutting-edge products to improve innovation in major defense acquisition programs.

Indian Incentive Program (IIP)

While Native Americans have a long history of contributing to the U.S. military, Indian reservations and Alaska Native Villages suffer some of the worst poverty in the country. In an effort to strengthen Native American economic development, Congress authorized Federal contracting agencies to encourage the use of Native American owned subcontractors. The Indian Incentive Program (IIP) incentivizes contracting with Indian Organizations, Indian-Owned Economic Enterprises, Native Alaska and Native Hawaiian Small Business Concerns by providing a five percent incentive to prime and sub-tier contractors who subcontract with eligible firms. Since FY2015, the IIP has funded more than 650 rebates totaling $100 million in incentive payments, which leveraged more than $2 billion in subcontract performance by Native-owned firms.

FY2020 Overview

Project Spectrum: In FY2020, OSBP partnered with US Cyber Command to develop Project Spectrum, an initiative designed to provide training and conduct risk assessments to enhance awareness of cybersecurity threats among small manufacturers and universities in the DIB. Its three main elements include:

1. The ecosystem of government partners and stakeholders pooling resources and working collaboratively to increase cybersecurity in the DIB;

2. Awareness and training of the DIB, including preparedness for the Department's latest cybersecurity requirements; and

3. Tools and services that lower the barrier to small and medium-sized companies obtaining and maintaining cybersecurity compliance.

To date, 20,000 small businesses have received training and more than 35 cybersecurity tools were evaluated.

Cybersecurity Education Diversity Initiative (CEDI): The CEDI Project is a collaboration between the National Security Agency's National Centers of Academic Excellence in Cybersecurity (NCAE-E) Program Management Office and the MPP program. It assists Minority Serving Institutions (MI) and Historically Black College and Universities (HBCU) with no existing cybersecurity programs with obtaining access to consultation and educational resources from designated NCAE-E institutions, thus expanding access to quality cybersecurity education and mentoring to students in all 50 states. This collaboration allows the OSBP MPP to provide participating protégés with technical assistance on cybersecurity at HBCUs and MIs.

Small Business Training Week: In September 2020, OSBP hosted the largest-ever virtual Small Business Training Week for the acquisition community. 1,056 attendees represented Small Business Professionals, Program Directors, Contracting Officers, and Program Managers. The training week's theme was "Refocus on Rebuilding a More Resilient Small Business Community," emphasizing the Department's direction to better align the small business industrial base to the DoD's mission. Topics aligned with current innovation gaps and provided practical ways for small business professionals and the broader acquisition workforce to understand their roles and take action.

Coronavirus Pandemic Response

The DoD OSBP team addressed the effects of COVID-19 early on in the pandemic, retooling the office's functions and outreach efforts. USD(A&S) Ellen Lord, referred to OSBP as the "Information Hub," providing up-to-date information to the small business industrial base. OSBP established industry calls and webinars with industry association partners to maintain a pulse on the private sector and provide direct information to small businesses on a broad range of topics including: COVID-19 resources, cybersecurity, foreign investment, and successful teleworking practices. OSBP also reinvigorated its outreach to industry. The OSBP website, defense.business.gov, became the central communication portal for DoD small business resources and updates, and social media channels were used to quickly disseminate information to the widest possible audience.

Industrial Base Analysis and Sustainment

Objective

The Industrial Base Analysis and Sustainment (IBAS) Program strengthens the DIB in the era of great power competition. It works to create a modern Industrial Base with the capacity to respond at will to national security requirements. IBAS investments fortify and forge traditional and emerging sectors to improve IB readiness. These investments are strategically catalyzing in critical areas that lack momentum.

IBAS Program Priorities:

- *Ready the Modern DIB:* Advance and sustain traditional defense manufacturing sectors

- *Prepare for the Future:* Identify, attract, and cultivate emerging defense sectors

- *Assess and Shape the Risk:* Mitigate supply chain vulnerabilities within the Global DIB

- *Build and Strengthen:* Build partnerships in the Global DIB

Investment Strategy

The IBAS office directs investment by identifying strategy/focus areas, obtaining resources, and overseeing the execution of projects to strengthen the defense industrial base by ameliorating industrial base and manufacturing issues. All projects are evaluated for industrial base risk using a framework of risk assessment methodologies and tools, including fragility and criticality risk criteria to develop feasible and effective course of actions. Key areas of IBAS investment include:

- Advancing and sustaining traditional and emerging defense manufacturing sectors

- Preserving critical and unique manufacturing and design skills

- Supporting and expanding reliable sources, and

- Identifying and mitigating supply chain, cyber, manufacturing, and trade skills vulnerabilities

---

Overview

Legislative Authority: 10 U.S. Code § 2508. Industrial Base Fund

Established: FY2014

Oversight: Industrial Policy

Cornerstone

The Cornerstone Other Transaction Authority (OTA) is a government-run, integrated contract vehicle used to create dynamic relationships across the DIB using the IBAS authorities. The Cornerstone OTA authority originates from 10 U.S. Code 2371b - Authority of the DoD to carry out prototype projects. Cornerstone focuses on "prototype" projects, capabilities, and capacities in support of a range of defense industrial base requirements across 19 sectors.

FY2020 Investments

In FY2020, IBAS continued to address issues from the E.O. 13806 report findings and priority programs, partnering on investments and shared interest areas.

IBAS FY2020 Budget

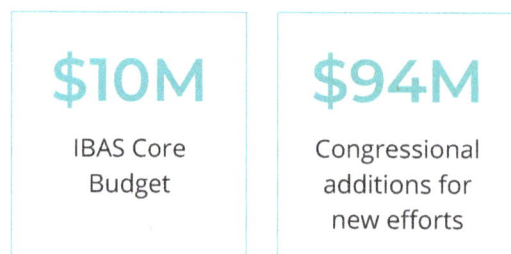

$10M	$94M
IBAS Core Budget	Congressional additions for new efforts

IBAS Investments

Boron Carbide	Expand DIB by establishing second U.S. source to mitigate foreign supply chain risk
Heavy Rare Earths Elements Supply Chain Resiliency	Establish U.S. capacity to mitigate foreign supply chain risk. Engineering study to inform production scale up
Rare Earth Elements from Coal Ash	Prototyping effort for rare earth elements extraction from coal ash *(in negotiations)*
DE Supply Chain Analysis and Readiness Study	Establish resilient DE supply chain
Radar Affordability Working Group Land & Sea Systems	Expand DIB suppliers for critical radar subcomponents to mitigate risks to cost and readiness
Silicon Interposer	Establish secure domestic production capability
Lead-Free Electronics	Establish public-private partnership-led electronics manufacturing consortium. First task: establish standards to mitigate risks of using lead-free electronics in high-performance systems *(in negotiations)*
Critical Energetics Working Group	Support to Joint Army, Navy, NASA, Air Force (JANNAF) Executive Committee
Advanced Armor-Piercing Penetrators	Improve supply chain resiliency for tungsten penetrators used in munitions
Machine and Advanced Manufacturing: America's Cutting Edge (ACE)	Joint DoD-DOE machine tool hub to improve U.S. machine tools competitiveness: advance machine tool capabilities for DoD-specific application; lower barriers to entry for small and medium manufacturers to adopt new machine tools
Automated Textile Manufacturing	Integrate automated manufacturing capability with advanced, high-end fibers
Supply Chain Analysis 1-3	Subscription services and tools to enable supply chain vulnerability detection and risk management efforts *(one award pending)*
Hypersonics Supply Chain Analysis and Readiness Study	Study support for Hypersonics War Room (R&E)
Mobile Nuclear Reactor Supply Chain Analysis & Readiness Study	Assessment of design elements, manufacturability, manufacturing process, and supply chain for mobile power source
Submarine Workforce Development	Public-private partnership with NE states to mitigate shortfalls within submarine-building supply chain
Interdisciplinary Center for Advanced Manufacturing	University-led consortium effort to reduce barriers preventing small and medium manufacturers from adopting advanced manufacturing capabilities and processes
Precision Optics Manufacturing	Effort to advance domestic precision optics manufacturing capability and workforce development pipeline *(in negotiations)*
Machine and Advanced Manufacturing: Workforce Component	Not-for-profit institute-led effort to develop and provide advanced machine tools training programs for small and mid-sized manufacturers
Manufacturing Engineering: Hypervelocity Prototype for Welding	Not-for-profit led regional welding workforce accelerated pipeline development for the ship/submarine sector
Manufacturing Engineering: Vermont	University-led regional engineering and critical manufacturing technician workforce pipeline development
Manufacturing Engineering: Texas Engineering Experiment Station	University-led regional manufacturing workforce pipeline development for Texas defense supply chain requirements
Manufacturing Engineering: System Engineering Technicians	University-led regional systems-engineering manufacturing technician workforce pipeline development
Manufacturing Engineering: Electronics Manufacturing & Technical Education	Small business-led electronics technician workforce pipeline development

*this table presents new IBAS FY2020 efforts (Note: Awards expected prior to report publication for those in negotiations or competition).

Warstopper Program

Objective

The Warstopper Program is the Department's primary program for consumable items in sustainment. It works to provide industry an incentive to support the sustainment of items that industry would otherwise not have a business case to support.

Warstopper Program Priorities:

- Sustainment readiness investments that allow for go-to-war material to be available during a surge.
- Preserve industrial capability for known go-to-war requirements of sustainment items that are in jeopardy of not being viable.
- Conduct DIB risk analysis for consumable items in sustainment to inform investment

Warstopper Program Criteria:

- Mission Critical Materials and Supplies
- Low Peacetime Demand – High Wartime Demand
- Limited Shelf Life – Long Production Lead Time

Investment Strategy

The Program provides an industrial strategy to meet go-to-war consumable items in sustainment. It is a deliberate strategy to off-set the buy and hold war reserve strategy as well as securing fragile consumable sustainment items with go-to-war requirements. This usually involves implementing contracting strategies for the following:

- Secure commercially available go-to-war material in the quantity and timeliness (example: pay management fees to guarantee the quantity and early delivery)
- Increase manufacturer and distributor capability to provide go-to-war consumable items material (example: stage raw material

Overview

Legislative Authority: Responds to requirements in E.O. 13603.

Established: FY1993 in response to FY1993 NDAA

Oversight: DLA

- and long lead time parts or provide additional equipment)
- Preserving cold production needed for go-to-war consumable items (example: fund a company's fixed cost to sustain a production line)

FY2020 Investments

In FY2020, Warstopper continued to provide risk mitigating investments for critical go-to-war items and sectors.

$72.7M

FY2020 Funding

Readiness Investments

Supply Chain	Project	Use	Impacted NSNs
Land	Preposition Steel Grade 9260	Aircraft Landing & Recovery Equipment (ALRE)	1
Maritime	Tungsten Rhenium Ingots	Electron Tube	119
Maritime	Generalized Emulation of Microcircuits (GEM)	Digital Microcircuits; 5V Logic Family Devices	445
Medical	Medical Corporate Exigency Contracts (CEC)	Pharma/Supplies/Equipment	7,223
Subsistence	UGR GFE Maintenance	Unit Group Rations	10
Subsistence	VMI Submarine Forces Pacific	Rations/Food Resupply of Pacific Theater	200
Subsistence	Buffer Stock Investment	Flameless Ration Heaters	1

Upstream Buffer Investments

Supply Chain	Material or Component	Usage	Impacted NSNs
Aviation	Steel Grade 300M	Torsion Bars and Aircraft Landing Gear	295
Aviation	Steel Grade M50; 440C & 52100	Bearings	942
Aviation	Titanium 6AL-4V & 5AL-2.5SN	Aircraft Structural Parts	8,611

Preservation of Capabilities/Capacities Investments

Supply Chain	Initiative/Targeted Systems	Impacted NSNs
Aviation	Aircraft/Aerospace	2,001
Aviation	Bomber/B-1, B-52	5,474
Aviation	Engine/TF-33, B-52	1,500
Energy	Launch/Gaseous Nitrogen	1
Energy	Satellite/Hydrazine	1
Energy	Satellite/Dinitrogen Textroxide (N204)	1

Small Business Innovation Research & Small Business Technology Transfer

Program Objective

The statutory purpose of the SBIR program is to strengthen the role of innovative Small Business Concerns (SBCs) in Federally-funded research or research and development (R/R&D) to:

- Stimulate technological innovation
- Involve small business to meet Federal R/R&D needs
- Foster and encourage participation by socially and economically disadvantaged SBCs, and by women-owned SBCs, in technological innovation;
- Increase private sector commercialization of innovations derived from Federal R/R&D to increase competition, productivity, and economic growth.

In addition to the broad goals of the SBIR program, the statutory purpose of the STTR program is to stimulate a partnership of ideas and technologies between innovative SBCs and non-profit Research Institutions. By providing awards to SBCs for cooperative R/R&D efforts with Research Institutions, the STTR program assists the U.S. small business and research communities by supporting the commercialization of innovative technologies.

Small Business Innovation

SBIR encourages domestic small businesses to engage in Federal R/R&D on initiatives that have the potential for commercialization. Through a

competitive awards-based program, SBIR enables small businesses to explore their technological potential, provides the incentive to profit from commercialization, stimulates high-tech innovation from non-traditional contractors, and encourages entrepreneurial spirit as the Federal agencies meets its specific R&D needs. As required by statute, each Federal agency with an extramural budget for R/R&D in excess of $100,000,000 must participate in the SBIR Program and reserve a minimum percentage of its R/R&D budgets for small business R/R&D contracts.

Small Business Technology Transfer Program

The Small Business Technology Transfer Program (STTR) is intended to stimulate a partnership of ideas and technologies between innovative SBCs and non-profit Research Institutions. By providing awards to SBCs for cooperative R/R&D efforts with Research Institutions, the STTR program assists U.S. small business and research communities by supporting the commercialization of innovative technologies. STTR expands funding opportunities in the federal innovation R&D arena. Central to the program is expansion of public/private sector partnerships to include joint venture opportunities for small businesses and non-

PHASE I	PHASE II	PHASE III
Project Feasibility—determines the scientific, technical, and commercial merit and feasibility of proposals.	Project development to prototype (the major R&D effort)—funding the prototyping and demonstration of the most promising Phase I projects.	Commercialization (the goal of each SBIR/STTR effort)—Phase III work must be funded by sources outside the SBIR/STTR Program.
~1,300 awards/year	**~950 awards/year**	**Funding exceeded $15B**

profit research institutions. Unique to the STTR program is the requirement for the small business to formally collaborate with a research institution in Phase I and Phase II. STTR's most important role is to bridge the gap between basic R&D and commercialization of resulting innovations. STTR is regulated by the same statue as SBIR, requiring participation based extramural budget for R/R&D.

FY2020 Overview

- In June 2020, the Office of Small Business Technology Partnerships (SBTP) office launched the OSD Transitions SBIR/STTR Technologies Pilot Program, which will help enable and accelerate the incorporation and transition of SBIR/STTR Phase II technologies to the Warfighter. Since June, the program has funded $39.4M on 24 projects

- In August 2020, the DoD SBIR/STTR Innovation Portal integrated with Login.gov to increase security, efficiency, and user experience for Small Business Concerns.

- In October 2020, the SBTP Office hosted its inaugural DoD SBIR/STTR Virtual Symposium. The Symposium appealed to a broad audience aiming to do business with the Department. Registrants and participants represented all 50 states and the territories of Puerto Rico and the U.S. Virgin Islands. Participants included: government personnel, large business, prime contractors, small business, support contractors, and university/academia. Approximately 1,110 unique visitors logged in to view and participate in the symposium.

4,367
Total Contracts Awarded in FY2020

$2.06B
Total Amount Awarded in FY2020

*These figures are accurate based on FY20 contract actions as of the date of preparation of this document and do not reflect final numbers for the 2020 Fiscal Year

FY2021 Goals

The Small Business and Technology Partnerships (SBTP) office's primary goal is to increase awareness of the SBIR and STTR Programs within the Department and encourage small innovative businesses to work with DoD to solve National Security challenges. The following objectives will help achieve this goal:

- Implement legislative changes to the SBIR/STTR programs in accordance with the FY2020 NDAA;

- Engage with other DoD and Federal stakeholders on SBIR/STTR best practices;

- Participate in outreach events across the country to educate the small business community on the SBIR/STTR programs;

- Enhance the Defense SBIR/STTR Innovation Portal (DSIP) based on feedback from users and stakeholders;

- Identify and establish relationships with new partners.

COVID-19 Response

March 2020, SBTP formed a COVID-19 Response working group. The group's purpose was to strategize on how the SBIR/STTR programs could utilize funding to quickly respond to the coronavirus pandemic and determine if funding through as the CARES Act could be utilized to fund COVID-19 related research and development. The Missile Defense Agency and Defense Logistics Agency, respectively, provided additional funding to companies e-Spin Technologies and AAPlasma, who converted their current SBIR technologies for use in PPE gear. The SBTP office provided $7.38 million to DARPA to further develop COVID-19 technologies in partnership with the Texas Air National Guard. Additionally, the office is reviewing $13.5 million in potential funding for COVID-related projects from the Defense Health Agency.

Rapid Innovation Fund

Objective

The Rapid Innovation Fund (RIF) operated via Congressional Add until funding ceased in FY2020. There is no expectation the RIF will receive future funds or be reinstated. The RIF continues to be managed by OUSD(R&E) Small Business and Technology Partnerships (SBTP) through closeout.

The RIF was established as a competitive, merit-based program designed to rapidly transition innovative technologies into defense acquisition and use. Projects are drawn from Small Business Innovation Research/Technology Transfer (SBIR/STTR) initiatives, defense laboratory and academia efforts, and other non-conventional sources. The RIF is a major benefactor to small businesses and SBIR/STTR follow-on efforts, acting as a direct-to-Phase III conduit. Program objectives include:

- Accelerating or enhancing a military capability,
- Reducing development, acquisition, sustainment, or lifecycle costs of defense acquisition programs or fielded systems,
- Reducing program technical risk, and
- Improving timeliness and thoroughness of test and evaluation.

In FY2018, the RIF re-aligned objectives to address critical security needs based on the 2018 National Defense Strategy (NDS). In FY2019, the RIF adapted requirements to cover the NDS modernization priority areas supported by OUSD(R&E). Prior efforts focused on general warfighting needs and Reliance 21.

Overview

Authority: National Defense Authorization Act, Public Law 116-92, Section 878

Established: 2011

Permanently Authorized: 2017

FY2011-FY2019 RIF Highlights

>$2.2B Invested in Department of Defense requirements from Air Force, Army, Navy & over 30 OSD organizations	**85%** Small Business Awards
	57% SBIR/STTR Phase III Awards
20,600 Whitepapers	**~1,500** Proposals
~1,000 Contract Awards	**$2.1M** Average Value

++ Financial statistics from TechLink "Defense Rapid Innovation Fund: An Assessment of RIF Effectiveness FY 2011-16"

RIF Source Selection Process

Individual projects limited to $3-6M* each and 24-month performance period

STEP I	STEP II	STEP III
Issue annual broad agency announcement for whitepaper (WP) solicitation	Invite highest-rated WPs for full proposals	Award highest-rated full proposals

* Higher cost projects cannot exceed 25 percent of the total budget

Recent Accomplishments

SBTP delivered milestone RIF FY2020 National Defense Authorization Act Congressional report on FY2017 through FY2019 RIF efforts and overall program effectiveness in June 2020

- Data from a TechLink study determined RIF is highly successful at meeting program objectives, transitioning approximately 60 percent of projects to-date with more than three times return on investment

Streamlined financial process to shorten timelines

- Simplified funds request paperwork and process

- Implemented financial deadlines: Check-ins at 30, 60, 90 day marks; award within 90 days

- Awarded contracts on average within 74 days

Increased RIF Office oversight from proposal through contract award phases

- Cradle-to-grave project tracking to link program and financial team efforts

- Monthly financial updates to decrease risk from contract issues

- Quarterly updates from RIF Office to program managers

- Quarterly performance project performance reviews with all RIF program managers

Awarded FY2019 selections from Army, Air Force, Navy, and OSD-affiliated Organizations, including selections by OUSD(R&E) Modernization Principal Directors

- Awarded over 60 percent of FY2019 funding to projects within OUSDR&E modernization priority areas

Modernization Principle Director Projects		
AI/ML	6 awards	$15.8 M
Autonomy	6	$13.8 M
Cybersecurity	7	$13.1 M
Directed Energy	4	$11.2 M
Hypersonics	4	$8.9 M
Microelectronics	3	$8.9 M
Networked C3	8	$20.3 M
Space	2	$6 M
Total	**40**	**$98 M****

Services and OSD Projects		
AI/ML	6 awards	$11.9 M
Autonomy	4	$10.7 M
Biomedical & Human Systems	4	$9.3 M
Cybersecurity	2	$3.8 M
Energy & Power	4	$9.7 M
Materials & Manufacturing	7	$18.8 M
Microelectronics	3	$8.9 M
Networked C3	6	$16.6 M
Platforms: Air, Ground & Sea	4	$8.3 M
Sensors	9	$22.9 M
Weapons Tech	2	$3.1 M
Other	3	$6.8 M
Total	**54**	**$131 M**

** Funding does not include project administration costs

FY2019 Investments

$250M	2,212	153	94	~$2.4M
Total FY 2019 appropriations	Whitepapers	Proposals	Awards	Average award value

Manufacturing Technology Program

Objective

The DoD ManTech Program was created to further national security objectives through the development and application of advanced manufacturing technologies and processes. The program strives to reduce the acquisition and supportability costs of defense weapon systems and reduce manufacturing and repair cycle times across the life cycles of such systems.

DoD ManTech comprises component ManTech investment programs operated out of OSD, Army, Navy, Air Force, Defense Logistics Agency, and Missile Defense Agency. The OSD ManTech Office is responsible for administering the DoD ManTech Program by providing central guidance and direction to the component ManTech programs.

Overview

Legislative Authority: Title 10, U.S. Code §2521

Established: 1956

Oversight: OUSD(R&E), Office of Strategic Technology Protection and Exploitation

The various ManTech programs collaborate to identify and integrate joint requirements, conduct and develop joint program planning and strategies, and avoid duplication. While the Military Services invest in more targeted projects, OSD ManTech focuses on cross-cutting defense manufacturing needs – those that are beyond the ability of a single service to address – and stimulates the early development of manufacturing processes and enterprise business practices concurrent with science and technology development.

Investment Priority Areas

	Long Range Precision Fires; Next Generation Combat Vehicle; Future Vertical Lift; Network; Assured Positioning, Navigation, and Timing; Air and Missile Defense; Soldier Lethality; Synthetic Training Environment
	Metals Processing and Fabrication; Electronics Processing and Fabrication; Composites Processing and Fabrication; Manufacturing Enterprise; Energetics Manufacturing
	Advanced Concepts; Future Factory; Digital Enterprise; Additive Manufacturing; Low-Cost Attritable Systems; Networked Command, Control, & Communications (C3) Systems; Hypersonic Strike
	Advanced Microcircuit Emulation; Battery Network; Castings/Forgings; Military Unique Sustainment Technology; Subsistence Network; Defense Logistics Information Research; Additive Manufacturing
	High Temperature; Refractory Alloys; Thermal Protection Systems; Advanced Ceramic Composites; Printed Sensor Microsystems; Next Generation Electronics; Flexible Hybrid; Electronics; Biocarbon-based Supercapacitors; Additive Manufacturing
	Metals; Electronics; Composites; Advanced Manufacturing Enterprise; Energetic Materials; USD(R&E) Modernization Priorities: 5G, Artificial Intelligence and Machine Learning, Autonomy, Biotechnology, Cyber, Directed Energy, FNC3, Hypersonics, Microelectronics, Quantum Science, Space

DoD Manufacturing Innovation Institutes

The OSD ManTech Office also sponsors nine manufacturing innovation institutes (MII) with headquarters and hubs across the country. Each institute is a public-private partnership designed to overcome the challenges faced by manufacturing innovators in a variety of technology areas. The DoD MIIs connect organizations and activities to enable the affordable and rapid transition and delivery of defense-essential technologies. While each institute operates in its own unique ecosystem, the institutes offer common capabilities that:

- Provide access to state-of-the-art tools and equipment that are otherwise beyond the reach of most businesses,

- Implement targeted education and workforce development training programs, and

- Encourage project investments in applied research & industrially-relevant manufacturing technologies.

Industry partners, commercial manufacturers, start-up businesses, higher education institutions, and state and local economic developers join as members of the institutes for the opportunity to collaborate with each other and DoD in a pre-competitive environment.

The DoD Manufacturing Innovation Institutes bring new technologies to U.S. warfighters through:

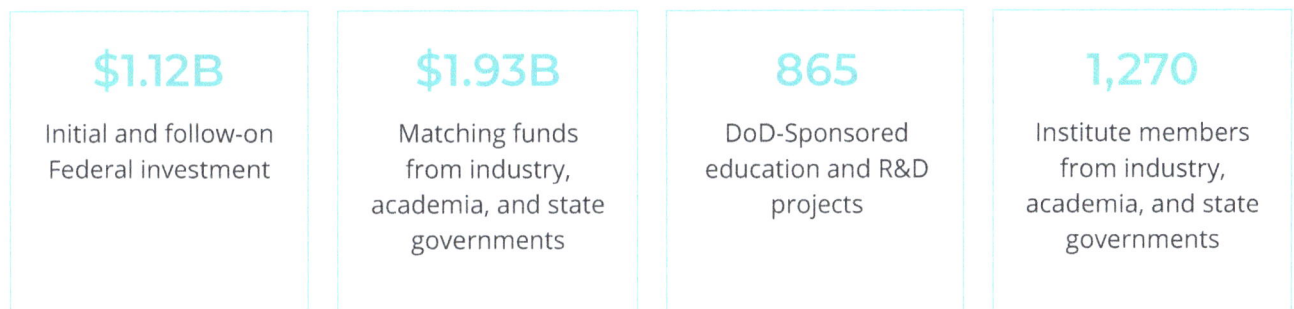

$1.12B	$1.93B	865	1,270
Initial and follow-on Federal investment	Matching funds from industry, academia, and state governments	DoD-Sponsored education and R&D projects	Institute members from industry, academia, and state governments

Hart-Scott-Rodino

Objective

The Hart-Scott-Rodino (HSR) Act was established to avoid some of the difficulties and expenses encountered when challenging anticompetitive mergers and acquisitions after the fact. It is often impossible to restore competition fully once a merger takes place, and any attempt to reestablish competition is usually very costly for the parties and the public.

The HSR Act requires parties to certain mergers or acquisitions notify the Federal Trade Commission (FTC) and the Department of Justice (DoJ) before consummating a proposed acquisition. Once FTC and DoJ are notified, the parties must wait a specific period of time (generally 30 days) while these enforcement agencies review the proposed transaction. The review period enables the FTC and DOJ to determine which acquisitions are likely to be anti-competitive and to challenge them at a time when remedial action is most effective.

Determining Reportability

The HSR requires both acquiring and acquired persons to file notifications under the Program if all of the following conditions are met:

1. As a result of the transaction, the acquiring person will hold an aggregate amount of voting securities, non-corporate interests (NCI) and/or assets of the acquired person valued in excess of $200 million (as adjusted), regardless of the sales or assets of the acquiring and two acquired persons;

2. As a result of the transaction, the acquiring person will hold an aggregate amount of voting securities, NCI and/or assets of the acquired person valued in excess of $50 million (as adjusted) but at $200 million (as adjusted) or less;

Overview

Authority: Hart-Scott-Rodino Antitrust Improvements Act of 1976, 15 U.S.C. 18a. 7a of the Clayton Act

Effective: September 5, 2978

3. One party has sales or assets of at least $100 million (as adjusted); and

4. The other party has sales or assets of at least $10 million (as adjusted).

Case Study

In June 2019, Raytheon and United Technologies Corporation (UTC) two major defense suppliers announced their pending merger of equals with the transaction valued at $121 billion, resulting in the creation of one of the largest defense contractors by revenue. Both companies served as prime contractors and subcontractors to multiple customers within the DoD, notably the Army, Navy, Air Force, and the U.S. Special Operations Command. Shortly after announcing their intent to merge, the companies filed the HSR premerger review documents. The DoD worked closely with the DoJ, the lead antitrust agency for the case, during the entirety of the review to meet with the companies and other industry members to gauge the impact on competition, as well as facilitate discussions with DoD stakeholders to examine all identified overlapping capabilities. The review, including review of divestitures, carried into FY2020.

The review revealed that the overlap in three of the companies' businesses would present a potential threat to competition within the defense industrial base, specifically for airborne radios, military GPS, and Electro-Optical/Infra-Red sensors. As a result, one companyRaytheon was required to divest its airborne radios business, and another companyUTC was required to divest its GPS business and its optics business. The investigation was carried out by both the DoD and DoJ to approve potential buyers for the divested businesses. In January 2020, it was announced that a major global defense firm BAE Systems would purchase the airborne radio and military GPS businesses. In April 2020, it was announced that a technologyAmergint company would purchase the optics business. Following the second request in March 2020, DoJ filed a consent decree, approving the merger on the condition that the pending divestitures be completed. The merger officially closed in April 2020 with the airborne radio, military GPS, and Optics divestitures closing in May 2020, July 2020, and September 2020.

FY2020 HSR Actions

- In FY2020, the DoD assessed 23 transactions as part of the HSR premerger review process. Of those 22 transactions, 20 were investigations initiated in FY2020 and two were continuing investigations or mitigation efforts from previous fiscal years. There was a slight decrease in overall transactions between FY2019 and FY2020, possibly due to the impact of the coronavirus pandemic.

- Two transactions assessed in FY2020 were abandoned: Hexcel/Woodward and Carlisle Companies/Draka Fileca.

- The average value of the transactions (disclosed financial terms included) was $622 million, excluding United Technologies' $120 billion merger with Raytheon, which was announced in FY2019 and completed in FY2020.

- The large majority of the transactions involved companies in the Aerospace and Defense sector. Three transactions involved companies in the Industrials sector and two transactions involved companies in the Services sector.

- Major HSR actions from FY2020 include: United Technologies/Raytheon (announced in FY2019), CPI/GD SATCOM (announced in FY2019), Huntington Ingalls/Hydroid, and Leidos/Dynetics.

Trusted Capital

Program Objective

The Trusted Capital program connects companies critical to the defense industrial base with vetted trusted capital and capability providers.

Companies critical to the DoD require access to rapid funding from capital providers at key development stages. Without this funding, capability providers in the DoD supply chain become susceptible to strategic funding from adversaries that leverage capital to exploit technology transfer.

The Trusted Capital Marketplace is a forum to convene trusted sources of private capital with innovative domestic companies. The companies have been down-selected by the military services and operate in emerging technology sectors critical to the U.S. defense industrial base – strengthening domestic manufacturing through, and limiting foreign access to, critical technology. Trusted Capital Marketplace participants include:

- AFWERX
- Army Futures Command
- Defense Innovation Unit
- NavalX
- U.S. Special Operations Command

Capability Providers: Capability Providers are companies that specialize in developing and providing products and services in key technology sectors and subsectors. These companies offer key capabilities and have been down selected by the military services or the DoD innovation programs for inclusion in the Trusted Capital program so they can raise additional investment funding for growth.

Capital Providers: Capital Providers are vetted sources of strategic capital. Capital providers invest in companies to increase the capability of the defense industrial base to support the DoD production needs and the availability of emerging technologies.

Overview

Oversight: OUSD(A&S)/Chief Information Security Officer

Website: https://www.acq.osd.mil/tc

Established: 2020

Sectors Of Focus

- Advanced Computing
- Advanced Conventional Weapons Technologies
- Advanced Engineering Materials
- Advanced Manufacturing
- Advanced Sensing
- Aero-Engine Technologies
- Agricultural Technologies
- Artificial Intelligence
- Autonomous Systems
- Biotechnologies
- CBRN Mitigation Technologies
- Communication and Networking Technologies
- Data Science and Storage
- Distributed Ledger Technologies
- Energy Technologies
- Human-Machine Interfaces
- Medical and Public Health Technologies
- Quantum Information Science
- Semiconductors and Microelectronics
- Space Technologies

Why Trusted Capital?

The 2018 National Defense Strategy called for the DoD to strengthen its military advantage through three lines of effort: Lethality, Partnerships, and Reform.

The Trusted Capital program is aligned with the NDS:

- Trusted Capital Marketplace increases Lethality
- Innovation Tours with Industry build Partnerships
- Incentives for Capital Providers supports Reform

The Trusted Capital program's lines of effort will cultivate new partnerships with the private sector to provide opportunities for innovation, ensuring a more efficient, lethal force and enduring competitive edge.

How do I participate in the DoD Trusted Capital program?

Capital Providers will be able to apply via the Trusted Capital Marketplace website. Capability Providers will have the ability to submit white papers through the Trusted Capital Website and then must be down selected by a DoD Military Service through their acquisitions processes. Once a company has been down selected, the Military Service may offer the company the opportunity to apply to the Trusted Capital program and will provide companies with a link to access the online Trusted Capital application portal.

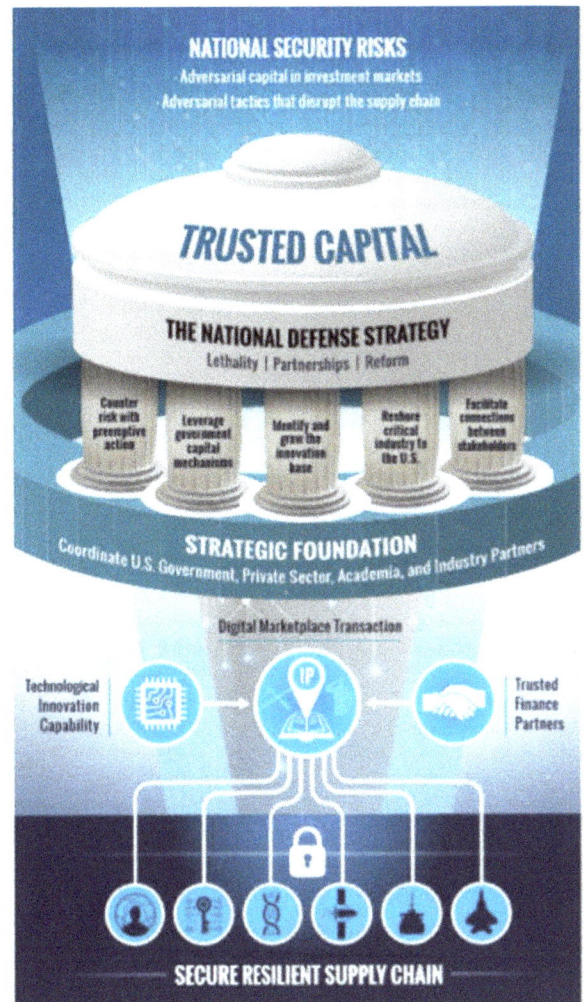

APPENDIX

Appendix A: Industrial Base Map

This appendix contains controlled unclassified information, and business confidential and proprietary content, and will be provided to Congress as an annex to this report.

Appendix B: Industrial Base Studies and Assessments

This appendix contains controlled unclassified information, and business confidential and proprietary content, and will be provided to Congress as an annex to this report.

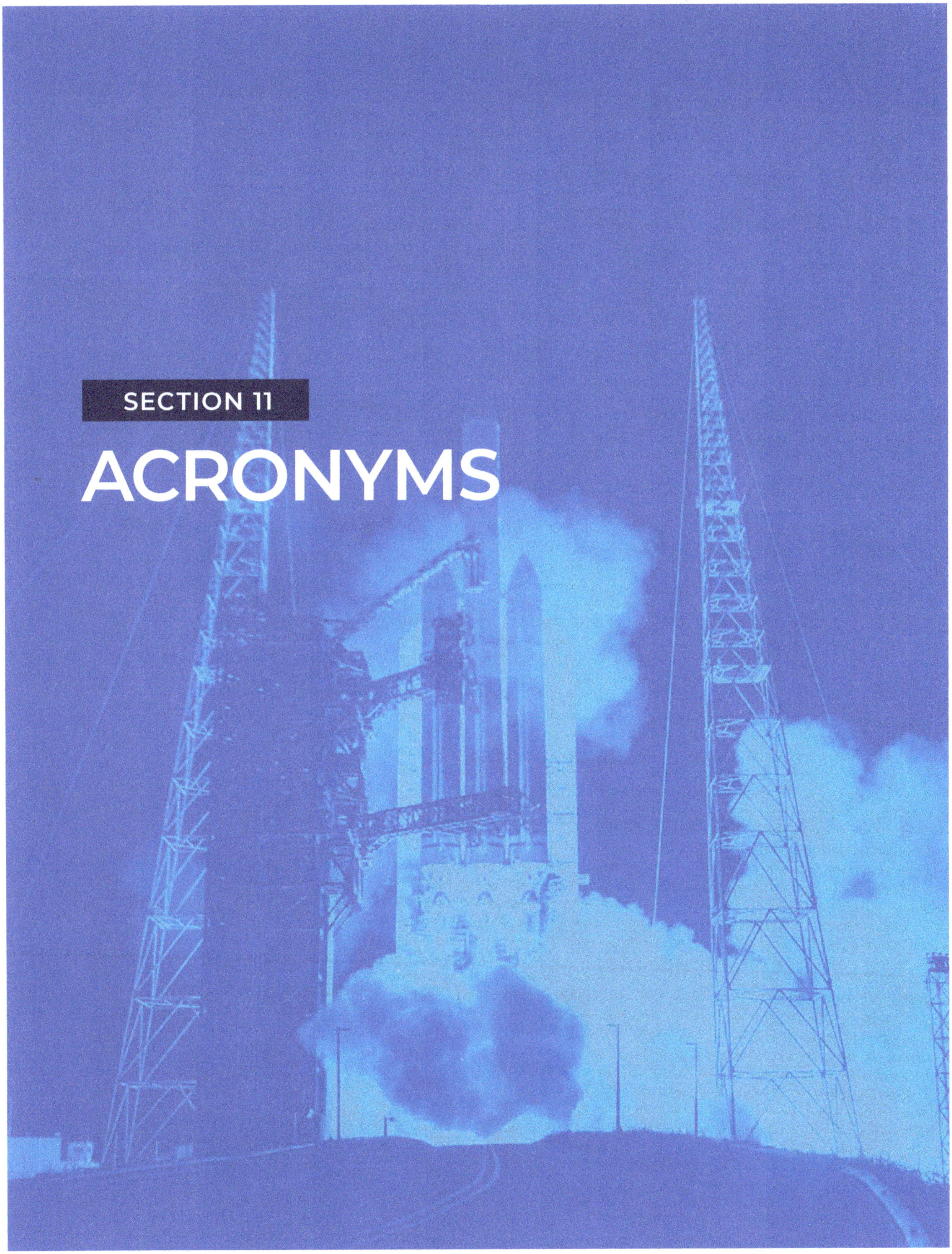

SECTION 11

ACRONYMS

11. ACRONYMS

5G	Fifth generation
A&D	U.S Aerospace and Defense Industry
ACE	America's Cutting Edge
AESA	Actively Electronically Scanned Array
AFRL	Air Force Research Laboratory
AI	Artificial intelligence
AMT	Association for Manufacturing Technology
ARM	Advanced Robotics for Manufacturing Institute
ASIC	Application-specific integrated circuits
C2	Command and Control
C3	Command, Control, and Communications
CAGR	Combined Annual Growth Rate
CARES Act	Coronavirus Aid, Relief, and Economic Security Act
CBC	Chemical Biological Center
CBDP	Department of Defense Chemical and Biological Defense Program
CBRN	Chemical, Biological, Radiological, and Nuclear
CBRND	Chemical, Biological, Radiological, and Nuclear Defense
CDI	Covered defense information
CEMWG	Critical Energetic Materials Working Group
CFIUS	Committee on Foreign Investment in the United States
CHIPS	Creating Helpful Incentives to Produce Semiconductors
CIO	DoD's Chief Information Officer
CITE	Center of Industrial and Technical Excellence
CMMC	Cybersecurity Maturity Model Certification
CO	Cyberspace Operations
CUI	Controlled Unclassified Information
CV	Combat Vehicles
DARPA	Defense Advanced Research Projects Agency
DCMA	Defense Contract Management Agency
DE	Directed Energy
DevSecOps	Development, security and operations
DEW	Directed Energy Weapon
DFARS	Defense Federal Acquisition Regulations Supplement

DFC	U.S. International Development Finance Corporation
DIB	Defense industrial base
DISA	Defense Information Systems Agency
DIU	Defense Innovation Unit
DLA	Defense Logistics Agency
DMS&T	Defense-Wide Manufacturing Science & Technology
DMSMS	Diminishing manufacturing sources and material suppliers
DoC	Department of Commerce
DoD	Department of Defense
DOE	Department of Energy
DoJ	Department of Justice
DPA	Defense Production Act
DTTI	Defense Technology and Trade Initiative
EB	DPAS Enterprise Board
EBITDA	Earnings before Interest, Tax, Depreciation, and Amortization
EM	Electromagnetic
EMS	Electronic manufacturing service
EO	Executive Order
EW	Electronic Warfare
FAANG	Facebook, Amazon, Apple, Netflix, and Google
FEMA	Federal Emergency Management Agency
FGPA	Field-programmable gate arrays
FIR	Foreign Investment Review
FIRRMA	Foreign Investment Risk Review Modernization Act
FNC3	Fully Networked Command, Control, and Communications
FTC	Federal Trade Commission
FY	Fiscal Year
FYDP	Future year defense program
GaN	Gallium Nitride
GOCO	Government-owned, contractor-operated
GOGO	Government-owned, government-operated
GPU	Graphics processing units
HBCU	Historically Black College and Universities
HEL	High energy lasers
HHS	Department of Health & Human Services

HPM	High power microwaves
HSR	Hart-Scott-Rodino Act
HSWR	Hypersonics War Room
IAG	Defense Contract Management Agency's Industrial Analysis Group
IB	Industrial Base
IBAS	Industrial Base Analysis & Sustainment Program
IBC	Industrial Base Council
IC	Integrated circuit
IC	Intelligence Community
IoT	Internet of things
IP	Intellectual Property
IPT	integrated product team
ISR	intelligence, surveillance, and reconnaissance
IT	Information technology
JADC2	Joint All-Domain Command and Control
JATF	Joint Acquisition Task Force
JGPD-HME	Joint General Purpose Decontaminant for Hardened Military Equipment
JIBWG	Joint Industrial Base Working Group
JRIBWG	Joint Radar Industrial Base Working Group
LEP	Life Extension Program
LOE	Line of effort
LSRM	Large solid-rocket motor
M&A	Mergers & Acquisitions
M2M	Machine, machine teaming
ManTech	Manufacturing Technology Program
ME	Microelectronics
MI	Minority Serving Institution
MII	Manufacturing Innovation Institutes
MILDEPS	Military Departments
MINSEC	Microelectronics Innovation for National Security and Economic Competitiveness
ML	Machine Learning
MMIC	Monolithic Microwave Integrated Circuits
MOA	Memorandum of Agreement
MUM-T	Manned-Unmanned Teaming
NACE-E	National Centers of Academic Excellence in Cybersecurity

NASA	National Aeronautics and Space Administration
NAVSEA	Naval Sea Systems Command
NCI	Non-corporate interests
NDAA	National Defense Authorization Act
NdFeB	Neodymium Iron Boron
NDS	National Defense Stockpile
NDS	National Defense Strategy
NIST	National Institute of Standards and Technology
NSS	National Space Strategy
NTIB	National Technology and Industrial Base
ODASD(MR)	Office of the Deputy Assistant Secretary of Defense for Materiel Readiness
ODIN	Optical Dazzler Interdictor
OEA	USD(A&S) Office of Economic Adjustment
OECD	Organization for Economic Co-operation and Development
OIB	Organic Industrial Base
OLED	Organic light emitting diode
OSAT	Outsourced semiconductor assembly and test
OSBP	Office of Small Business Programs
OSD	Office of the Secretary of Defense
OTA	Other Transaction Authority
OUSD(A&S)	Office of the Undersecretary of Defense for Acquisition and Sustainment
OUSD(R&E)	Office of the Under Secretary of Defense for Research and Engineering
PBA	Pine Bluff Arsenal
PLAA	People's Liberation Army
PLAN	People's Liberation Army Navy
PPBE	Planning, programming, budgeting and execution
PPE	Personal protective equipment
PPP	Public Private Partnership
PrCB EA	DoD Executive Agent for Printed Circuit Board and Interconnect Technology
PrCB	Printed circuit board
PrCBA	Printed circuit board assembly
QA	Quality Assurance
R&D	Research & Development
R/R&D	Federal Research/Research and Development
RAMP	Rapid Assured Microelectronics Prototypes

RDT&E	Research, Development, Testing, and Engineering
RF/OE	Radio frequency and optoelectronic
RIF	Rapid Innovation Fund
RSRP	Radar Supplier Resiliency Plan
S&T	Science and technology
SBC	Small Business Concern
SBIR	Small Business Innovation Research Program
SBTP	Office of Small Business Technology Partnerships
SHIP	State-of-the-Art Heterogeneous Integration Prototype
SIBWG	Space Industrial Base Working Group
SLP	Substrate-like printed circuit board
SMM	Small and medium-sized manufacturers
SOTA	State-of-the-art
STEM	Science, technology, engineering, and mathematics
STTR	Small Business Technology Transfer Program
sUAS	Small Unmanned Aircraft Systems
SWAP	Software Acquisition and Practices
TEA	Technical execution area
TKA	Tail Kit Assembly
TMIB	Technology, Manufacturing, and Industrial Base
TWTA	Traveling Wave Tube Amplifiers
TWV	Tactical Wheeled Vehicles
U.S.	United States
UAE	United Arab Emirates
UAS	Unmanned Aircraft Systems
UAV	Unmanned Aerial Vehicle
USD(A&S)	The Undersecretary of Defense for Acquisition and Sustainment
WG	Working group
YTD	Year-to-date

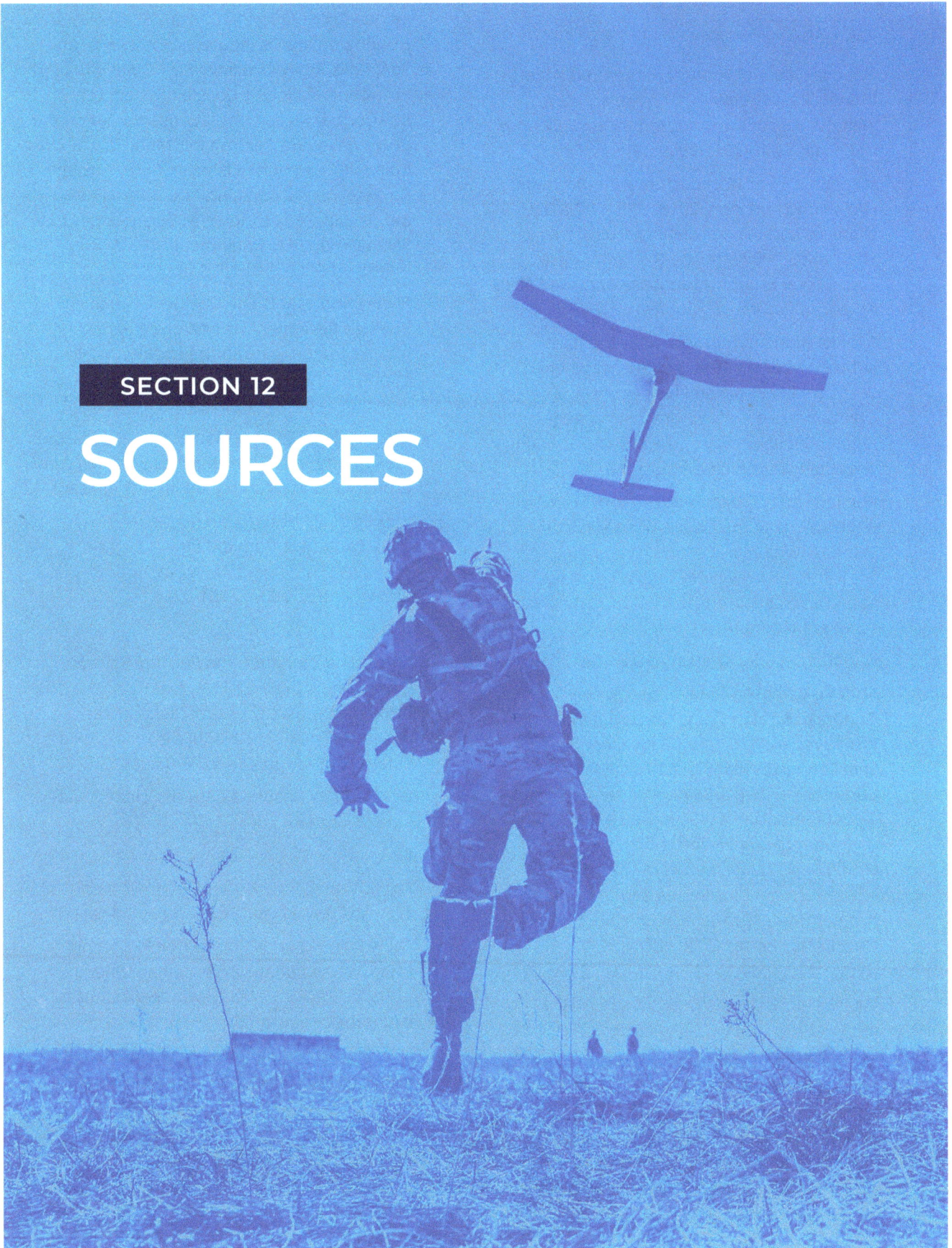

SECTION 12

SOURCES

12. SOURCES

1. National Security Strategy of the United States of America, December 2017, https://www.whitehouse.gov/wp-content/uploads/2017/12/NSS-Final-12-18-2017-0905.pdf

2. Stephen J. Rose, Manufacturing Employment: Fact and Fiction, April 2018, URBAN INSTITUTE (citing its author's calculations from 1960, 1980, and 2000 censuses, the Conference Board Total Economy Database Data, and 2015 American Community Survey)

3. An evolution often described as the "Last Supper," after the Pentagon dinner where Secretary Les Aspin and his deputy (and eventual successor) William Perry urged greater consolidation of the already-shrinking post-Cold War defense industry.

4. Public Remarks, Deputy Secretary of Defense Robert Work at the Royal United Services Institute, Whitehall, London, September 2015, https://www.defense.gov/Newsroom/Speeches/Speech/Article/617128/royal-united-services-institute-rusi/

5. National Security Strategy, December 2017.

6. Antonio Varas, Raj Varadarajan, Jimmy Goodrich, & Falan Yinug, "Government Incentives and U.S. Competitiveness in Semiconductor Manufacturing," Boston Consulting Group & Semiconductor Industry Association, (September 2020), Caution-https://web-assets.bcg.com/27/cf/9fa28eeb43649ef8674fe764726d/bcg-government-incentives-and-us-competitiveness-in-semiconductor-manufacturing-sep-2020.pdf

7. Defense Production Act Title III, https://www.businessdefense.gov/Programs/DPA-Title-III/

8. 25 Mid-Tier includes: a combination of 25 U.S. and Foreign based U.S. DoD Suppliers that are publicly traded. Compiled using FPDS data on prime obligations and Defense News Top 100 list of defense suppliers based on revenue for 2020 (Companies: L3Harris Technologies Inc, Leidos Holdings Inc, Airbus SE, Thales SA, Huntington Ingalls Industries Inc, Leonardo SpA, Rolls-Royce Holdings PLC, Qinetiq Group PLC, General Electric Co, Elbit Systems Ltd, Ball Corp, Science Applications International Corp, ViaSat Inc, Textron Inc, Moog Inc, Curtiss-Wright Corp, Oshkosh Corp, Aerojet Rocketdyne Holdings Inc, TransDigm Group Inc, Singapore Technologies Engineering Ltd, Serco Group PLC, Rheinmetall AG, Melrose Industries PLC, Saab AB, Safran SA)

9. "How Important Is The U.S. Government To Boeing's Revenue?," https://dashboards.trefis.com/no-login-required/pFxcKTVr/How-Important-is-the-US-government-to-Boeing-s-Revenue ?fromforbesandarticle=ba200102

10. "Drone Manufacturer Market Shares: DJI Leads the Way in the U.S.," https://www.droneii.com/dronemanufacturer-market-shares-dji-leads-the-way-in-the-us

11. "May Passenger Demand Shows Slight Improvement," https://www.iata.org/en/pressroom/pr/2020-07-01-02/

12. Ibid.

13. "U.S-China Economic and Security Review Commission The 13th Five-Year Plan," https://www.uscc.gov/ sites/default/files/Research/The%2013th%20Five-Year%20Plan_Final_2.14.17_Updated%20(002).pdf

14. 2017 County Business Patterns, United States Census Bureau

15. Ibid.

16. NSWC Crane, Counterfeit Electronic Part Trends, Created using ERAI-provided data

17. "New Rule Expands Counterfeit Reporting", https://www.nationaldefensemagazine.org/articles/2020/1/13/new-rule-expands-counterfeit-reporting

18. U.S. Department of Commerce, U.S. Bare Printed Circuit Board Industry Assessment 2017, Data updated in 2020 by DoD Executive Agent for Printed Circuit Board and Interconnect Technology.

19. "EMS 2019 in Review: Trade Wars Batter Supply Chains, Profits,"

20. Benchmark, Space Systems, https://www.bench.com/space

21. "TTM Tecnologies, Inc. Announces Opening of Advanced Technology Center in Chippewa Falls, Wisconsin," https://www.globenewswire.com/news-release/2020/02/25/1990456/0/en/TTM-Technologies-Inc-Announces-Opening-of-Advanced-Technology-Center-in-Chippewa-Falls-Wisconsin.html

22. "Aerospace and Defense Deals Insights: Midyear 2020," https://www.pwc.com/us/en/industries/industrial-products/library/aerospace-defense-quarterly-deals-insights.html

23. "Summit Interconnect, INC. Acquires Integrated Technology LTD. (ITL Circuits)", https://www.summit-pcb.com/press-releases/summit-interconnect-inc-acquires-integrated-technology-ltd-itl-circuits/

24. "NTI-100 2019: A Not-So-fabulous Year for Fabricators", https://www.pcdandf.com/pcdesign/index.php/editorial/menu-features/14933-a-not-so-fabulous-year-for-fabricators

25. "2020 Trends in Electronics Sourcing," https://www.businesswire.com/news/home/20200519005327/en/Supplyframe-Electronics-Sourcing-Report-Highlights-Innovation-Imperative-Amid-COVID-19.

26. Ibid.

27. "The Impact of the Coronavirus (COVID-19) Epidemic on Electronics Manufacturers: March Update," https://www.ipc.org/emails/gr/corona-virus-report2.pdf.

28. "Department of Defense Announces $197.2 Million for Microelectronics," https://www.defense.gov/Newsroom/Releases/Release/Article/2384039/department-of-defense-announces-1972-million-for-microelectronics/

29. "DOD Can Lead Microelectronics Manufacturing Back to U.S.", https://www.defense.gov/Explore/News/Article/Article/2320194/dod-can-lead-microelectronics-manufacturing-back-to-us/.

30. World Electronic Circuits Council (WECC), WECC Global PCB Production Report for 2015.

31. World Electronic Circuits Council (WECC), WECC Global PCB Production Report for 2018.

32. GP Ventures, "199", http://gp-ventures.com/199-2/

33. "Do Trade Wars and Mergers Portend a Coming Changing of the Guard?", https://www.circuitsassembly.com/ca/editorial/menu-features/31430-ems-top-50-1906.html

34. Ibid.

35. "EMS 2019 in Review: Trade Wars Batter Supply Chains, Profits", https://www.circuitsassembly.com/ca/editorial/menu-features/33470-ems-2019-in-review-trade-wars-batter-supply-chains-profits.html

36. "Mid-2019 PCB and EMS M&A Round-up", http://gp-ventures.com/mid-2019-pcb-and-ems-ma-round/, 08/22/2019

37. Semiconductor Industry Association Brief to OSD Industrial Policy, June 2020.

38. "Global Semiconductor Sales Increase 5.8 Percent Year-to-Year in May; Annual Sales Projected to Increase 3.3 Percent in 2020, 6.2 Percent in 2021", https://www.semiconductors.org/global-semiconductor-sales-increase-5-8-percent-year-to-year-in-may-annual-sales-projected-to-increase-3-3-percent-in-2020-6-2-percent-in-2021/

39. "Worried About Chinese Backdoors, Lord Pushes for New Tech Strategy", https://breakingdefense.com/2020/09/worried-about-chinese-backdoors-lord-pushes-for-new-tech-strategy/

40. Comparison of Global Machine Tool Producing and Consuming Nations by Value, https://www.gardnerintelligence.com/report/world-machine-tool

41. Ibid.

42. "When the machine stopped: A cautionary tale from industrial America," ISBN-10: 0875842089

43. "Trade Balances for Machine Tool Sector Nations," https://www.gardnerintelligence.com/report/world-machine-tool

44. "The Hazards of Global Supply Chains," https://www.asme.org/getmedia/82c9f3bd-9622-4677-97a8-0cff5a4c3a8d/ps20-13-asme_hazards_of_global_supply_chains.pdf

45. "Net Orders for U.S. Consumption of Manufacturing Technology," https://www.amtonline.org/article_display.cfm?article_id=205180

46. Language contained in the NDAA for FY2019 directs the Secretary of Defense to deliver a comprehensive strategy to the congressional defense committees for improving the depot infrastructure of the military departments with the objective of ensuring that the depots have the capacity and capability to support the readiness and material availability goals of current and future DoD weapon systems. The language requires that the strategy include a review of the current conditions and performance of each depot, a business-case analysis comparing the minimum investment necessary required under Section 2476e of title 10, United States Code, with the actual investment needed to execute the planned mission and a plan to improve the conditions and performance utilizing this data.

47. See https://media.defense.gov/2018/oct/05/2002048904/-1/-1/1/assessing-and-strengthening-the-manufacturing-and%20defense-industrial-base-and-supply-chain-resiliency.pdf.

48. 2020 Department of Defense China Military Power Report

49. World Steel Association, https://www.worldsteel.org/

50. Ibid.

51. Assessing and Strengthening the Manufacturing and Defense Industrial base and Supply Chain Resiliency of the United States, https://media.defense.gov/2018/oct/05/2002048904/-1/-1/1/assessing-andstrengthening-the-manufacturing-and%20defense-industrial-base-and-supply-chain-resiliency.pdf

52. Executive Order on Assessing and Strengthening the Manufacturing and Defense Industrial Base and Supply Chain Resiliency of the United States, https://www.whitehouse.gov/presidential-actions/ presidential-executive-order-assessing-strengthening-manufacturing-defense-industrial-base-supply-chainresiliency-united-states/

53. "STEM crisis or STEM surplus? Yes and yes", https://doi.org/10.21916/mlr.2015.14

54. Report was provided in response to Senate Report 115-290, Pages 199-200, Accompanying S.3159, the Department of Defense Appropriations Bill for Fiscal Year 2019

55. 2018 "Deloitte and The Manufacturing Institute skills gap and future of work study," http://www. themanufacturinginstitute.org/~/media/E323C4D8F75A470E8C96D7A07F0A14FB/DI_2018_Deloitte_MFI_ skills_gap_FoW_study.pdf

56. "STEM Occupations: Past, Present, and Future", https://www.bls.gov/spotlight/2017/science-technologyengineering-and-mathematics-stem-occupations-past-present-and-future/pdf/science-technologyengineering-and-mathematics-stem-occupations-past-present-and-future.pdf

57. Under Secretary of Defense for Acquisition and Sustainment, Software Acquisition Pathway Interim Policy Review, https://www.acq.osd.mil/ae/assets/docs/USA002825-19%20Signed%20Memo%20(Software).pdf

58. DoD Enterprise DevSecOps Initiative, https://software.af.mil/dsop

59. U.S. and Global STEM Education, https://www.nsf.gov/statistics/2018/nsb20181/digest/sections/u-s-andglobal-stem-education

60. Report was provided in response to Senate Report 115-290, Pages 199-200, Accompanying S.3159, the Department of Defense Appropriations Bill for Fiscal Year 2019

61. "The Importance of International Students to American Science and Engineering," http://nfap.com/wp-content/uploads/2017/10/The-Importance-of-International-Students.NFAP-Policy-Brief.October-20171.pdf

62. "In the wake of Northrop-Orbital merger, Aerojet's solid rocket engine business teetering on the brink", https://spacenews.com/in-the-wake-of-northrop-orbital-merger-aerojets-solid-rocket-engine-businessteetering-on-the-brink/

63. Avon Rubber Completes Acquisition Of 3m's Ballistic Protection Business," https://www.avon-rubber. com/media-centre/press-releases/press-releases1/avon-rubber-completes-acquisition-of-3m-s-ballisticprotection-business/#currentPage=1

64. Russian Ministry of Defense, http://eng.mil.ru/en/news_page/country/more.htm?id=12071791@egNews

65. Ibid.

66. "'Iron Man' Suit To Fall Short Of Its Goals (Updated)," https://www.nationaldefensemagazine.org/articles/2019/2/6/special-ops-iron-man-suit

67. World Bank, https://data.worldbank.org/, Central Intelligence Agency, https://www.cia.gov/library/publications/the-world-factbook/rankorder/rankorderguide.html

68. Defense Space Strategy Summary, https://media.defense.gov/2020/Jun/17/2002317391/-1/-1/1/2020_DEFENSE_SPACE_STRATEGY_SUMMARY.PDF?source=email

69. "Evaluation of China's Commercial Space Sector," https://www.ida.org/research-and-publications/publications/all/e/ev/evaluation-of-chinas-commercial-space-sector

70. "The Global Commercial Market for Orbital Launch Services." Distribution C. April 2020.

71. "The Contest for Innovation: Strengthening America's National Security Innovation Base in an Era of Strategic Competition," https://www.reaganfoundation.org/media/355297/the_contest_for_innovation_report.pdf

72. Award summaries available at https://www.oea.gov/Defense-Manufacturing-Community-Support-Program

73. Office of the Undersecretary for Defense for Research & Engineering, Modernization Priorities, https://www.cto.mil/modernization-priorities/

74. M. Zatman, Fully Networked Command, Control, and Communication: Infrastructure Supporting the National Defense Strategy (NDS), 2020

75. Ibid.

76. Ibid.

77. M. Zatman, "FNC3 Road to Dominance Overview (Workshop Opening Remarks)," 2020

78. M. Zatman, Fully Networked Command, Control, and Communication: Infrastructure Supporting the National Defense Strategy (NDS), 2020

79. Office of the Undersecretary for Defense for Research & Engineering, Modernization Priorities, https://www.cto.mil/modernization-priorities/

80. Ibid.

81. "2020 State of the U.S. Semiconductor Industry," https://www.semiconductors.org/wp-content/uploads/2020/06/2020-SIA-State-of-the-Industry-Report.pdf

82. "CHIPS for America Act Would Strengthen U.S. Semiconductor Manufacturing, Innovation," https://www.semiconductors.org/chips-for-america-act-would-strengthen-u-s-semiconductor-manufacturing-innovation/

83. "DOD Adopts 'Zero Trust' Approach to Buying Microelectronics," https://www.defense.gov/Explore/News/Article/Article/2192120/dod-adopts-zero-trust-approach-to-buying-microelectronics/.

84. "Emerging Military Technologies: Background and Issues for Congress," https://crsreports.congress.gov/product/pdf/R/R46458

85. Maintaining Technology Advantage, "Artificial Intelligence TAPP Appendix A-1," 2020.

86. " Maintaining the Competitive Edge in Artificial Intelligence and Machine Learning." https://www.rand.org/pubs/research_reports/RRA200-1.html

87. " Artificial Intelligence and National Security," https://crsreports.congress.gov/product/pdf/R/R45178/9

88. "Big Data at War: Special Operations Forces, Project Maven, and Twenty-First-Century Warfare," https://mwi.usma.edu/big-data-at-war-special-operations-forces-project-maven-and-twenty-first-century-warfare/

89. "AI To Fly In Dogfight Tests By 2024: SecDef," https://breakingdefense.com/2020/09/ai-will-dogfight-human-pilots-in-tests-by-2024-secdef/

90. "Army advances learning capabilities of drone swarms," https://www.army.mil/article/237978/army_advances_learning_capabilities_of_drone_swarms

91. " Keeping Top AI Talent in the United States," https://cset.georgetown.edu/wp-content/uploads/Keeping-Top-AI-Talent-in-the-United-States.pdf

92. " Artificial Intelligence and National Security," https://crsreports.congress.gov/product/pdf/R/R45178/9

93. "Recommendations on Export Controls for Artificial Intelligence," https://cset.georgetown.edu/wp-content/uploads/Recommendations-on-Export-Controls-for-Artificial-Intelligence.pdf

94. "Executive Summary of the Defense Science Board Report on Applications of Quantum Technologies."

95. "USD(R&E) Technology Roadmap Quantum Science" Briefing, May 20200

96. OUSD(R&E)/ST&E/S&T, Quantum Technology Area Protection Plan, September 2020

97. "USD(R&E) Technology Roadmap Quantum Science" Briefing, May 2020

98. "Fiscal Year 2019 Industrial Base Capabilities ' Report to Congress."

99. OUSD(R&E)/ST&E/S&T, Quantum Technology Area Protection Plan, September 2020

100. "USD(R&E) Technology Roadmap Quantum Science" Briefing, May 2020

101. "Understanding Gartner's Hype Cycles," https://www.gartner.com/en/documents/3887767/understanding-gartner-s-hype-cycles

102. Assessing and Comparing the Robustness of the U.S. Industrial Base in Quantum Technology: Kickoff Briefing Addendum."

103. "MITRE Statement of Work: DIB Workforce Assessment," October 2020

104. "Emerging Military Technologies: Background and Issues for Congress," https://crsreports.congress.gov/product/pdf/R/R46458

105. "Maintaining Technology Advantage, 2020 Directed Energy TAPP Appendix A-1."

106. "Advancing High Energy Laser Weapon Capabilities."

107. "The ODIN Shipboard Laser: Science Fiction No More." https://jnlwp.defense.gov/Press-Room/In-The-News/Article/2213173/the-odin-shipboard-laser-science-fiction-no-more/

108. AFRL gives warfighters new weapons system."https://www.whs.mil/News/News-Display/Article/2138161/afrl-gives-warfighters-new-weapons-system/

109. Ibid.

110. "Emerging Military Technologies: Background and Issues for Congress," https://crsreports.congress.gov/product/pdf/R/R46458

111. "Advancing High Energy Laser Weapon Capabilities."

112. Ibid.

113. Ibid.

114. "DoD Drafts Guidelines for Laser Design," https://breakingdefense.com/2020/08/dod-drafts-guidelines-for-laser-design/

115. "Army Rapid Capabilities and Critical Technologies Office Manufacturing Technology Overview."

116. Office of the Undersecretary for Defense for Research & Engineering, Modernization Priorities, https://www.cto.mil/modernization-priorities/

117. IEEE 5g and Beyond Technology Roadmap White Paper," https://futurenetworks.ieee.org/images/files/pdf/ieee-5g-roadmap-white-paper.pdf .

118. Ibid.

119. Ibid.

120. Ibid.

121. "FCC 5G," https://www.fcc.gov/5G

122. "DOD Kicks Off World's Largest Dual-Use 5G Testing Effort," https://www.defense.gov/Explore/News/Article/Article/2378047/dod-kicks-off-worlds-largest-dual-use-5g-testing-effort/

123. Ibid.

124. "Defense Department Press Briefing on 5G Communications Technology Testing and Experimentation," https://www.defense.gov/Newsroom/Transcripts/Transcript/Article/2208939/defense-department-press-briefing-on-5g-communications-technology-testing-and-e/ (accessed 16 Oct 2020)

125. "Report of the Defense Science Board Summer Study on Autonomy." Undersecretary of Defense (USD), Acquisition, Technology, and Logistics (AT&L).

126. "Manned-Unmanned Teaming: A Great Opportunity or Mission Overload?" https://www.japcc.org/manned-unmanned-teaming/

127. "Army robots get driver education for difficult tasks," https://www.army.mil/article/237248/army_robots_get_driver_education_for_difficult_tasks (accessed October 8, 2020)

128. "The Army's got a Universal Robot Driver," https://breakingdefense.com/2019/11/the-armys-universal-robot-driver/

129. "AI Chips: What They Are and Why They Matter," https://cset.georgetown.edu/research/ai-chips-what-they-are-and-why-they-matter/

130. "New Challenges Facing Semiconductors," https://irds.ieee.org/topics/new-challenges-facing-semiconductors

131. "Artificial Intelligence and National Security," https://crsreports.congress.gov/product/pdf/R/R45178/9

132. "Joint Chiefs of Staff Publication 3-12, Cyber Operations," https://www.jcs.mil/Portals/36/Documents/Doctrine/pubs/jp3_12.pdf

133. Office of the Undersecretary for Defense for Research & Engineering, Modernization Priorities, https://www.cto.mil/modernization-priorities/

134. "2018 National Cyber Strategy," https://www.whitehouse.gov/wp-content/uploads/2018/09/National-Cyber-Strategy.pdf

135. "Defense Primer: Cyberspace Operations," https://fas.org/sgp/crs/natsec/IF10537.pdf

136. "2017 National Security Strategy of the United States of America,"https://www.whitehouse.gov/wp-content/uploads/2017/12/NSS-Final-12-18-2017-0905.pdf

137. "Cyberspace Solarium Commission Report," https://www.solarium.gov/report

138. Ibid.

139. "The Defense Production Act of 1950: History, Authorities, and Considerations for Congress," https://crsreports.congress.gov/product/pdf/R/R43767

IMAGE SOURCES

Page

Cover   Photo By: Joshua Armstrong, Air Force
https://www.defense.gov/observe/photo-gallery/igphoto/2002085551/

7   Photo By: Air Force Senior Airman Keith Holcomb
https://www.defense.gov/observe/photo-gallery/igphoto/2002556357/

8   Photo By: Navy Petty Officer 2nd Class Taylor DiMartino
http://www.defense.gov/observe/photo-gallery/igphoto/2002460143/

21   Photo: by Senior Airman Franklin R. Ramos, U.S. Air Force/Released
https://www.flickr.com/photos/39955793@N07/12234809043/in/photolist-29QD6SM-2gfJxj7-2gfK3JR-SV81N5-p6VUva-nknxXp-oYAEyU-KoTXjk-ps1jtf-VynNBa-p68mPW-p4jVME-p67tke-TCrQfB-dtmgHo-LYDrrQ-L4TkLU-Uh2fmS-p68oV9-JGXTLk-popuxw-ps2Zni-VHE4eb-MQ9Qxy-ojhQLN-2guVzva-daEqmD-ddHWY5-e4U6b4-pMDyJv-LeGao3-jD9Atv-VVZvtA-e5ZAgk-Lt3vp7-p7Jmn9-bGVyun-p7JUo1-oR2K59-e5a8Gk-e13pAK-bEwYun-daEoLx-bNQuAH-bDd6va-bDhAtr-9dycGi-85sNFD-84GAhq-7gPNde

22   Photo By: Air Force Staff Sgt. Trevor McBride
http://www.defense.gov/observe/photo-gallery/igphoto/2002554084/

25   Photo By: Air Force Airman 1st Class Jacob B. Wrightsman
https://www.defense.gov/observe/photo-gallery/igphoto/2002477835/

26   Photo By: Army Sgt. Sarah Sangster
http://www.defense.gov/observe/photo-gallery/igphoto/2002559196/

31   Photo By: Joshua Armstrong, Air Force
https://www.defense.gov/observe/photo-gallery/igphoto/2002526348/

32   Photo By: Marine Corps Lance Cpl. Mackenzie Binion
https://www.defense.gov/observe/photo-gallery/igphoto/2002456042/

35   Photo By: Army Sgt. John Schoebel
http://www.defense.gov/observe/photo-gallery/igphoto/2002557041/

36   Photo By: Navy Petty Officer 3rd Class MacAdam Weissman
http://www.defense.gov/observe/photo-gallery/igphoto/2002559799/

39   Photo by: Ens. Jalen Robinson
https://www.flickr.com/photos/39955793@N07/32853273557/in/photostream/

40   Photo By: Marine Corps Cpl. Brennan Beauton
http://www.defense.gov/observe/photo-gallery/igphoto/2002559200/

49   Photo By: Air Force Senior Airman Bryan Guthrie
https://www.defense.gov/observe/photo-gallery/igphoto/2002557114/

50   Photo By: Navy Petty Officer 3rd Class Nicholas Huynh
     http://www.defense.gov/observe/photo-gallery/igphoto/2002353486/

115 Photo By: Navy Petty Officer 1st Class Devin Langer
     https://www.defense.gov/observe/photo-gallery/igphoto/2002508788/

116 Photo By: Todd Maki, Air Force
     https://www.defense.gov/observe/photo-gallery/igphoto/2002551733/

163 Photo by Sgt. Jesse Pilgrim
     https://www.flickr.com/photos/39955793@N07/48631270737/

167 Photo By: Jeff Spotts
     https://www.defense.gov/observe/photo-gallery/igphoto/2002551086/

173 Photo: by Sgt. Dustin D. Biven
     https://www.flickr.com/photos/39955793@N07/48631279807/

139 Photo By: Army Master Sgt. Becky Vanshur
     https://www.defense.gov/observe/photo-gallery/igphoto/2002558184/

www.ingramcontent.com/pod-product-compliance
Lightning Source LLC
Chambersburg PA
CBHW080331270326
41927CB00014B/3180